The Young Internationalists

THE EAST-WEST CENTER—formally known as "The Center for Cultural and Technical Interchange Between East and West" —was established in Hawaii by the United States Congress in 1960. As a national educational institution in cooperation with the University of Hawaii, the Center has the mandated goal "to promote better relations and understanding between the United States and the nations of Asia and the Pacific through cooperative study, training, and research."

Each year about 2,000 men and women from the United States and some 40 countries and territories of Asia and the Pacific area work and study together with a multi-national East-West Center staff in wide-ranging programs dealing with problems of mutual East-West concern. Participants are supported by federal scholarships and grants, supplemented in some fields by contributions from Asian/Pacific governments and private foundations.

Center programs are conducted by the East-West Communication Institute, the East-West Culture Learning Institute, the East-West Food Institute, the East-West Population Institute, and the East-West Technology and Development Institute. Open Grants are awarded to provide scope for educational and research innovation, including a program in humanities and the arts.

East-West Center Books are published by The University Press of Hawaii to further the Center's aims and programs.

The Young Internationalists

Edited by Thomas A. Hiatt
and Mark Gerzon

AN EAST-WEST CENTER BOOK
The University Press of Hawaii
Honolulu

Copyright © 1973 by The University Press of Hawaii
All rights reserved
Library of Congress Catalog Card Number 70-188981
ISBN 0-8248-0218-7
Manufactured in the United States of America
Designed by Eileen Cufley Williams

DEDICATED

To Karl Jaeger, for his foresight

To Dr. Lerner and Dr. Gorden, for their direction

To the young people of the world, that we may come together
in peace to solve our common problems

Contents

Foreword

It began on a fine Saturday morning, 29 September 1968, at San Francisco International Airport. We had gathered together—thirty-nine souls of diverse provenance—for a flight to Honolulu. For thirty-two college students, mainly juniors, and for two professors and their families, it was a momentous meeting. During the next eight months we were to travel around the world together as a peripatetic academy called the International Honors Program, Class of 1969 (IHP '69). Before the trip was over we had become a family as well as an academy.

IHP '69, the tenth in this unique program of study years abroad, culminated a decade of educational experimentation and innovation. In some important ways, IHP '69 was like no other class, and I shall soon speak of its singularity. But we were also the beneficiaries of the successful IHP format that had been evolved over the years. Like all IHP classes, we traveled by air—although there was nothing "jet set" about us. We studied in seven countries over periods ranging from three to six weeks, with short stopovers in several countries along our route. Despite the brevity of our visits, we absorbed experiences of incredible quantity and quality in each study center. This was due in large measure to the excellent IHP blend of localism with globalism. In each country our logistics were prearranged by experienced local representatives; our classrooms and libraries were provided by local colleges; perhaps most significant, our students lived with local families. Such continuous contact with local people gave us insights into the ways and means of each scene, and contributed its share to our education in the lifeways of world humanity.

Our pace was rapid, but not frenetic. True, we rarely left a country without wishing we had spent more time there. But equally true, we never left a country without some ability to handle its language, some sense of its culture, some feel for its people. In this respect, we were the most diligent and intelligent tourists that could be wished for. Our high level of aspiration and achievement was noted with warm favor, and some surprise, in every country. People abroad were often unprepared to find American students today "like that" —meaning "that good."

But enlightened tourism was only part of our purpose. For us, this was primarily a *study* year. Where tourism was teacher, we learned all we could absorb. But if we played hard, we worked even harder. Our IHP academic schedule averaged ten classroom sessions per week; often we spent even more time in class as worthwhile local lecturers became available to us; and we were perpetual students of the peoples and cultures around us. In every major study center, our students completed an original paper based on independent study plus field work. This volume contains the students' most characteristic papers, as selected by their two editors.

This book is the tangible evidence of their *academic* achievement. Some of these papers were promptly recognized as valuable contributions to knowledge of their own countries by eminent scholars, who asked me for permission to publish them. Some papers have been accepted for journal publication in this country, including winners of the Phi Beta Kappa Prize and other national honors for undergraduate contributions to scholarship. Each is the product of a fine young mind exploring a new aspect of the world. Collected like this, the record of these productive "young internationalists" is a stimulating, even inspiring, example of what able young people can accomplish when they are encouraged to seek rational and empirical answers to the deeper questions about the world we live in.

Since their academic achievements speak for themselves in this book, I wish to add a note of gratitude to them personally. Although their origins were varied—they came to IHP from Laredo and Whitehorse, from Boston and Los Angeles, from great private universities and small state colleges, from rich and poor families—their unity was shaped by their excellence of mind and character. They refreshed the spirit of an old teacher and persuaded me, in my year as their "dean," that no civilization is moribund which produces such young people as these. After a few months with them in our IHP year, I was writing home enthusiastic letters to the effect that "these kids are the best news I've had about America in many years." Two years later, after sustained contact with them as they went their separate ways, I still believe this.

The students have chosen to entitle their book *The Young Internationalists*. This is a very appropriate designation, for none could have undertaken such a study year with better will toward the peoples and places of the world. Nor have any world travelers, in my experience, made better use of their opportunities to encounter and evaluate our world. This book reveals the unique blend of good heart and hard head which may, eventually, make genuine internationalism the way of the world. I am proud to have been associated with them in this enterprise.

It remains only to thank those who made IHP '69 so memorable an experience. Our first thanks must go to the students themselves. Next we thank Karl Jaeger, whose creative vision and philanthropy over the past decade have provided the IHP format and made good its deficits. Indispensable was the contribution of our field director, Professor Morton Gorden, and the warm participation of our faculty families. All of us are grateful to the host families and local institutions who nourished the bodies and souls of the "young internationalists." Each of us is permanently richer by this unique experience.

DANIEL LERNER
Ford Professor of Sociology and
International Communication,
Massachusetts Institute of Technology

The Students

BONNIE ACKER, *Sarah Lawrence College*

JOHN A. ALMSTROM, *University of British Columbia*

HAROLD W. BORKOWSKI, *Colgate University*

MARCIA J. CARPENTER, *Colorado Woman's College*

LAWRENCE S. COOLEY, *Colgate University*

MARSHA N. CHALMUS CUNNINGHAM, *Sarah Lawrence College*

GEORGE W. COOPER, *Holy Cross College*

DAVID J. H. DEAN, *Austin College*

CORNELIA DELLENBAUGH, *University of Pennsylvania*

KATHY SUE WILLIAMS DONER, *Stetson College*

MARK GERZON, *Harvard University*

BARBARA S. HANCOCK, *Radcliffe College*

THOMAS A. HIATT, *Wabash College*

JONATHAN JAY, *University of Texas*

VIDAR J. JORGENSEN, *Harvard University*

ALAN KIRSHENBAUM, *University of Pennsylvania*

LORRAINE BENVENISTE KIRSCHENBAUM, *Alfred University*

RICHARD LANDES, *Harvard University*

EDWARD M. LEBOW, *Harvard University*

LOUISE A. LERNER, *Radcliffe College*

THOMAS H. LERNER, *Princeton University*

JOHN MACKIE, JR., *Claremont Men's College*

SUSAN MEISELAS, *Sarah Lawrence College*

WILLIAM B. MICHAELCHECK, *Southwestern College at Memphis*

JOHN V. MOLLER, JR., *Colgate University*

LEWIS PERRY III, *Harvard University*

JEFFREY B. PETERS, *Harvard University*

RONALEEN RICCIUTI, *Allegheny College*

DAVID P. RUBIN, *Lehigh University*

MICHAEL S. SIEGAL, *Harvard University*

CANDACE SLATER, *Pembroke College*

JOHN H. ZAMMITO, *University of Texas*

The Itinerary

1968–1969

The Young Internationalists

MARK GERZON

Harvard University

Introduction

He was standing alone near a ping-pong table in the lounge of a dorm. We were in the East-West Center at the University of Hawaii, and I had just begun the first leg of our trip. I was not even outside American borders, though it almost felt like it. All I could tell from his black hair and eyes was that he was Asian and that he was looking for someone to play ping pong with. I offered to play and introduced myself. "I am Huan," he answered. As we began to volley I asked him where he was from. He said, "Vietnam."

For the first time I felt far away from home. And bewildered. In Indianapolis I did not run into real Vietnamese, though they were in the newspapers and on TV. At that point I had been opposed to the Vietnam war for about two years, and had read a great deal of criticism of American foreign policy.

That didn't make things any easier, and my first urge was to say, "I am not an American." That, I decided, was lying. Then I almost said, "I'm sorry." Meaningless. "North or South?" Irrelevant. "What can I do?" Cowardly. "I have done something to try to stop it." Inconsequential.

Still in shock, I said simply, "Let's play."

My smashes worked well. But his returns were consistent.

He won the match.

After the ping-pong game I reflected on the events that had led up to our arrival in Honolulu. I remembered that sometime during the summer months before we had left the continent, each of us had received a booklet containing pictures and profiles of the other thirty-two students with whom we would be traveling. How, I had wondered then, looking through the booklet, would these students —from homes as different as a Manhattan apartment and a Pecos ranch—get along? Why are they all going?

My curiosity continued even when we all met for the first time on 29 September 1968 at San Francisco International Airport, and so I decided to talk with each of my fellow travelers during our journey about their backgrounds and objectives.

My hunch was that we had all decided to make the IHP trip because each of us had already experienced a geographical uprooting —changing family residence, traveling abroad, going away to school —which had made us feel more independent and aware, and that we were again seeking personal and intellectual encounters.

I soon realized, however, that my hunch by no means encompassed the range of motivations, that our group was as diverse as any collection of capable American college students.

Some of us had searched diligently for the program; others were approached by college deans. Some were financed by scholarships, some by summer-job earnings, and some by their parents. Some sacrificed an editorial position on a college paper or participation in an active political movement; others gave up merely an unwanted coming-out party or a lovingly overhauled motorcycle.

Despite these differences, some common concerns emerged in our conversations which I believe reveal a great deal about American students in general.

The four basic questions I asked the other students were these:
1. What were your major change-inducing experiences before this trip?
2. Why did you come on the IHP trip?
3. How have you changed as a result of the trip?
4. How do you see America differently now?

WHAT WERE YOUR MAJOR CHANGE-INDUCING EXPERIENCES?

Most students described their previous development as a series of *discontinuities*—personal, geographic, or institutional—which first produced inner stress but ultimately produced personal growth.

Some placed these wrenching experiences as early as grade school; more frequently, though, the events occurred during high school, with its expanded social world, greater intellectual demands, and other areas where new competence was required. Among these experiences, travel was often mentioned. Some thought high school foreign-exchange programs had a powerful impact on their growth —one student felt going to Austria had "dwarfed" his Midwestern experience; another believed being overseas had taught him he could not impose his way of life on other people. Other students had the same reaction in simply changing schools—moving from Colorado to New Jersey, from Long Island to Colorado, from a small cow-town in Texas to a large industrial city. Whatever the change, the common reaction was that one's previous strengths could not cope with it. It demanded, and most often fostered, further growth.

For nearly everyone, however, the leap from high school to college triggered an explosively expanding awareness. Going from "big wheel to small wheel" (as a Harvard North Carolinian put it); caught between home-town and college friends ("Who was my best friend then?" asked a Rutgers student. "I'd have to say, 'My best friend *where*?' "); having to adapt from the country or small town to the big city ("I'm rural no longer," said a Yukon classmate attending college in Vancouver); and exposure to "educationally minded" people (the phrase of a former small-town Tennesseean)—these factors began a process of personal and intellectual questioning which the students believed was immensely valuable.

WHY DID YOU COME ON THE IHP TRIP?

Perhaps the simplest reply was: "Why not?" Indeed, an opportunity for world travel seems hard to pass up.

But in fact many college students might very well pass it up, and many more would not actively seek it out. By his junior year a student has spent two years of study in his department, in cultivating friends, or in developing a college activity. Compared to pursuing these interests, IHP might offer little perceptible gain. What made the juniors in our group different?

Asked why they came along, they expressed their replies almost as deeply felt convictions:

"To get an understanding of people which I can't get sitting back home."

"To see how people order their lives when faced with circumstances different from my own."

"To experience the world through another person's vision."

"To gain a little relativity."

The theme that emerged was that the students felt a personal need to search for a *nonethnocentric, empathic understanding* of the *relativity of cultures*. Because of their own earlier experience of discontinuity, of learning that the world is always larger than one imagines, they were impelled once again to reach out for the widest exposure to diversity, to encounter the world itself.

Most students had already acquired a kind of relativism. But as a Texan expressed it, looking back on his high school years, the relativism merely meant "if it's not like home it must be like Mexico." For others, the relativism meant a simple dualism between their "conservative" home towns and their "liberal" universities, and they realized that they needed more perspective on the process by which political views are shaped. And one Southern student, who had always prided himself on his unprejudiced (as opposed to his neighbors' racist) views of blacks, found he had to confront his own prejudices in dealing with Japanese, Indians, or Russians.

Thus, our reasons for traveling were motivated by a yearning for exposure to the complex patterns of cultural diversity, for an emotional, intellectual, nonpharmacological trip through the different realities of mankind.

HOW HAVE YOU CHANGED
AS A RESULT OF THE TRIP?

At various points on our trip I asked the members of the group how their experiences had affected them—a deceptively simple question which was actually terribly difficult because of the unprecedented images, ideas, and information that overwhelmed us.

My friends' responses revealed a need to sort out and order the perceptions which engulfed them:

"I have had to see myself from a different angle."

"I am taking myself through a whirlwind of diversity to see how I change."

"I am having to get outside myself, to rediscover what I believe, to see what lasts."

"I am discovering my illusions, and so I'm losing all my values that are culture-bound."

"I felt I was slowing down, failing to change."

These remarks reveal more than simple, adolescent rebellion and certainly more than purposeless alienation. For most of us the trip was, I believe, a serious attempt to develop a life style of *continuous self-change*. Each of us hoped, by exposing himself to cultural diversity, to become an *open, empathic personality,* the necessary precondition for understanding other cultures—and our own.

Many students felt college itself was not enough. As a Sarah Lawrence girl put it, "I needed to place myself in situations where I had to commit myself emotionally, not just rationally." And as a Penn student said, "I had a lot of growing up to do that college just wasn't making me do."

This search for a perspective on college life, this unwillingness to become part of a routine made by somebody else, is not unusual. Kenneth Keniston considers it characteristic. Youth, he believes, is a time of life when "enormous value is placed upon change, transformation, *movement*. . . ." Thus, he writes:

To change, to stay on the road, to retain a sense of inner development and/or outer momentum is essential to the youth's sense of active vitality. The psychological problems that afflict youth are experienced as most overwhelming when they seem to block change. Thus, youth abhors . . . the feeling of "getting nowhere," of "being stuck in a rut," or "not moving." It is during youth that we see the most strenuous, self-conscious, and even frenzied efforts at self-transformation, using whatever religious, cultural, therapeutic, or chemical means available.

IHP, we felt, was better than LSD, ROTC, ITT, GOP, or $\beta\theta\pi$ as a way of accomplishing our own self-change. If cars represented social change to our parents, our travel-jets and the COMSAT television satellites represented it to us.

To cope with the changes in our lifetimes (some of us may live to the year 2020), to understand them and guide them or to criticize and defy them, we do indeed, as one girl told me, "need another spurt of growth."

HOW DO YOU SEE AMERICA DIFFERENTLY NOW?

This question, of course, had as many answers as there were students. Economics majors noted America's enormous production and voracious consumption. Religion and philosophy students remarked on how secular our society is compared to others (including communist). ("The Puritans," said one, "set out to found a religious state. Something happened.") Psychology majors observed the peculiar blend of individualism and conformity distinguishing the American character.

Again, the answers seemed to indicate that the students wanted to relate their ideas and life styles to a broader frame of reference than family expectations, community standards, or college counterculture values, that they wanted to encompass the attitudes other cultures have of us. Just as previously each of our experiences had made our last one obsolete, so too did our encounter with other cultures make many earlier opinions seem ethnocentric and shallow.

We had much to unlearn. Bumming cigarettes is not cause for guilt in an Israeli kibbutz, where cigarettes are free to all. Concern for the poor is not shared by the Indian middle-class. Living in bamboo homes on stilts does not mean Thais are miserable in their poverty or hate Americans for their wealth. Socialism may be beneficial and democratic in a technological nation like Sweden. Americans may have more leisure, but that does not mean they know how to enjoy it.

The trip was far too complex to be called either "radicalizing" or "conservatizing." It raised questions as often as it answered them, fatigued as much as rejuvenated, made some pessimistic, some optimistic. All that can be generalized is this: we each learned more about what, as Americans, we did *not* know. Specifically, this meant that we learned to recognize the *limitations* as well as the potentialities of our cultural identities and our academic disciplines.

One student, for instance, who was previously critical of the competitive individualism of American education and economics developed "a new respect for the integrity we place on each human life and the freedom that this makes possible." But another traveler who had thought Americans hospitable and warm came home and was aghast at the omnipresence of police and the prevalence of fear in public life. Students sensitive to American imperialism were made to confront—perhaps by an Istanbul chemical company using American equipment, perhaps at a New Delhi Ford Foundation meeting —the possibility that our country may help other economies after all. Others, unaware of the exploitativeness of American capitalism

were thunderstruck that the USA, a nation of bounty, could com-
mandeer a nation's primary resources and thereby wield enormous
power over its political and cultural life. Some of us who had felt
we would be without common ground with the families we were to
stay with, in Japan, India, or wherever, marveled at how much of
la vie quotidienne was shared by the middle-classes the world over.
Others of us, convinced of the "global village," brothers of all mankind, became conscious of how deeply rooted we were in our native
culture and how fearful we could be of foreigners.

Of course, we did not always disprove our preconceptions—much
of the intellectual baggage we left with from San Francisco flew in
with us nine months later at JFK. Nor did we discover that everything is relative—the psychological costs of isolated individualism,
the effect of advanced technologies on less developed economies,
and the emergence of a world culture of shared characteristics all
have empirical aspects that defy vacillating relativism. The point is
this: our immersion in eight cultures around the skirts of Asia, in
central Europe, and in Scandinavia forced us to recognize what we
had projected onto other cultures and what we had overlooked in our
own. This act of cultural introspection was required if we were to
make order out of our intercultural experience, an act that many of
our contemporaries—whether die-hard conservatives, pleasant liber-
als, or flaming radicals—have yet to experience.

This does not mean that we arrived home as noncommital middle-
of-the-roaders. As a group, we were against a lot of things: the Indo-
china war, the buildup of weaponry, the politics and style of the Cold
War. We were dissatisfied with President Nixon (elected stealthily
in our absence, as if to summon us back to abandoned barricades).
We were also for many things: more openness toward China and the
Soviet Union in hopes that, with America, they could aid underdeveloped countries; a redefinition of American priorities so that our
way of life would attract young governments; an educational renais-
sance that would make men aware of dilemmas before mankind,
rather than emphasizing the problems between nations. We did have
and still have definite political views.

The difference is that our country believes you are either a part
of the problem or part of the solution—and we returned knowing
that we were part of both and can't really solve anything until we
realize it. We accepted our identity as Americans and even stood up

for America when it was more comfortable not to. But we also learned that to accept that identity wholeheartedly we would have to change America, raise its consciousness, so that its skills, money, and power would be used in humane ways, so that we could at last say with pride: We are Americans.

Why is it, after this trip, that I cannot rhapsodize on America's freedom and affluence or write lyrical poems on Kansas wheatfields and California ports? Perhaps it is because I am haunted by memories of a world not seen by most Americans—in particular, memories of young men like Huan, with whom I played ping pong, and Ramu.

Ramu was only one of a group of sixty Indians waiting to greet us at the New Delhi airport. Still, when I saw his handsome face with deep-set, piercing eyes, I thought: I hope *he* is going to be my "family" here.

To my pleasure, he was, and he was every bit as kind and intelligent as his eyes had shown. We returned to his rather simple home. He told me he had just passed his civil service examination and was working for the government.

As I sat in a wicker chair sipping the Fanta orange drink he had bought to welcome me, he asked me a question about America. "In New York City, I am told, there are many millionaires and there are many people who do not have enough food. How is this possible?"

I began to try to answer, explaining and qualifying, but his face reflected the inadequacy of my explanations.

The following night, as Ramu was driving us to a party, a speeding bus hit us, its square front plowing into the door on Ramu's side, throwing me out of the car. At the same moment my head was being slammed unconscious against the pavement the bent steering column was piercing Ramu's chest.

The next day—Christmas Day—he died.

At his funeral I cried. I cried for him, his grieving family, and because I could not answer his question.

Give me words, America, for Huan and Ramu, and then I will pledge my allegiance.

Chapter One | Changing Personalities

Traveling through many cultures tempts one to speak of groups and in generalities. Our impulse to do so, however, was somewhat restrained because we lived in families whose lives were set amidst important cultural and economic transformations. Instead of being Hilton tourists or visiting scholars, we were "sons" and "daughters" in the families of Japanese businessmen, Indian printers, Turkish civil servants, and Yugoslav farmers. We could not help but see that the tortuous changes called "modernization" were essentially changes in individual personalities.

The papers in this chapter are concerned with this human dimension of change. The first essay, "What is 'Modern'-ization?" asks whether American social science too often forgets that the economic and social indicators on which it relies refer to *people* like ourselves; and who are we to judge what is "modern" and what is not? Cross-cultural observation should make the traveler aware that he began in his own culture, that he sees other cultures from that vantage point, and that he had better do some soul-searching before he passes judgment on other national characters. In "Childhood and Culture in Japan" Lewis Perry shows how early in life one's culture affects his personality; he endeavors to describe—not to judge—family child-rearing practices quite different from ours. It is the task of nations to come to terms with each other *despite* their deep-rooted cultural separation, argues Ronaleen Ricciuti in "National Images and Personal Prejudice"—a task not only for government officials but for every citizen, a goal not only of politics but of education.

Increasing numbers of Americans in government, business, science, and education deal personally with people of other cultures or affect professionally the affairs of other nations through the decisions they make. On both levels Americans must forge a new ethic free of the historical pattern in which powerful countries, often for the noblest reasons, exploit weak ones. Before this internationalist ethic can be widely accepted and practiced, however, some men and women in all countries must defend the ethic before it appears practical.

Otherwise it never will be.

MARK GERZON

Harvard University

To be radical means to go to the root, and the root is man himself.

—KARL MARX

What is "Modern"-ization?

Social scientists agree that underdeveloped countries search for a model among the "modern" countries, and that, as Marx put it, the developed countries present the less developed with an image of their own future. Today, however, there are clearly multiple and conflicting images. Japan, America, the Soviet Union, Sweden, Yugoslavia—all provide different models. But how are we to compare them? Which nations are really modern? We cannot assess these models of modernity by examining social indicators (GNP, per capita income, literacy level) alone. Our judgments must also account for human, or psychological, factors.

If we begin by comparing some traditional with some totalitarian societies for their most salient psychological features, we may learn how human growth can be controlled.* Then, by applying this

MARK GERZON *is from Indianapolis, Indiana, and joined IHP from Harvard University. At Harvard, Mark's major interests were social and clinical psychology as well as writing; as a sophomore he authored* The Whole World Is Watching. *After IHP, Mark returned to Harvard and graduated in 1971, with honors and as a member of Phi Beta Kappa. Recently returned from Asia, Mark is presently on the staff of the Carnegie Council on Children in New Haven, Connecticut.*

---

* Traditional societies, as the name implies, are illiterate, agrarian, and economically underdeveloped; totalitarian societies are characterized by an authoritarian, centralized government.

method to ourselves, it will become clear that, although our society is neither traditional nor totalitarian, we cannot call ourselves modern—not if we define modernity as Marx did, as

a society in which the full and free development of every individual becomes the ruling principle [and] in which the free development of each is the condition for the free development of all.[1]

I

In terms of authority patterns, the major traditional societies we visited were strikingly similar. When Kazamias wrote that Orthodox Islam was not merely a religious unity but a political, social, and cultural one as well, since "it minutely regulated even the interpersonal relations of the members of the society,"[2] he could just as well have been speaking of traditional religion in early Japan or China or India. The following quotation could apply equally well to any of those societies.

The traditional Ottoman Islamic pattern was based on an authoritarian normative pattern. This was reflected in the relationship between the individual and the "government" . . . between man and woman, husband and wife, father and son, older and younger brother, and so on. In all interpersonal relationships, there was the same deferential attitude by those of "inferior" to those of "superior" status. These patterns of relationship were regulated in no small degree by the Islamic religion.[3]

These societies had not yet "escaped from freedom" because personal freedom did not yet exist. This is the psychosocial base from which all modern societies have risen.

Marx and Engels were decidedly removed from the "ideology" of traditional society. Devoting themselves to such ideals as democracy, freedom, and self-respect, opposing such bastions of traditionalism as religion, monarchy, and paternalism, they identified themselves as critics of fixed hierarchical authority.

It was the men of coercion, however, not Marx and Engels, who molded totalitarian communism. Unlike their intellectual predecessors in whose name they acted, these leaders were caught in a dangerous transition: modern enough to identify with the ideals of socialism, but traditional enough to retain the same hierarchical authority of feudal and prefeudal society.

According to Philip Selznik's analysis of Leninism in *The Organization Weapon,* a primary contribution of Lenin to Marxism was the fear of spontaneity: (1) the proletariat cannot be allowed to decide upon its real interests unguided; (2) only a highly trained, strictly disciplined elite (or "vanguard") can lead the proletariat to fulfill its historical destiny; (3) hence, the workers should be subjected to the centralized authority of the party.[4] What this accomplished, in fact, was the subjugation of the majority to the coercive power of the party.

So Marxism-Leninism had much in common with traditionalism, after all. The vanguard was but a modern version of the medieval priests (or, for that matter, the Anatolian *hojas*), and the same superior-inferior status prevailed. Lenin's fear of spontaneity was not unlike the clerics' fear of the people themselves actually reading the word of God and interpreting it without guidance.

Unlike bourgeois conservatism and clericalism, which denied the masses independence and equality for aristocratic or religious reasons, Lenin denied the proletariat its independence on the ground that only the vanguard could correctly guide the revolution—which was, after all, for the People. As Erich Fromm put it: "The crucial point in Lenin's position was the fact that he had no faith in the spontaneous action of the workers and peasants, and he had no faith in them because he had no faith in man. It is the lack of faith in man which . . . clerical ideas have in common with Lenin's concept."[5]

Moreover, as Jules Monnerot wrote: "The party structure is vertical and business proceeds exclusively along vertical lines."[6] With ruthless efficiency under Stalin, authority was further centralized, and along these vertical lines each inferior was dependent on his superior, for the very structure prevented group action on a single status-level. This was true not only within the Soviet Union but in the struggling communist cadres in Europe, as well. They, too, took direct orders from Moscow, and it was those revolutionaries who accepted this hierarchy that rose to power in the late Forties.

Implicit in this is the issue of "ideological posture." Just what types of opinions can be sanctioned? The most rapid method to persuade a traditional population to adopt a formal national ideology is to offer them a comparable structure. By providing a new hierarchy that resembles the old traditional structure, only ideological *content* must be changed; the ideological *posture* may remain. This is the method of totalitarian revolutions: they are limited only by technical problems (means of communication, organization, coercion) and not by social character, which remains basically traditional even though the ideological idiom has changed.

Brzezinski and Huntington write that in the initial phase of Soviet rule, the task of the youth organization was "breaking the youth's social and psychological relations with the 'past' society."[7] Ostensibly, the revolution was designed to make radically new men out of postrevolutionary generations. But, by strictly defining what is ideologically correct, by instituting a new infallible authority to replace the discarded religious one, and by rigidly controlling information, postrevolutionary generations are, in effect, given a new tradition—as uniform and dogmatic as the one they had to reject.

Totalitarianism fails quite tragically. It is beyond traditionalism in that it recognizes the question of social transformation and deals with more complex social phenomena. Totalitarianism attempts to organize society on the basis of traditional psychology, and so traditional psychology reappears as modern pathology. The traditional hierarchical pattern of dominance-submissiveness on the village and family level, when enlarged and distorted by communications, coercion, and totalitarian ideology, becomes a stark pattern of authoritarian control and destructive dependency.

Destructive dependency is important here because it is the situation in which the overwhelming majority of the members of totalitarian society find themselves. Erich Fromm concludes that in Stalinism (as in fascism) "the individual is made to feel powerless and insignificant, but taught to project all his human powers into the figure of the leader, the state, the 'fatherland' to whom he has to submit and whom he has to worship. He escapes from freedom into a new idolatry."[8]

These men are, literally, party products. They are the ones Trotsky called "fundamentally imitative" and "the adaptable type in search of protective color." It is, paradoxically, the bland and the submissive who become the bureaucracy for the revolution; or, as Monnerot puts it:

The communist politicians . . . are well aware that every man is most easily caught by playing on his weakness; the *weak point* of the individual becomes the *strong point* of the party.[9]

The totalitarian organization's strength is ensured by the individual's weakness; conversely, it would be challenged by his autonomy.

These are some of the social and psychological parallels between traditional and totalitarian societies. If we examine these societies in terms of human growth, however, the contrasts are marked.

In traditional society, human growth is characterized by *continuity*. Transitions from one stage to the next—from childhood to adolescence, for example—are managed with traditional rituals, the *rites de passage,* which ensure continuity. A child's personality (the *thesis*) is formed in a society which does not change, and his transition to adulthood is smooth.

In terms of social (not Freudian) psychology, the individual need not resist this transition (the *antithesis*), since his society remains ordered by unchanging rituals, symbols, and relationships. The adult personality (the *synthesis*) contains little more than the unfolding of the psychological thesis of childhood.

In the origins of totalitarian society, human growth is characterized by stark *discontinuity*—and here the antithesis, formed during youth, plays an important, if not dominant, role. Those who call themselves revolutionaries are always from societies which are changing, and almost always have backgrounds which attest to the primary significance of the antithesis.[10] Without the traditional *rites de passage* which helped the child to adapt to the existing traditional society, young revolutionaries experience intense antithesis— instead of adapting, they plan a whole new society.

The totalitarian avoids the problem of discontinuity by making it absolute (or, to use Erikson's phrase, "totalist"), by creating an "anti-tradition" which serves the same psychological purpose as the one it superseded. As Lifton says, " 'Hate your past to win your future' is the call of the totalitarians. But they might well have added, 'Do not hate it so much that you cannot bring us its sense of filial dedication.' The reformed intellectual was expected to be, as before, loyal, self-disciplined, obedient—now a filial son of the communist regime."[11] Men were asked to change their ideology, but not to change their servile relationship to it.

Because the totalitarian must resolve the conflict between old and new ideologies, he opts for one infallible dogma. Rather than attempt a social or personal synthesis, he imposes a set of fixed beliefs on himself just as he imposes an authoritarian control on his subordinates.

Both society and the self reflect the totalitarian's dialectic—both are repressive and authoritarian, both fail to achieve the "unity of contradictions" essential for human or social development. There is certainly a "dialectic process which results from growing individualism,"[12] in modern societies, but this can lead to freedom or to tyranny, to harmony or to a cacophony which the silence of traditional society could never imagine.

Bertrand Russell wrote in 1920, after a brief but intense affair with Bolshevism, that there is no *swift* way for a traditional society to achieve any *desirable* form of socialism.[13] His statement was not based on an underestimation of science and planning, nor on a misunderstanding of the possible means for accelerating social change. It was based on his acute understanding of human psychology.

When Russell and other humanists speak of socialism, they conceive of a society where every man has the maximum possibilities for autonomy. It is impossible, Russell is saying, for a society accustomed to rigid authority and unchanging dogma to be transformed swiftly into a free, egalitarian one. We would be fortunate indeed if we knew how to accelerate the coming of Trotsky's vision of a society in which the common man rises to the heights of an Aristotle, a Goethe, or a Marx. However, it is all too clear that ardent revolutionaries, attempting to accelerate too fast, become totalitarians and make that future society even more elusive.

In totalitarian communism this defect can be traced to Lenin's organizational weapon: his fear of spontaneity in the masses and his decision to have the vanguard work "in the People's interest." This demonstrates a disregard for human development. Marx himself wanted to eliminate the social hierarchy (aristocracy over peasants) and destructive dependency (worker upon capitalist owner); but totalitarian communism merely reinforces the old static structure. In his *1844 Manuscripts* Marx denied that communism itself is the goal of human development, and defined that goal as "the emancipation and rehabilitation of man," or autonomy.

This totalitarian disregard for the human factor can also be described in terms of the dialectics of human growth. The revolutionaries themselves give full credence to the antithesis, not only in their social philosophy but in their personal development. They view it as inevitable that they as young men rebelled against the social order.

"Rebellion is justified." But these same men permit no further rebellion, no more antithesis, social or personal. One distinctive feature of totalitarian societies is the sameness of views expressed by
youth organizations and adult authorities. It is a reversion to the
traditional pattern of unchanging human development, not a stride
forward.

The Soviet Union has developed its economy and technology, increased education, and met several criteria of modernity. But to decide whether Soviet society is really "modern," we must take a hard
look at the human aspect of modernity. Otherwise, statistics could
be made to show that the Soviet Union ranks as high as second
among the "modern" nations of the world.

The following section will focus on this problem. The point to be
made here is simply this: totalitarianism severely debilitates a society, not only during the transition from a subsistence to an industrial economy, but also during the transition from authoritarian to
autonomous personality. These transitions do not always coincide:
it depends on the society, and we must analyze both transitions to
understand their relationship. If it is our aim to find a durable and
meaningful definition for "modernization," then, in my opinion, we
must pay more attention to human, and less to economic, growth.

II

Although we moderns may debate what kind of modernity is pref-
erable, few of us would question the worth of modernity itself. Yet
modernity can have often unnoticed side-effects. Some of David Mc-
Clelland's findings underline this point. He considers that "certain
institutional and ideological changes carried out in Turkey since the
Revolution have indeed undermined the strong domination of the
Turkish father,"[14] and offers this as one explanation of the fast economic development of Turkey.

Normally, this social change would be considered positive (more
modern) because it raised the level of productivity. If we looked at
the standard social indicators, we would see only "economic
growth." But using McClelland's human indicators, we observe not
just "economic growth" but also the decline of the "authoritarian
father" and the "obedient son" syndromes and the weakening of
other "changeless social values." Thanks to McClelland's and similar studies, we get a fuller picture.

We moderns may still feel that the change is positive. We consider the loss of such authoritarian parent-child relationships to be as much in the interest of modernity as the economic growth itself. So it is possible to examine *both* human and social indicators in this case and without altering our conclusion that the overall change is positive. Since both the loss of authoritarianism and the gain in productivity are positive, the human and social indicators agree.

In speaking of human (or psychological) indicators, I refer to the indicators which give direct information about individual personality, in contrast to social indicators, which yield information about certain social attributes of the individual but fail to establish the human effects of these attributes. The use of human indicators runs the risk of being called unscientific, but if the aim is to understand the human aspect of social change, the social science approach is also vulnerable to this criticism.*

Social indicators provide information about the circumstances in which people live; and from this the human effects of these circumstances are inferred. These unscientific inferences did not suffer extensive criticism when researchers dealt with underdeveloped societies, and quite rightly. To infer that a man is now better off because he has enough to eat does not need extensive proof. But for us to infer that A is better off than B because he earns and spends twice as much, even though B has more leisure, a gratifying job, and an adequate income, is asking too much of social indicators. Such inferences can be made only with the use of human indicators.

The procedure of applying human and social indicators becomes much more complex as soon as we leave traditional society. In fact, economic and technological development in a totalitarian society may be based upon an *increase* of authoritarianism rather than, as in a traditional society, a decrease. Individuals may be exhorted to demonstrate their unreserved loyalty to leader or party by becoming technical wizards. And they can be made to reach even greater levels of productivity by rendering them more submissive to authoritarian control.

---

* As Albert Einstein observed: "Science cannot create ends and even less instill them in human beings; science, at most, can supply the means by which to attain certain ends. But the ends themselves are conceived by personalities . . . [and] we should be on our guard not to overestimate science and scientific methods when it is a question of human problems."[15]

But economic growth, as we have seen, is only part of the picture. If we apply a behavioral approach to the study of totalitarian society, we might well learn that the economic gains were achieved at the expense of human development. "Modernization" can no longer be a synonym for *socio-economic* "growth" or "development": it has to signify *human* growth and development as well.

The method we have applied to "traditional" and "totalitarian" societies must now be applied to "democratic" societies. Critics of democratic societies have fired a battery of charges against "grey-flanneled," "organizational," "automated," "conformist," "alienated," "consumer" society. Yet few such criticisms are as objective as those which can be made of totalitarian and traditional societies. Could we not use an integrated set of human and social indicators? Just as we achieved a clearer understanding of totalitarianism by analyzing both the human and the economic consequences of development, could we not apply a similar approach to the modern democracies?

Much as a political scientist compares political mechanisms in different governmental systems, the behavioral scientist would compare socio-psychological mechanisms. For example, both Fromm and Monnerot stress that the strength of the totalitarian organization is based on the weaknesses of its individual members, and that genuine individual autonomy would disrupt the system.

This observation applies equally well to modern democracies: genuine autonomy, for example, would disrupt the advertising business. If we still wish to shape a society which allows maximum autonomy, we cannot ignore this striking parallel between thought reform and advertising. Advertising firms, which inform the citizen that he is not sexy enough or that he won't be promoted or that he won't have friends unless he buys a certain product, create a similar psychological stress. Advertising success depends on the suggestibility of the individual; it undermines his sense of self-confidence or well-being by exploiting his self-doubts.

It can be argued, of course, that the individual himself actually wanted, or even needed, the product in question, and that he did not purchase it because his virility, sociability, or status was in doubt. But the point is this: the human effects of the psychological stresses created by advertising have not been systematically studied. Who knows how harmful such stresses are? Is it not disturbing that research on the human effects of advertising is thought somehow to be peripheral, purposeless, or even slightly subversive?

Once again, we have no assurance that the results yielded by human indicators would agree with those gained from social indicators. For example, on the basis of simple observation, it seems that young adolescents who have a warm home life and genuine personal relationships are less likely than their insecure counterparts to succumb to advertising. In terms of standard social indicators, which herald the creation of a "new market" as a result of increased youth-oriented advertising, this is an unambiguous step towards modernity. Yet a behavioral approach to this phenomenon might produce quite contradictory results. What is disturbing, once again, is the tacit assumption that when social indicators are positive, the human indicators need not be so closely studied; in other words, that the method which must be applied to totalitarian society need not, for some reason, be so rigorously applied to our own.

This concern with human indicators for modernity prompts Price to say: "In a saturation economy of science it is obvious that the proper deployment of resources becomes much more important than the expensive attempts to increase them."[16] And Galbraith writes that in a saturation economy "not the total of resources but their studied and rational use is the key to achievement." He adds that in the future the test of modern societies "will be less the effectiveness of material investment than the effectiveness of investment in man."[17]

Such "humanistic" warnings as these become widespread in America because of the point America has come to occupy on economists' S-curve, a graph which represents the percentage increase in annual GNP. Until recently, the economic development curve seemed to imply a similar curve of human development. Such an implicit analogy would now be ludicrous: the economic curve is leveling, yet the potential for human development is greater than ever before! So the relation between economic growth and human growth, at this level of productivity, can no longer be assumed; it has yet to be established. Yet the assumption seems to persist that the two factors increase in direct relation to each other at every point in the growth curve. Criticisms naturally arise when we are faced with the "logical" conclusion that human development must be "leveling off" as well.

III

Just as traditional and totalitarian societies inhibit autonomy, although in different ways, so would truly modern societies encourage autonomy. In the traditional society, the individual identifies with the absolute ideology on which his unchanging society is based. In the totalitarian society of the revolutionary generation, the individual identifies during adolescence with an absolute ideology opposed to the ideas of his childhood. And in the totalitarian society of the post-revolutionary generations, the individual identifies with the new totalitarian "tradition." Thus, both traditional and totalitarian societies produce an adult personality which remains fixed and immobile after youth and which perpetuates an authoritarian-submissive structure of relationships. But, the truly modern pattern would lead to an adult personality which is pluralistic—the individual would explore multiple and conflicting systems of ideas, and continue throughout adulthood to integrate them into a coherent, autonomous personality and social outlook, much as a truly egalitarian and pluralist political system would manage diverse interest groups.

Unlike the totalitarian, the truly modern adult neither hates nor denies his past, but integrates it. He recognizes no infallible source; he has a high tolerance of ambiguity. Moreover, he sees himself as the locus of decision-making, capable of coping with diversity through the exercise of his critical faculty and independent judgment. He prefers relationships based on equal status, finding the superior-inferior situation inimical to open communication. He considers individual participation, undiluted by "deference to authority," to be the basis of sound social organization. And he finds a pluralistic society —one in which divergent ideas and interests are allowed to compete freely—the best assurance of development. His highly developed empathy ensures his tolerance of diversity, for his own flexible personality absorbs multiple and conflicting traditions, perspectives, and experiences.

Young people in modern societies feel discontinuity, "a break in their sense of connection with the past" (Lifton), when they confront a world quite different from that their parents prepared them for. This is inevitable. What can be largely prevented, however, is their tendency to blame this discontinuity on someone's dishonesty or malice. Most of our childhood is spent learning a fixed system of ideas as if we still lived in a traditional or transitional society. Little if any consideration is given to *planning*—human, not economic—for the inevitable encounter with multiple and conflicting systems of ideas. The childhood thesis, in retrospect, seems narrow and exclusive: hence, the feeling of discontinuity and the suspicion of dishonesty or hypocrisy. If the same concern for planning were found in the educational as in the economic sphere, in dealing with human instead of material resources, the young would be better equipped to forge the all-important synthesis. Until planning is applied with the same vigor in human as in social development, "modern" lives will be disrupted by inefficient reform and violent personal revolution—and so, consequently, will "modern" societies.

To complete this transition from authoritarianism to autonomy, the individual must be taught to cope with competing ideas without reverting to authoritarian psychology—whether in the name of "law and order" or of "liberation." Adorno and his colleagues state that the political and social outlook of the authoritarian is characterized by "a desperate clinging to what appears to be strong and a disdainful rejection of whatever is relegated to the bottom."[18] In totalitarians the outlook is some form of the converse: a single-minded championing of whatever is "relegated to the bottom" and a virulent contempt for those in authority. Ideological content is changed, ideological posture is not; authoritarians substitute prejudice for empathy, and stereotypes for synthesis.

It is in keeping with our traditional overemphasis on quantitative indicators that we seek to make a pluralistic *society,* and simply expect that individuals will be properly molded. We should also seek to shape—through the media, education, and political style—a pluralistic *personality,* open to new ideas and capable of infusing a democratic society with them.

If we consider this factor of human growth, we clearly cannot yet speak of modern societies, societies in which all men are free to develop their potential. It is this factor—the human factor—which we need to make our concept of modernization durable. And it is the task of behavioral scientists to make it meaningful. Only by planning the human aspect of development can they approach the radical perspective which is now, as always, necessary; for only then will they have gone to the root—which is man himself. If they balk at this task, because the human factor defies scientific procedure or because their style and aim are confined to empty discourse, others whom they feel are less constructive might have to define what that radical perspective is.

NOTES

1. Quoted by Dwight MacDonald, *The Root Is Man* (Alhambra, Calif: Cunningham Press, 1953).
2. Andreas M. Kazamias, *Education and the Quest for Modernity in Turkey* (Chicago: University of Chicago Press, 1966), p. 196.
3. Ibid.
4. Philip Selznick, *The Organizational Weapon; A Study of Bolshevik Strategy and Tactics* (Glencoe, Ill.: Free Press, 1960).
5. Erich Fromm, *Sane Society* (New York: Holt, Rinehart & Winston, 1955), pp. 209, 220–221.
6. Jules Monnerot, *Sociology of Communism* (London: Allen & Unwin, 1953), p. 75.
7. Zbigniew K. Brzezinski and Samuel P. Huntington, *Political Power USA-USSR* (New York: Viking Press, 1965).
8. Fromm, *Sane Society,* p. 208.
9. Monnerot, *Sociology,* p. 117.
10. This was discussed in Japan with reference to the radical outlook of Zengakuren, whose youth had been caught in the conflict of pre- and postwar Japan, and in China with reference to Mao's own adolescence. Further, Bertrand Wolfe's *Three Who Made a Revolution* shows a strikingly similar pattern in the adolescence of Lenin, Trotsky, and Stalin.
11. Robert Lifton, *Thought Reform and the Psychology of Totalism* (New York: W. W. Norton & Co., 1961), p. 379.
12. Erich Fromm, *Escape From Freedom* (New York: Holt, Rinehart & Winston, 1941), p. 21.
13. Bertrand Russell, *Practice and Theory of Bolshevism* (New York: Simon & Schuster, 1967), p. 67.
14. Kazamias, *Education and the Quest for Modernity in Turkey,* pp. 197–200.
15. "Why Socialism?" *Monthly Review,* 1949.
16. Derek J. De Solla Price, *Little Science, Big Science* (New York: Columbia University Press, 1963), p. 112.
17. John Kenneth Galbraith, *The Affluent Society* (Boston: Houghton Mifflin Co., 1958), pp. 255, 352.
18. Theodor W. Adorno et al., *The Authoritarian Personality* (New York: W. W. Norton & Co., 1950), p. 971.

LEWIS PERRY III

Harvard University

Childhood and Culture in Japan

Japanese culture has long fascinated Westerners, and for good reason: Japanese society, religion, and art are based on premises directly opposed to the Western sensibility, and as a result Japanese behavior frequently seems "inscrutable" and "contradictory" to Western eyes. American interrogators during World War II were astonished at the cooperation of the same soldiers who, mere hours before, had resisted defeat and capture with fanatic fury. Western businessmen are appalled at the extent to which considerations of personal loyalty and group consensus will cause a Japanese to override obvious "business sense." European visitors are struck by the gentle kindness of Japanese within the home—and their brutal insensitivity on the street. In this essay I will attempt to explain these and other behavioral paradoxes by showing how they are consistent with certain psychodynamic patterns underlying Japanese culture.

LEWIS PERRY III *is from Colorado Springs, Colorado, and was enrolled in the English honors program at Harvard University before he became a member of the IHP group. At Harvard, Lewis was active in musical and dramatic performances and in writing, and planned for an eventual doctorate in cultural anthropology. Lewis resumed his studies at Harvard after IHP, and graduated in 1970. He is presently singing lead tenor professionally for the New England Regional Opera and the Boston University Opera Workshop.*

The most striking difference between Japanese and American child-rearing premises is that Americans try to develop children who exhibit "independent" characters, whereas Japanese parents try to raise children whose characters depend on external approval for decision making. Whereas Americans see life in dramatic terms, as the struggle of individuals against their fate, Japanese see life in organic terms, as the reconciliation of the leaf to the tree, and the tree to the forest. The Japanese child is taught to feel Freud's "oceanic feeling" as he acquires a sense of willing integration into an intricately, hierarchically organized universe, and to feel such an intense corporate identity with the groups with which he interacts that he will evaluate his achievements not as an individual production, but as a manifestation of Japan in one of its aspects.

The roots of Japanese dependency lie in the mother-child relationship in infancy and in early childhood. The central fact of the Japanese mother-child relationship is indulgence. A Japanese infant spends nearly every waking hour under the luxuriant attention of his mother. The mother takes great enjoyment in holding and cuddling her infant. When she does housework she rarely allows her infant to stray more than a few feet away, humming and chattering to him as she works, never relegating him to a playpen. When she goes to market, her baby is strapped loosely to her back. She eats with her infant on her lap, bathes with him on her knees, and sleeps with him in her arms. A Japanese child is never left to "cry himself to sleep" (unlike Western babies, whose mothers are afraid of pampering them too much) but is always immediately picked up and cuddled, whatever the cause of distress. Toilet training is lax.[1] Moreover, a Japanese mother virtually never strikes her infant, and is apt to be shocked at what appears to be Western cruelty in this respect.

Oral gratification for a Japanese infant is very great. He is fed whenever he is hungry rather than at fixed hours. Weaning is extremely late, often taking place only after the birth of a subsequent child, or when the infant has become two-and-a-half or three years old. Since the breast is not withheld on the basis of a fixed timetable, the separation of the self and the breast (and the mother) in the infant's psyche does not take place as early nor with as much pain as happens with Western babies. Since the mother is extremely indulgent, there is not the early object-division of the mother into the "gratifying mother" and the "withholding mother," as occurs in the

early development of the Western child, who is seemingly more separated and superficially more gratified than the Japanese child. It is
significant to note here that psychosis and paranoid schizophrenia,
which are related to maternal and oral deprivation, are statistically
insignificant problems in Japan, whereas in American mental hospi-
tals patients with these disorders fill forty-three of every hundred
beds.[2]

To understand the Japanese method of rearing a child, it is important to understand first the relative roles of the mother and father.
In Japan, for child-rearing purposes, the relationship within the
household between the father and mother corresponds exactly to
the pre-Meiji relationship between the Emperor and the Shogun.
Where the Emperor was owed a total mystical respect and allegiance, corresponding to the filial duty of Japanese children toward
their father, all of the actual administration of the country was in the
hands of the Shogun. Similarly, although the Japanese father maintains economic control within the household, and social dominance
outside the household, he is revered as an honored guest within the
home, and felt to be outside the intimate circle of the mother and
her children. He is almost entirely peripheral to the administration
of the household, and the discipline and training of the children is
entirely in the hands of the Japanese mother. This division of powers
has a vital significance to the Japanese child, because it means that
he cannot play off one parent against the other. Since the Japanese
father is typically reserved with his wife and children, in contrast to
the mother's indulgent intimacy, the child is forced into deeper dependency on the mother.

Simply in physical terms, Japanese childhood tends to foster dependency. A child is dressed by his mother through grade school.
More significantly, the Japanese family tends to sleep in the same
room until the children reach adolescence. The youngest child
sleeps on the mattress with his mother, the next oldest sleeps with
the father, and any older children with the grandmother or grand-
father. Much of the child's early life has been spent as an extension
of the mother's lap, arms, back, and face, without the experience of
such separations as playpens or cribs. Naturally, this intimacy reinforces a person's sense of corporate identity, since from early childhood he has had little chance to develop a sense of self.

Before discussing the role of shaming in increasing a child's sense of dependency, it would be useful to discuss the interaction of identification and dependency. Shame is an effective sanction only on someone who feels dependent on external approval, and such a dependency is possible only if the person identifies strongly with larger groups. The sanction works thus: "They are a part of me, and I of them; they are ashamed of me, so I too, must be ashamed." Since in the child-rearing process the parents' expectations have an enormous effect, it is crucial that the Japanese assume that a child is basically good, and that if made to understand he will incorporate the social process in the literal sense of making his body and mind a part of it.

Whereas Westerners emphasize the roles in society, the Japanese emphasize the totality of which these roles are a part. Westerners assume that a child has a "will of his own" and that only by firm and consistent sanctioning can he learn to obey and to submit his will to discipline. This assumption is early communicated to the child, who, internalizing the value of "will" and the expectation that to obey is to sacrifice his will, begins a lifelong struggle to win independence and gratification against the powers that act against him (starting with the parents) to limit his will.

Japanese parents begin with no such assumption. Rather, they see an infant or child as a helpless creature without a coherent "will" or differentiated self, his mind a *tabula rasa,* his dissent a function of naïveté rather than willful disobedience. Furthermore, Japanese culture does not place a premium on personality or uniqueness; a famous proverb goes: "The nail that sticks up must be hammered down." Consequently, the Japanese mother communicates to the child her hovering fear that he might become separated from "the way of the family" (*katuu*) and "the way of the world" (*ninjo*) and fall into certain disaster. There is not, therefore, the dichotomy that exists in the American child-rearing process, between the parents' wish for a strong-willed, independent child and their insistence on obedience. To the Japanese, mere obedience is of little value; what is important is that the child "understand."

As a consequence, the Japanese mother is extraordinarily objective in her responses to her child's behavior, being not at all ego-involved in the obedience/disobedience dimension of child-rearing.

Rather, she expects the child to trust her judgment, indulges him whenever possible, and gives in if he insists on something with a tantrum. The mother who does not give in to intransigence will be criticized for failing to understand the importance of the complaint to the child. Thus, it is not at all unusual on shopping days in the major Japanese cities to see a child pleading with his mother for a toy until, faced with a real tantrum, she gives in.

The resulting intimacy between mother and child further reinforces the child's identification with and dependency on his mother. The intimacy is further developed through the mother's openness to criticism, and especially to demands from her children. In a survey taken in Tokyo's eastern district, Asakusa, 200 mothers were asked to write dialogues depicting their relationships with their children.[3] Of the 142 questionnaires returned, 53 dealt with situations in which the children were critical of their mothers, and in 49 of these, the mother admitted her mistake. The following, from the forty-year-old mother of an eleven-year-old girl, is typical:

M: Change your clothes and get in bed now, Hanako-san.
D: *(Continues to stand.)*
M: What are doing?
D: *(Starts sobbing.)*
M: What are you crying for? How do you expect me to know? Tell me the reason or I can't sleep.
D: Mother, you talked to me so harshly that I felt miserable. I want you talk to me in a nicer way.
M: Yes, that's true. I'm sorry. I'll be careful to speak more gently from now on. Will you forgive me?

The objectivity of the mothers sampled was shown by their failure to chastise for noncompliance, their acceptance of guilt when criticized, and their use of "reasoning" to bring results. Mere recognition as the superior, or final, arbiter is not their interest.

Dependency is not merely an outcome, it is a sanctioned goal of Japanese child-rearing. The most powerful sanctions used to enforce dependency are shaming and the threat of desertion. These really work together, since in the shaming the mother builds up an intense fear of the outside world and of other people. Thus, two well-known Japanese proverbs are, "Outside your house lie seven enemies" and "Consider every stranger as a robber." Such a cultural view is reinforced in the shaming sanction: in the same study cited earlier, 67 percent of the respondents dwelled on the theme of "people will laugh at you" or "the whole world will laugh." Naturally, the implication is that proper behavior is not based on principles that are independent of persons (the Judeo-Christian ethic, for instance), but rather that public opinion is the salient criterion for behavior. What develops out of this is an extreme sensitivity to the approval of others, and a morality of relationship and particularism rather than of principles and universalism.

This dependency on others has further roots in the desertion phobia that is richly exploited by Japanese parents. Thus, a mother will create instant hysteria when she threatens to desert a child at the market. Whereas the Western child is threatened with being made to "stay home," the Japanese child is threatened with being locked out. A frequent sanction against a child who misbehaves in front of a guest is for the mother to ask the guest to take the child away and sell him.[4] Japanese shame and dependency derive their force from the sharp swing between total indulgence (not earned achievements) and the terror of separation.

Westerners have frequently assumed that "shame" is less deep in some sense than guilt, but this is not the crux of the difference. Rather, the crucial difference lies in the orientation of the sanction. Whereas guilt deals with violated principles, shame deals with real or imagined social consequences. Guilt presupposes a self-confident optimism that one might have done otherwise: "I should not have done this." Shame is more pessimistic, more an admission of helplessness and failure, and more nearly total: "I am incompetent." It may be interesting to note that American shame centers about tasks and occupations, since the child is made to feel that he must earn his parents' love through achievement; his inner-directed ego is stronger in social situations.

For Japanese it is the reverse. Parents' love is assumed in childhood; hence, tasks are not seen as self-definitions. However, shame is great in the sphere of social relations because one feels that he is as he is perceived by others. His identifications with various groups and his consequent sense of great dependency on their indulgence and benevolence can either gain him the sense of what the Japanese love to call *deru kuji*—being "completely enveloped"—or else a despairing sense of helplessness. Thus, as one observer has written: "Shame is man's grief at his separation from his origin. It is a feeling of inadequacy rising out of a fundamental separation from the ground of being. Shame is deeper than remorse."[5] One need only comment here that for the Japanese the "ground of being" is society.

Now that we have noted some of the psychodynamic forces at work in Japanese culture, we are in a better position to understand the seemingly paradoxical behavior of Japanese cited at the beginning of this essay. The captured soldier's cooperation with the Allies can be understood in terms of the soldier's shame-oriented sense of a totalistic, all-or-nothing identification with Japan. His sense of shame at being captured was so great that he felt he was irrevocably separated from the "ground of being"—that is, his nation, or his family, society, and past. Thus, nothing he could do or say could bridge this separateness. This action expressed his particularism and dependency-need. An American might be his enemy in principle, but this particular American was his superior; therefore, to preserve satisfactory inferiority-superiority relations, he cooperated.

This same principle of particularism explains the apparent contradiction in the gentleness and graciousness of Japanese within the home as opposed to their appalling insensitivity on the street—pushing in subways, cutting ahead in lines, and so on. It is well to remember that the generosity of Japanese receiving guests is based not on an ethic of hospitality but on a feeling of extreme dependency on the approval of the guest. The typical way of handling this is for a Japanese to establish himself as the inferior and thus bring out his guests' benevolence and indulgent approval. In striking contrast to the Chinese, whose proverbs reflect a preference for being feared rather than for being loved, the Japanese much prefer the role of the indulged inferior or the accepted group member to any decisive leadership capacity. Japan's leading psychoanalyst has written that most of Japan's leaders suffer from a sense of being surrounded by hostile critics.[6]

It is well to remember that aggression is very often a reaction to frustration. Hence, any person in a superior role in Japanese society will be the object of hostile feelings according to how much he frustrates the desire for benevolence and indulgence of those who feel dependent on his approval. Conversely, Japanese psychiatrists frequently find that the hostility of their patients toward specific individuals is a disguise for their secret desire to be loved, indulged, and taken care of by that person.[7]

In evaluating cultural change in Japan under the process of modernization, we must be aware of the possibilities for individuation; that is, an expansion of the role and importance of the individual in society. But individuation is not necessarily the inevitable outcome: expanding capitalism has increased Japanese mobility and broken down traditional hierarchies, notably that of the extended family. However, the inner-directed character, which sociologist David Riesman predicted would become modal in an expanding economy, has not in fact emerged in Japan. Although the reasons are not entirely clear, perhaps it is that Japanese "groupism" has simply adapted to capitalist conditions. Moreover, with increased communications and increasingly self-conscious youth peer groups, it is quite likely that Japan will skip directly to Riesman's stage of "other direction" from "tradition direction," bypassing the period of "inner direction" and individualism. In fact, some observers fear that Japanese children will grow up depending on others for their self-evaluation, yet also greatly suspicious of others, because of the breakdown of hierarchies and institutions and because economic individuation will create more possibilities for personal choice. In other words, modernization would free the individual but destroy his *deru kuji*—his sense of being "completely enveloped"—without replacing it with a sense of personal worth.

NOTES

1. Betty Lanham, "The Mother-Child Relationship in Japan," *Monumenta Nipponika*, 21, nos. 3–4, Sophia University, Tokyo. Miss Lanham describes in fascinating detail the manner in which the Japanese mother toilet-trains by anticipating the bowel movement, taking the infant to the toilet at the right moment, and then rewarding profusely for defecation. Sanctioning almost never occurs.
2. James Clark Moloney, *Understanding the Japanese Mind*, (Tokyo: Charles Tuttle Press, 1954). Although Moloney's figures date back to 1954, Dr. Takeo Doi, director of psychiatry for St. Luke's Mental Hospital in Tokyo, assured me that Moloney's findings were still accurate statistically with respect to Japanese patients. Dr. Graham Blaine, director of psychiatry at the Harvard University Health Services, substantiated Moloney's 43/100 statistic for American patients.
3. Lanham, p. 3.
4. Takeo Doi, "Amae: A Key Concept for Understanding Japanese Per-

sonality Structure," in *Aspects of Social Change in Modern Japan* ed.
R. P. Dore (Princeton, N.J.: Princeton University Press, 1967).
5. Dietrich Bonhoeffer, *Ethics* (Glencoe, Ill.: Free Press, 1954), p. 22.
6. The psychiatrist referred to is Dr. Takeo Doi (see note 2 above) the only
Western-trained psychoanalyst in Japan of Japanese nationality. His findings are based on his private practice and on a private study of the personal
writings of various Japanese leaders.
7. This is another of Dr. Doi's unpublished findings; at a recent conference of
Japanese psychiatrists and psychologists, one of the recurrent signs that a
patient was improving (substantiated by a great number of specialists at the
conference) was the patient's discovery of a long-repressed wish to be
indulged and loved by the object of long hostility.

BIBLIOGRAPHY

Ballon, Robert J., ed. *Doing Business in Japan.* Tokyo: Sophia University
Press, 1968.
Benedict, Ruth. *The Chrysanthemum and the Sword.* New York: Meridian
Books, 1946.
De Vos, George. "The Relation of Guilt toward Parents to Achievement in
Japanese Children" *Psychiatry,* Vol. 23, 1960.
Dore, R. P. *City Life in Japan.* Berkeley, Calif.: University of California
Press, 1967.
Lanham, Betty. "The Mother-Child Relationship in Japan," *Monumenta
Nipponika,* 21, nos. 3–4, Sophia University, Tokyo.
Moloney, James Clark. *Understanding the Japanese Mind.* Tokyo: Charles
Tuttle Press, 1954.
Norbeck, Edward, and Margaret Norbeck. *Personal Character and Cultural
Milieu.* Los Angeles, Calif.: University of California Press, 1965.
Reischauer, Edwin O. *The United States and Japan.* Cambridge, Mass.: Har-
vard University Press, 1957.
Smith, Robert, and Richard Beardsley, eds. *Japanese Culture.* Chicago: Al-
dine Publishing Co., 1962.
Vogel, Ezra F. *Japan's New Middle Class.* Berkeley, Calif: University of
California Press, 1963.

RONALEEN S. RICCIUTI

Allegheny College

Appearances to the mind are of four kinds. Things either are what they appear to be; or they neither are, nor appear to be; or they are and do not appear to be; or they are not, and yet appear to be. Rightly to aim in all these is the wise man's task.—EPICTETUS, *Discourses*

National Images and Personal Prejudice

Before 1950, what research there was on international behavior dealt primarily with national stereotypes, attitudes toward war and peace, and public opinion on foreign policy problems. Few researchers examined the actual interaction of nations and peoples. Few specialized in the psychological dimension of international relations, since most observers were more concerned with description. Few tried to explain the development of images and attitudes on the basis of interactions among nations or to explain the linkage between national stereotypes and foreign policy.

Recently, however, scholars have emphasized, as one put it, "the social psychology of international relations,"[1] a discipline which overlaps the interests of political science, sociology, and psychology and concentrates on the individual as a participant and respondent

RONALEEN RICCIUTI *is from Erie, Pennsylvania, and joined IHP from Allegheny College, Meadville, Pennsylvania, where she was majoring in political science and international studies. At Allegheny, Ronnie was an Alden Scholar and was involved with the theater. After IHP, Ronnie returned to Allegheny and graduated in 1970 cum laude, a member of Phi Beta Kappa. She is currently working on the research staff of* Changing Times *magazine, specializing in investment and taxes, and is also studying Japanese at American University in Washington, D.C.*

in his particular milieu. Political science thereby became concerned with, in the words of one political scientist, "(1) a more conscious consideration of context, with emphasis on environmental factors reflecting interdisciplinary findings; and (2) more systematic, more objective, handling of data which are 'observable and measurable.' "[2] This approach followed World Wars I and II as a reaction to the "states-as-sole-actors" approach which itself came into prominence following the Napoleonic Wars, when the idea of "nation-states" replaced images of princes and kings as sovereigns. Both the "individuals-as-actors" and the subsequent "decision-making" approach humanized international politics by calling attention to the human factor. However, the aim of replacing abstract notions of "state" with actualities of human "minds, wills and hearts" succeeded in replacing one set of abstractions with another. After all, it is equally abstract to study the individual plucked from the context of political acts which surround him.[3]

The following essay is based chiefly on studies I conducted in Japan in November 1968 and in India in January 1969. In each of these studies I circulated a questionnaire among high school students to discover any relationships between the students' opinions of a foreign country, the way the students ranked foreign nations in relation to their own, and the benefits students felt foreign countries could offer their country. In short, my purpose was to study the psychological and sociological factors affecting the images through which the ordinary man views the world.

I

It is well known in the social sciences that as Kenneth Boulding observes, people "do not respond to the 'objective' facts of the situation, whatever that may mean, but to their 'image' of the situation. It is what we think the world is like, not what it is really like, that determines our behavior."[4] Likewise, as Hans Morgenthau says of world affairs, the "foreign policy of a nation is always the result of an *estimate* [emphasis added] of the power relations as they exist among different nations at a certain moment of history and as they are likely to develop in the immediate and distant future."[5] Thus, the study of images is valuable because people, whether the leaders or the led, act in terms of them.

What, exactly, are images? As have other subjective concepts, images of nations have been defined in a variety of ways and with varying degrees of complexity. The more superficial approaches often refer to unsystematic collections of fragmentary impressions left by movies, stories, and accounts about other lands which we may never know personally. However, through research, more sophisticated approaches have been developed. Kenneth Boulding views images as highly structured products of past messages formed partly by "inputs and outputs of information" and partly by the inherent characteristics of the images themselves.[6]

In my study the Japanese characterized themselves as "careful, honest, moral, and hardworking" and the same students, regarding the United States as the nation with the most military attitude, viewed Americans as "wealthy, materialistic, aggressive, and practical." The Indian students were lavish in their praise of themselves as "philosophical, brave, artistic, strong, and hardworking." They assigned more negative characteristics to the Communist Chinese, who they felt had the most military attitude: "dishonest and aggressive." The Pakistanis were similarly described. These characterizations support the hypothesis that war expectancy tends "to be associated with a dislike of nations or the perception of them as dangerous."[7]

Further evidence indicates that the attribute of power "is a subjectively enduring aspect of a nation-image and that this quality too may be generalized over a variety of nation-objects."[8] But we must distinguish between the views of a direct participant and those of one who is only marginally involved. In considering the "cold war" between the United States and the Soviet Union, the Canadians who tended to feel apprehensive about one side in the struggle also tended to feel apprehensive about the other side. But the same concerns over both sides is not felt by the citizens of either of the two major powers confronting one another. In the views of the major participants, "our" side would be in the right, "their" side in the wrong.

In such a reciprocal (or mirror-image) view, each side regards the other as the aggressor; as having a government which exploits and deludes the people; as having a population unsympathetic to the government; as untrustworthy; and as advocating policies verging on madness.[9] Thus, it appears that power, a frequently applied attribute of national images, can involve as many different aspects and points of view as nations and individuals.

The basis for the formation of any image is rooted in perception.

Perception, commonly defined as the ways in which an individual deals with incoming information, has characteristics that apply with little modification to the way we view people or nations.

Social perception involves the *organization* of information about persons and the *attribution of properties* to them, often on the basis of only sketchy cues. These properties manifest *constancy,* in spite of observed variation, and are *selectively* attributed in the sense that they are influenced by the perceiver's psychological states. The processes by which information is organized are *flexible*; the same body of information is subject to patterning in different ways. Thus social perception refers to a set of processes that intervene between the presentation of information about a person and awareness of him.[10]

We perceive according to our training and experience, according to our mental set, our mental expectations, and according to our desires. For example, the Japanese smile when amused but also when they are forced to relate something unpleasant or when they are being scolded. In the first case, not wishing to burden others with unpleasantness and make them unhappy, the Japanese may smile, thus appearing harsh and cold to misunderstanding Westerners. In the latter case, smiling serves the purpose of smoothing over an otherwise unpleasant situation, although it appears to us that the Japanese is being insolent.[11]

According to Boulding, we eliminate error in perception by a process whereby our image of the past is shown to be correct or incorrect. This reality-testing and the subsequent alteration of images by processes of day-to-day "folk-learning" or by scientific observation is least effective in what he terms "the world of literary images," which is exactly where he places most theorizing about international matters.[12] Boulding seems to feel that reality cannot be tested on the abstract "literary" level.[13] Thus, reality-testing is an important concept in image alteration. Mirror-images of opposite international sides can be partially eliminated by direct contact and improved communication.

II

It is evident that individuals usually share the prevailing opinions of the group to which they belong, using that group as a standard by which to evaluate their own actions and those of others. Reference groups may be actual or desired, positive or negative; but in general it appears that people whose sociological characteristics are similar are more likely to feel favorable toward one another than those whose characteristics differ. This leads inevitably to a process of ethnocentric perception—the tendency to see and judge external occurrences in terms of the values, wishes, and expectations acquired as a member of a particular community. Just as we form stereotypes, we tend to project our frames of reference onto others; the great need here is to realize that our frame is as relative as the frames of others.

Closely related to ethnocentric perception is the concept of nationalism. The development of nationalism—in essence the feeling of "homeland"—is apparently the result of a long process which begins in early childhood and continues to about the age of twelve. This process is marked by a broadening of the world view and, it may be assumed, a relative broadening of the value system.[14] The home, the school, and the mass media are all sources of nationalism which, in combination with various psychological factors, act against "reciprocity of thought and action which is vital to the attainment of impartiality and affective understanding."[15] Nationalism also has a hint of irrationality about it that presents an obstacle to the development of empathy for peoples in other lands.

According to George Bernard Shaw, the Golden Rule should be reversed to read: "Do not do unto others as you would they should do unto you. Their tastes may not be the same."[16] The transformation of foreign lands by Western innovations may not be received with the warm thanks that Western developers expect if the people concerned have different "tastes." The social psychologist defines empathy as "taking the role of the other," and implies that this is an emotional, perhaps intuitive process whereby one person identifies with another.[17] Perception appears to be a necessary but not sufficient condition for empathy. More than simple perception is involved: we may empathize with a disaster victim known only through the media; yet we may not empathize with people we meet face-to-face for a brief time. Ideal empathy, permitting one to understand the motives and values of others, is spontaneous. Merely projecting one's own needs, interests, and attitudes upon another as if they were his is not empathy, but ethnocentrism.

III

The mass media, rather than creating new stereotypes and images, tend to reinforce the status quo. The media shape for us a picture of the world with which we have little contact, and can affect our attitudes, our knowledge, and even our behavior.

Society can provide direct contact with aspects of a foreign nation but there is no guarantee that direct contact will result in greater friendliness or understanding. The nature of the interaction between groups in direct contact is in large part determined by the reciprocal interests and goals of the groups involved. Thus, the aims of the contact are vital if positive reactions are to ensue. One of the most diligently researched and highly significant areas of direct contact is cross-cultural education—"the reciprocal process of learning and adjustment that occurs when individuals sojourn for educational purposes in a society that is culturally foreign to them, normally returning to their own society after a limited period."[18] In terms of William Scott's analysis of image formation, "cross-cultural education should be of a kind that would increase the probability of broadening the basis of an individual's self-esteem, reality-testing, self-knowledge, and range of compassionate concern for others."[19] In short, since there is no single successful type of cross-cultural education, it should at least attempt to permit sufficient broadening so that stereotypes can be eliminated and empathy encouraged.

Whether the goal of the specific program is to promote international understanding, technical training, or personal growth or education, each visitor brings to it his own preconceptions and expectations, his own motivations and national background—all of which tend to cause differing perceptions based on his experiences in the host country.[20] Moreover, it has been observed that

. . . as a consequence of previous socialization, sojourners learn value orientations which provide a framework for evaluating behavior in role interactions. The result is that when two members of particular social systems are interacting each can anticipate the other's responses with sufficient accuracy so that his behavior is likely to elicit the results he desires. This complementarity of role expectations generally becomes disturbed when an individual moves from one social system to another where differing value orientations and normative expectation are characteristic.[21]

An interesting aspect of this phenomenon involves the assignment of status to visitors in a host country. The fact that a student comes from a country he recognizes as low in status does not, in itself, mean that his attitudes of the country he is visiting will be unfavorable. But if a student compares his idea of his country's status with the ideas of the hosts and finds that the hosts place it much lower, his attitudes of the country are more likely to be unfavorable.[22] Unfavorable attitudes are also more likely if the visitor has few close friends. It has been found that Europeans visiting America are much more likely to have bad impressions.[23]

After returning home, a student's attitude can change depending on the social conditions and his expectations of the home culture. The security of the student's position on return seems particularly important here. For example, a Japanese student desiring to study abroad must consider his career stage at that moment. Close personal relationships, promising future career opportunities, are formed in prep school and university. The student going abroad, therefore, may well be leaving his career behind him.[24] To avoid problems on returning to the home culture, the most productive students sometimes remain in a foreign country.

Since most national images are based completely on second-hand information, one has few opportunities to test the reality of the image. Thus, the influence of group norms as standards of judgment are invaluable; it is here that the school, the home, the church, and other such institutions play their important roles. The communication media and political parties are similar shapers of national images—but these institutions often find it advantageous to build simplistic, undifferentiated images.

IV

In conclusion, I feel I must add a few words emphasizing the potential value of studies of "international behavior" conducted by the social sciences. Cases where the behavioral sciences have contributed directly to foreign policy are few and in those that can be found, the relationships are often tenuous.[25] However, social scientists seem to agree with government officials, who allocate funds each year for furthering behavioral studies, that the behavioral sciences can contribute to international relations and to foreign policy.[26]

At present there are several reasons why greater use is not made of recommendations from the behavioral sciences. Some of the reasons are: (1) most foreign policy decisions are made swiftly, and behavioral information often comes much too slowly; (2) the language of the social sciences is often "impenetrable" for foreign policy personnel; (3) in the past the social sciences ignored historical and political contexts; (4) the advice of behavioral scientists, when requested, is often too theoretical; (5) government security makes certain studies difficult; and (6) there appears to be a prejudice against the behavioral sciences among foreign policy personnel, especially the old guard.[27]

However, the barriers are slowly being removed. In the first place, the behavioral sciences have recently begun to focus on specific issues. Moreover, there now appears to be more of a chance for constructive change in the private and academic spheres than in the governmental sphere with its complex bureaucracy. In any case, international relations research is needed in the areas of conflict resolution, the personal bases of aggression, national imagery, public opinion, the psychological basis of national involvement and sovereignty, and the social and psychological conditions necessary for international governing bodies.[28]

My research abroad, and this more theoretical essay, were undertaken to help meet these needs. In a world of nuclear armies, understanding how nations perceive each other is no longer a merely academic concern. Other nations must gain a more accurate image of us, and we of them. The United Nations' Economic and Social Council recognizes the importance of national imagery in the Preamble of its Constitution: "Since war begins in the minds of men, it is in the minds of men that the defenses of peace must be constructed." Our system of public education, our news media, and our governmental agencies—the foremost shapers of national images—must ensure that the impressions we form of other nations are based on objective information rather than the prejudices of the misinformed or the propaganda of political expediency. Only by seeing other cultures more clearly, and by helping other nations better understand us, can the defenses of internationalism be universally established in the minds of men.

NOTES

1. Herbert C. Kelman, "Social-Psychological Approaches to the Study of International Relations: Definition of Scope," in *International Behavior: A Social-Psychological Analysis,* ed. H. C. Kelman (New York: Holt, Rinehart & Winston, 1965), p. 3.
2. Marian D. Irish, "Advance of the Discipline?" in *Political Science: The*

Advance of the Discipline, ed. Marian D. Irish (Englewood Cliffs, N.J.: Prentice-Hall, 1968), p. 13.

3. Arnold Wolfers, "The Actors in International Politics," in *Theoretical Aspects of International Relations,* ed. William T. R. Fox (Notre Dame, Ind.: University of Notre Dame Press, 1959), pp. 83–84.
4. Kenneth E. Boulding, "National Images and International Systems," *Journal of Conflict Resolution* 3 (June 1959): 120.
5. Hans J. Morgenthau, *Politics Among Nations: The Struggle for Power and Peace,* 4th ed. (New York: Alfred A. Knopf, 1967), p. 76.
6. Boulding, "National Images," p. 121.
7. William A. Scott, "Psychological and Social Correlates of International Images," in *International Behavior: A Social-Psychological Analysis,* ed. H. C. Kelman (New York: Holt, Rinehart & Winston, 1965), p. 73.
8. Ibid., p. 74. Some evidence for this statement can be found in the public opinion surveys. In 1959, responses of Canadians who felt that Russian power during 1960 would increase were found to be negatively correlated with the belief that Russian communism would fall by 1980. Also, a view that Russia had had a successful past decade was linked to the belief that its power would continue to increase. The Canadian results showed similar positive correlations concerning the future success of Russia, America, and Great Britain.
9. Urie Bronfenbrenner, "The Mirror-Image in Soviet-American Relations: A Social Psychologist's Report," *Journal of Social Issues* 17, no. 3 (1961): 46–48. An interesting comment on the importance of images is Dr. Bronfenbrenner's statement that "so long as we remain victims of the re-assuring belief that the Soviet Union can only acquire adherents by force, we are likely to underestimate the positive appeal, especially to economically backward countries, of communism not only as an ideology but as a technology that seems to work." Ibid., p. 53.
10. Theodore Newcomb, Ralph H. Turner, and Philip E. Converse, *Social Psychology: The Study of Human Interaction* (New York: Holt, Rinehart & Winston, 1965), p. 157. This is a paraphrase of a quote by C. E. Osgood in *Methodology and Theory in Experimental Psychology* (New York: Oxford University Press, 1953), pp. 193–194.
11. Otto Klineberg, *The Human Dimension in International Relations* (New York: Holt, Rinehart & Winston, 1964), p. 136.
12. Kenneth E. Boulding, "The Leanring and Reality-Testing Process in the International System," in *Image and Reality in World Politics,* ed. John C. Farrell and Asa P. Smith (New York: Columbia University Press, 1967), pp. 2–5.
13. Although Boulding demands reality-testing to revise images, he himself develops a friendliness-hostility guide which depends in part on the nebulous concept of power. Although he admits that his system is oversimplified, it appears to me to be totally inoperational, belonging only in the "literary world."
14. Jean Piaget and Anne-Marie Weil, "The Development in Children of the Idea of Homeland and of Relations with Other Countries," *International Social Science Bulletin* 3, no. 3 (Autumn 1951): 562.
15. Ibid., p. 578. A vivid description of nationalism is given by J. B. Priestley in "Wrong-ism," *New Statesman* 71 (25 February 1966): 253. "Nation-

alism, the rotten meat between two healthy slices of bread . . ." (the slices are regionalism and internationalism).

16. George Bernard Shaw, quoted in Klineberg, *Human Dimension*, p. 69.
17. Charles W. Hobart and Nancy Fahlberg, "Measurement of Empathy," *American Journal of Sociology* 70 (March 1965): 596.
18. M. Brewster Smith, "Cross-Cultural Education as a Research Area," *Journal of Social Issues* 12, no. 1 (1956): 3.
19. George V. Coelho, "Personal Growth and Educational Development through Working and Studying Abroad," *Journal of Social Issues* 18, no. 1 (1962): 62–63.
20. An example might be the Japanese student abroad. An old Japanese saying is, "If you love your child, send him on a journey." The purpose of the journey may not be only self-enrichment. From the Meiji era to the modern day, Japanese students were sent abroad often for Japan to reap the future benefits of their training. Secondary in importance during Japan's early development was promoting understanding. *See* T. Watanabe, "Social Aspects of Educational Travel in Japan," *International Social Science Bulletin* 8, no. 4 (1956): 642–644.
21. Gullahorn, and Gullahorn, "Extension of U-Curve," p. 34.
22. Richard T. Morris, "National Status and Attitudes of Foreign Students," *Journal of Social Issues* 12, no. 1 (1956): 20–25.
23. Claire Seltiz, Anna Lee Hopson, Stuart W. Cook, "The Effect of Situational Factors on Personal Interaction between Foreign Students and Americans," *Journal of Social Issues* 12, no. 1 (1956): 44.
24. Eugene Jacobson, Hideya Kumata, and Jeanne Gullahorn, "Cross-Cultural contributions to Attitude Research," *Public Opinion Quarterly* 24 (Summer, 1960): 215.
25. A more direct example would be the suggestion of social anthropologists that the Japanese Emperor be retained during the final days of World War II, and that his fate be left up to the Japanese themselves. This decision proved wise. *See* W. Philips Davison, "Foreign Policy," in *The Uses of Sociology*, ed. Paul F. Lazarsfeld, William H. Sewell, and Harold L. Wilensky (New York: Basic Books, 1967), p. 392.
26. Ibid., pp. 399–401. The Subcommittee on International Organizations and Movements of the House Foreign Relations Committee calls repeatedly for contributions from behavioral science to the psychological and ideological dimension of foreign policy. Several Federal agencies allocate funds for research and keep track of government and private studies. Also, in 1964, the Foreign Area Research Coordinating Group first met. It includes such agencies as the State Department, the Department of Health, Education, and Welfare, the Department of Agriculture, the Agency for International Development, the Central Intelligence Agency, and the US Information Agency.
27. Ibid., pp. 405–410.
28. Daniel Katz, "Current and Needed Psychological Research in International Relations," *Journal of Social Issues* 17, no. 3(1961): 69.

Chapter Two | # Changing Cultures

Individuals are bound together in cultures—but what is a culture? What is it that makes us feel more or less at home in America but decidedly out of place elsewhere? Is it the houses, the TV, the landscape, the flag? What could one take away and still have a singular culture distinct from all the rest? If American women wore *saris,* and Indian women wore minis, the two cultures would still be quite identifiable. If India were an industrialized state and America largely agricultural, however, could either culture still be called "American" or "Indian"?

Despite their different approaches, all the students in this chapter search for answers to fundamental questions about the cultures we studied. With a historical perspective, George W. Cooper examines the early sources of cultural change which swept through eighteenth-century China and drove the country to ultimate unification. As much as culture is a shared sense of history, however, it is also a shared set of values. In her essay on women, Marcia J. Carpenter writes about the values that societies place on womanhood, and discusses how changing perceptions of women's social and political status ultimately change the nature of a society itself. Language is clearly one of the most powerful bonds of culture. Louise A. Lerner's study of multilingual India outlines the impediments to uniform cultural change when men in the same country cannot communicate with one another in a common language to discuss their shared destiny. Finally, medicine is the sphere in which Kathy Sue Williams Doner searches for a definition of culture. When a question of medical treatment is involved, we can hardly afford to shut ourselves off from sources of understanding—whether from within our own culture, or from without.

History, sexual equality, language, medicine—these are but four aspects of culture. Communications, weapons, products, transportation—the children of technology—all enable America to influence other cultures with an impact never before possible. If this power is to be used not merely for our own aggrandizement but for the benefit of man, we must gain a new respect for other men, and determine what *they* can teach *us*. In the following essays on culture, we may learn more accurately what makes our culture American, and what we must do to understand those which are not.

We students learned that to exercise this cultural empathy is not, as is often supposed, a charitable act by which only others benefit. On the contrary, it is to our benefit as well. Within our borders we Americans view ourselves only in mirrors of our own construction, and much about us remains hidden by our own handiwork. When we go abroad, however, we may come to see reflections of ourselves which are far more illuminating, both when they are flattering and when they are not.

As patriotic government officials are always reminding us, we should not spare our foreign critics a swift, forthright reply. But neither should we proudly close our ears to the thoughtful cultural criticism which comes from abroad. Observation is sometimes more accurate at a distance—and few Americans have achieved this distance. Until we do, the eyes of our foreign neighbors provide a perspective which, though unrepresented in the poll booths at election time, will play a decisive role in our national future.

GEORGE W. COOPER

Holy Cross College

Civilizations decay in the measure that they become conscious of themselves.

—LAWRENCE DURRELL

China: The Collapse of the Middle Kingdom

I. THE PILLARS OF CHINESE CIVILIZATION

TRADITIONAL CHINA: THE MIDDLE KINGDOM

The great land mass of China is separated from the rest of Asia by wide deserts and rugged mountain terrain. It is in itself a fertile region with a great variety of climate and soil, fit to nourish and sustain a major culture almost wholly isolated from any other. Eastward of China stretches the Pacific. A few small islands, the larger Japanese and Philippine groups, are all that early man could hope to reach by voyaging on that sea. The sea was the end of the world, leading nowhere and linking nothing. The Mediterranean, the central sea and highway of the ancient Western world, has no counterpart in the Far East.

GEORGE W. COOPER, *originally from Arlington, Virginia, came to IHP from Holy Cross College in Worcester, Massachusetts, where he was enrolled in the economics honors program. He graduated from Holy Cross with honors in 1970 following his year with IHP, and is currently working toward a masters degree in Asian studies at the University of Hawaii. George is also a teaching assistant in a University of Hawaii survival program which concentrates on the methodology of organizing for ecology and peace, and is active in local political groups.*

For many centuries China was therefore a world apart, even when coasting voyages brought a slight contact with southern Asia, and when caravans crossed the central Asiatic deserts; yet even then the contacts were few and their effects delayed. The Chinese people developed the main features of their civilization alone and adapted themselves to their peculiar environment. It was not until the adaptation had long been made and its pattern set that foreign influences first seeped in to diversify the uniform character of Chinese culture. The basic elements of the Neolithic (or Stone Age) culture of the Western world are also found in China; but the next steps —the advance to literacy, the organization of government, the development of abstract ideas and religion—were taken in China by Chinese alone.

The circumstances of the ancient Chinese prevented the rise of the concept of nationality in the sense in which it appears at a very early period in the Western world. The Chinese distinguished between civilized and barbarous peoples, though they did not put all the latter into one category, nor did the names they gave them have the same semantic force as the term "barbarian" had to Greeks. As explained by C. P. Fitzgerald,

Northern nomadic peoples in the steppes beyond China were Jung, Ti, and later Hu. Southern forest dwellers who were rice cultivators like the Chinese, but backward, were Man. Western mountain people from the fringes of Tibet were Chiang. At a very early period the Chinese of the Central Kingdom knew themselves as Hsia, the term "All the Hsia" standing for the loose group of separate states, which although politically independent, were linked by culture and language.[1]

An economic reality lay behind this terminology. The nomadic peoples were not cultivators; the Chinese and the southern Man were not pastoralists. Therefore, the southern peoples could be absorbed, civilized, made into Chinese (Hsia), and gradually admitted into the circle of civilized states. But the northern nomads remained beyond the pale. Their steppes yielded no crops. It was profitless to conquer such a country; all that could be done was to keep its dangerous inhabitants from raiding into China. Thus the steppes, and later the Great Wall, set a limit to the bounds of northern civilization.

No such limit was imposed on southern expansion. The peoples of southern China emerged around 1000 B.C. grouped, like the older north, into states to whose rulers Chinese pedigrees were attributed, legitimizing them as now among the civilized. It was accepted and recorded that these southern peoples did not speak the same language as the northern peoples. Whether or not it was a different language, or a different dialect, cannot now be determined. But this fact did not make them foreign in the sense that the Chinese recognized the northern nomads as forever alien in their land. The contests of the warring kingdoms, north and south alike, were seen as the struggles of princely houses for supremacy, not as the conquest of one people by a foreign race. Statesmen, nobles, and warriors could change their allegiance, could travel the land in search of a just prince or a worthy master, as did Confucius. This would not have been betrayal of the home country.

The sense of unity, of belonging to a civilization rather than a state or nation, was thus very ancient. It transcended political allegiances. It formed in later times the foundation for the acceptance of the firm and enduring centralized government which first united the region in the third century B.C. It was an ideal which could be transmitted to the southern peoples as they were absorbed into the group of older civilized states. This sense of unity then, mightily supported by the absence of any rival center of civilization, gave the Chinese the concept of the Middle Kingdom.

Unity was further manifested and bolstered by a recognition of the supreme leadership of a king who was both ruler and priest. He was the sole priest of the highest deities, and the authority of his noblemen was measured by the right to perform certain sacrifices to certain deities. Only the lord of a territory might perform those to the gods of the soil and the crops; only the supreme king those to the deity of heaven. Thus, far back there arose the twin concepts of hierarchy and orthodox doctrine, both embodied in the concept of the Middle Kingdom. As we read in *The Sayings of Mencius*, "the king was a priest, the director of irrigation and flood conservancy, the general, and the expounder of sacred matters: arbiter of heaven and earth."[2]

Divine monarchy became the set pattern of government at an early period, and the form was not questioned until modern times. Chinese political philosophy never concerned itself with the form, but only with the content of government. Monarchy was never in dispute. How to train the monarch to perform his proper duty, what system of rule he should follow, who should be the instruments of his government—these were the problems which for centuries were hotly debated by the Chinese philosophers. These thinkers, men whose speculations upon the nature and purpose of the universe paralleled those of their contemporaries the Greeks, never engaged, like the Greeks, in disputation upon the form of government. No ancient Chinese terms meaning "democracy" or "aristocracy" ever existed. But the Chinese sages did contend, and very actively, for opposed systems of autocratic rule.[3]

The monarch was therefore at the pinnacle of civilization. Neither his position, nor the status of his elite literati, nor the value of the culture for which he mediated with heaven, was questioned in premodern China.

THE CONFUCIAN BUREAUCRACY

To rule the sprawling Chinese empire demanded a well-disciplined bureaucracy. Quite naturally, its manner of selection and formation, being deeply rooted in Chinese history, was distinctively Chinese. The roots were in the writings of a single individual, Confucius, the interpretation of whose thoughts became coterminous with civilization.

Confucianism was an ethical system which prescribed conduct according to social status. Its complex of rules stemmed from the Chinese perception of the relationship of man to nature, a relationship so intimate that human conduct is reflected in acts of nature. Man is so integral a part of the natural order that improper conduct on his part will throw the whole of nature out of joint. Therefore, man's conduct must be made to harmonize with the unseen forces of nature lest calamity ensue.

This was the rationale of the Confucian emphasis on right conduct on the part of the ruler, since the ruler was thought to mediate between men and the forces of nature (heaven). As the Son of Heaven, he maintained the universal harmony of man and nature by doing the right thing at the right time. It was therefore logical to assume that when natural calamity came, it was the ruler's fault. It was for this reason that the Confucianists became so important. Only they, by their knowledge of the rules of right conduct, could properly advise the ruler in his cosmic role.

The central point of this theory of government was the idea of virtue, which was attached to right conduct. To conduct oneself according to the rules of propriety, or *li,* in itself gave one a moral status or prestige. This moral prestige in turn gave one influence over the people. On this basis the Confucianists established themselves as an essential part of the government, especially competent to maintain its moral nature and so retain its legitimacy, the Mandate of Heaven. As interpreters of *li* they were technical experts, whose explanations of natural portents and of the implications of the ruler's actions could be denied or rejected only on the basis of the Classics, the ultimate repository of Confucian wisdom, of which they themselves were the masters. Entry into the ruling elite was thus a function of knowledge of the Classics.

An elaborate examination system testing one's knowledge of the Confucian Classics was developed as the means of formal entry into the imperial bureaucracy. It was designed with great consistency.

Every detail was thought out: a gradation of examinations from the provincial to the capital level; guarantees against cheating and outside help; objective valuation through identification by numbers instead of names; continual testing of an official on active service by means of annual achievement reports based on objective criteria, such as the population increase or decrease in the district concerned, or the number of criminals apprehended.[4]

Examination standards were very high. In some provinces of the Manchu period, ninety-eight percent of the candidates failed.[5] A carefully restricted staff of top officials, some chosen personally by the emperor, had the privilege of proposing candidates for advancement to the highest ranks, but they were obliged to guarantee the quality and good conduct of their candidates.

In this way an impressive system of unity arose, and one of its most striking elements was the underlying desire to open the doors of government employment to every kind of talent, regardless of social origin. In reality, of course, the system was not so democratic. Apart from the members of a few despised occupations (for example, merchants), anyone was free to apply for admission to the examinations. However, the knowledge required for them demanded years of study, something which only a minority could afford. Here the clan was vital, for it could provide stipends. The clan viewed the members that it supported as investments, and it was always worthwhile to have an active representative in the regional or, better still, the central administration. But here too the outsiders could not really compete with the wealth at the disposal of the well-established clans.

Despite its intricate bureaucracy, however, the empire was never feudal, as the term was used in the West. The Confucianists needed the centralized state and therefore had very serious antifeudal commitments. Furthermore, Confucian intellectuality ran counter to the feudal admiration of martial vigor. War was for the young, and the Confucian reply to a Western pantheon of heroes was a turn to the elders, to wisdom over courage, and to a system of examinations of learning as the ideal road to power and prestige, circumventing those guarantees of status which feudalism accorded to birth. And the examinations stressed a traditional learning, not original thought, because age over youth means not only counselor over warrior but old over new: "the rule of precedent and example."[6]

THE PEASANTRY

The Chinese peasantry was, and still is, the great heap of humanity beneath the ruler and his bureaucracy.[7] This huge class was the third pillar of the empire. Its function was simply to produce food and remain docile. Several quotes from Confucius (in the *Analects*) will help us to understand the peasants' position and their relation to the ruling class:

With the portion of mankind that is above average one may speak of the higher things; with those below it, one may not.

The people can be made to follow, but they cannot be made to understand.

On another occasion Chi-sun Fei inquired, "Suppose I slay those who do not follow [the] System, so that only the followers thereof are left?"

"Why do any slaying in your exercise of government? If you yourself desire competence, the people will indeed be competent. Excellence in the prince may be compared to the wind; that in the people to the grass. When the grass is put upon by the wind, it must bend."[8]

The peasantry's acceptance of a government was critical to the government's success. They could not be effectively controlled by force for they chose to be unruly only when compelled by conditions to choose rebellion and banditry or starvation. This desperate choice recurred throughout history, oftentimes as if according to Malthus. When it occurred, the bureaucracy would abruptly close ranks; for bureaucrats, due to their favored situation, were in a far better position to protect their personal interests and those of their clans than were the peasants, the suppliers of wealth. In times of relative scarcity, the bureaucracy would tend not to lessen their demands upon the peasants. Furthermore, the worsening of this problem would be accelerated by the tendency of the bureaucrats to increase taxation and to secure more administrative positions for their clansmen.

II. THE PASSING OF THE EMPIRE

THE MANDATE OF HEAVEN

Foreign invasion and civil strife are nothing new to the Chinese. They have spent a great deal of their history enduring agrarian uprisings, civil wars, and violent invaders. Indeed, so regularly has violence appeared and so often has the ruling dynasty been swept away by it that some historians have come to view these occurrences as cyclical—a patterned passing of the Mandate.

The theory of the Mandate of Heaven, the right of rebellion, has been called the Chinese Constitution. It is important to investigate who exercised this right, who rebelled successfully, and who failed to achieve the Mandate.

Rebellions in China, from the foundation of the centralized empire, fall into two classes: the great peasant risings, often associated with religious movements, and the insurrections of powerful generals. There have been many great peasant risings. There were two in the first empire, two during the Han (the next dynasty), another at the end of the T'ang dynasty (c. 900 A.D.). The founder of the Ming (c. 1400 A.D.) was the leader of such a movement; another dethroned his descendants. In the last century the T'ai P'ing rebellion conformed closely to this type. The Boxer movement at the beginning of the present century was essentially similar. Now with one exception all these great peasant uprisings that swept across the empire failed to overthrow the feeble and degenerate dynasties which they opposed. All the rest were ultimately defeated. They shook the throne soundly but could not overthrow it. In each case the weakened dynasty succumbed a few years later to some military adventurer who had risen either in the ranks of the rebellion or in the armies raised to suppress the rebels. The single exception was the peasant rebellion which drove the Mongols from the throne of China and founded the Ming dynasty.

Why did Ming Hung Wu succeed when all the others failed? It was certainly not through superior education.

Chu Yuan-chang, the man who reigned as Hung Wu (king) of the Ming, was born in the poorest dregs of society. He was left a famine orphan at an early age, became a beggar, a Buddhist monk, a bandit, and then a leader of rebels. For many years he fought his way slowly to the forefront of the nationalist movement against the Mongols, which eventually threw them out. His success was in part due to military ability, to skillful alliances with other rebels, and *above all* to the fact that, leading a movement of peasants risen against the perennial injustices of landlord and official exactions, he welcomed to his standard the scholars who resented their exclusion from the government by the Mongols.[9]

Ming Hung Wu, in fact, led more than a peasant rising: it was a national rising, one of the very few in Chinese history before modern times. His success was due to the alliance of scholars and peasants, the two classes upon which all Chinese government must rest. The first by virtue of their education are essential to the workings of government. The second must give their consent to be governed. If they withhold it no regime can stand; if the scholars withdraw, no system can work.

No other peasant rising commanded this dual support. The scholars "drew back from the religious rites and incantations" of the other peasant rebellions.[10] They would always rally around the throne, however bad, however weak, if the throne was willing to use them. When the peasants were beaten some general could be allowed to usurp the throne, since he would surely take over the civil service as a going concern, and the scholars for their part would ratify his act by declaring that the Mandate of Heaven had passed. The Mongols made the fatal mistake of both fleecing the peasants and excluding the scholars from employment and hopes of preferment. They thus raised up against them the irresistible combined force of both these classes and were destroyed.[11]

The Mandate of Heaven theory works out in practice as a justification for military insurrections which succeed with the blessings of the scholars. Rebellions contrary to the interests of that class did not succeed. The real character of Chinese rebellions is thus twofold: on the one hand there are peasant risings which do not succeed in founding new regimes; on the other, military usurpations which obtain the backing of the civil service. The Confucian scholar was certain that whatever king might reign, he would be called upon to serve, for he was essential to government. A Chinese change of dynasty was *not* a revolution. It was a change of government, sometimes carried out by force, more often by the exercise of superior power without bloodshed. Rebellions rarely overthrew dynasties, but when they did the scholars hastened to enlist under the banner of the victorious rebel and assure him of the Mandate of Heaven—provided he in turn was willing to use them and carry on the system of government they understood and served.

In the belief that this pattern of dynastic succession, which had endured so long, and so seldom suffered disturbance from the outside, would last forever, the Confucian scholar was content to serve even a decaying dynasty knowing that in due course it, but not he, would be replaced. So even when nomadic invaders, such as the Manchus, seized the throne, the scholars rested assured that they would be relied upon as much by these aliens as they would be by native Chinese.

THE WESTERN ASSAULT

Raymond Aron writes, "For the first time, all men share the same history."[12] The history to which he is referring is the one that grew out of Western Europe. It is the chronicle of the growth of the industrial society which has engulfed the world. All men are forced to share in it; its military and economic power have enabled its manipulators to spread their physical superiority far beyond their native countries. The world is being revolutionized in the attempt to cope with these agents. And the Chinese revolution—that is, the collapse of the Middle Kingdom—was the signal for the violent entry of the earth's largest nation into this shared history.

How did Western Europeans penetrate the Middle Kingdom? A good place to begin our investigation is the traditional Chinese system of handling foreign-initiated contact. The tribute system, the imperial method of handling nonmartial foreign affairs, was an application to foreign affairs of the Confucian doctrines by which Chinese rulers gained an ethical sanction for the exercise of political authority. It was the ruler's function to be compassionate and generous to the benighted barbarians. The barbarians, of course, had to humbly acknowledge their inferiority.

Once the barbarian had recognized the unique position of the Son of Heaven it was unavoidable that these reciprocal relations of compassionate benevolence and humility should be demonstrated in ritual form, by the ceremonial bestowal of gifts and tribute respectively. Tribute thus became one of the rites of the Chinese court. It

. . . betokened the admission of a barbarian to the civilization of the Middle Kingdom. It was a boon and a privilege, and not ignominious. As the original

Chinese culture island spread through the centuries to absorb barbarian tribes, the formalities of tribute relations were developed into a mechanism by which barbarian regions outside the empire might be given their place in the all-embracing Sino-centric cosmos.[13]

When Europeans first came to China by sea these formalities were naturally expected of them. They felt, however, that the humiliation of the tribute ceremony more than offset the imperial benevolence which they in turn received. The ceremony was the kowtow, three kneelings and nine prostrations which left no doubt in anyone's mind, least of all the performer's, as to who was inferior and who was superior. "Egalitarian" Westerners failed to appreciate that this humiliating gesture was a normal aspect of ceremonial life in a society of rigid status. The emperor kowtowed to Heaven and to his parents; the highest officials kowtowed to the emperor, and so on. From a tribute bearer it was therefore considered no more than good manners.

The trading states of eastern Asia presented tribute to the Chinese court in order to maintain their trade and friendly relations, and they were duly enrolled as tributaries. Certain ports and markets were designated for them. Canton, a southern seaport, served the southeast Asians who wished to trade with the Chinese, and it was there that the Europeans first made contact. Upon arriving they were similarly enrolled and, almost without realizing it, became part of China's tributary firmament. These first European traders, though a rather coarse bunch, did little or nothing to shatter the Chinese institution of tribute and the conviction of superiority which it signified.

"The old Canton trade in its heyday (c. 1760–1840) was carried on under a working compromise between the Chinese system of tributary trade and European mercantilism."[14] The British East India Company was the sole European participant at that time, for it was one of the few trading companies of the mercantilist era to survive the Napoleonic Wars and was subsequently able to beat out its rivals and establish a monopoly in the Chinese trade. The company was based in India and set up a very profitable triangular trade between India, England, and China.

Western expansion and free trade in particular disrupted the Canton system after the East India Company lost its monopoly of Britain's China trade in 1833. The last great age of European imperialism coincided with the scramble for colonies and markets. China intitially encountered this expansionism in the opium trade, a historical circumstance that has poisoned Sino-Western relations ever since. It remains for anti-imperialists a classic symbol of imperialist greed exploiting an inoffensive people. Furthermore, to deal in opium was to violate an explicit command of the emperor, thus sparking off the first major conflict with the traditional order. The barbarians, an unruly lot and lacking in court manners, were now in open defiance of the Son of Heaven. High Chinese officials tried to suppress the trade; the result was the Opium War in 1840–1842, a war which the British began with the stated intention of reopening Canton to free trade—the Chinese had tried to close it—and ended with a British expeditionary force being sent up the eastern coast to secure privileges of commercial and diplomatic intercourse on a Western basis of equality. The Treaty of Nanking in 1842 codified the newly won privileges.

The treaty satisfied neither side, however, and a second war was fought by the French and English against the Chinese which ended in a new treaty structure in 1858. The reluctant dynasty would not fully assent to it until the British and French occupied Peking itself in 1860. Again new treaties were signed, this time placing China wide open to the inroads of Western commerce and culture. A new system now came into being, that of extraterritoriality based on treaty ports, special ports where the new privileges held. These ports eventually totalled more than eighty.

Extraterritoriality was an invention by which foreigners were not subject to Chinese jurisdiction. It was thus a powerful tool for the opening of China. Now manufacturers, railroad builders, and missionaries poured into China, ultimately to undermine the entire traditional order. And their overwhelming power eliminated the need of demurring to the Son of Heaven. This demonstrable Western superiority was only in the military and economic spheres, it is true, but even that was an incredible reversal for the Chinese. This realization shook an already tottering dynasty, and ultimately caused it not only to pass the Mandate of Heaven but to cease to exist.

REVOLUTION

The dynasty of the Manchus, the Ch'ing, was manifestly declining in the nineteenth century. The endemic organizational problems hastened its deterioration. The bureaucracy's tendency to close ranks accelerated with the increasingly severe agrarian problems.

Ascertaining the exact size of China's population has always been extremely difficult. Nevertheless, demographers are now fairly certain that China, in the century that preceded large-scale Western contact, doubled its population with little concomitant increase of arable land. The final dissolution of the northern threat in the eighteenth century bringing peace, and the introduction of new and more nourishing foods bringing prosperity, seem to have resulted in this fantastic population increase.[15] The enormous pressure on the land, coupled with an increasingly unresponsive bureaucracy under the sponsorship of an alien and extremely cautious dynasty, produced an agrarian uprising in 1851. This revolt was the T'ai P'ing and it deserves some extensive mention.

The T'ai P'ing rebellion, or the "Great Peaceful Heavenly Kingdom" as the leader called the movement, was in some ways yet another great peasant uprising, coming, as before, when the dynasty was in decline, and using an exotic creed as its rallying point and inspiration. The difference was that this exotic creed was not some variant of an indigenous mysticism but a form of Christianity. The leader taught his followers the Christian religion as he understood it. He further claimed to be divinely inspired by visions in which he had conversed with Jesus. He took the title of "Younger Brother of Jesus Christ."[16]

The rebellion met with sweeping success in its early days. The rebels overran most of China and almost took Peking. Everywhere they went they preached their Christianity, utterly repudiating all other existing religions including Confucianism, the state religion. They fed on the misery that was then widespread among the peasantry, inciting them to a rebellion that had definite racial overtones since the Manchus were aliens. The T'ai P'ings asserted a claim to the Mandate and they seemed wholly justified, for the reigning dynasty seemed no longer fit to rule. Because prosperity or its absence was directly assignable to the emperor, he was held responsible for the increase of starvation and disease which accompanied the population increase, and, very importantly, he was accountable for all the evils the Western imperialists had brought with them: the undermining of cottage industries by Western manufacturers; the railroad tracks which ran over graveyards; the opium trade; and the unbearable humiliation which the forcible opening of China to their trade had caused. These outrages had aggravated an explosive frustration among all Chinese, but due to the initial manner of explosion the peasants did not receive the backing of the class whose support is essential to a successful revolt, the Confucianists. Chinese intellectuals were still Confucianists, and so the old pattern of loyalty held. They remained faithful to those who recognized their value and would employ them—namely, the dynasty in power.

The T'ai P'ing rebellion dealt the empire a blow from which it never recovered. The regime was almost wiped out militarily and financially, forcing them to ask for aid from the Western traders, a great humiliation.

The intellectual fruits of all this upheaval were beginning to ripen. As C. P. Fitzgerald writes:

At the time when the material power of the Empire was proved inadequate and antiquated, when its claim to universal sovereignty of the civilized world was manifestly disproved and when the age-old economic balance of population and food supply was evidently being upset, then suddenly came the still more terrible realization that orthodoxy (Confucianism) itself was neither infallible nor essential to civilization. There were whole worlds which knew not Confucius; great empires more powerful than China which derided her ethical and political system. The foreigner could point to defeat in war, to Chinese famine and poverty, and to the technical and scientific knowledge of the West and say, "How do you justify your claim to civilization, let alone to superiority?" [17]

Future historians may know the answer to this question. Perhaps they will reply that technical skills are not a good criterion of true civilization. Perhaps a desire for harmony in human society is better than restless change and searching for some undefined goal. Perhaps grace of living is more important than material comfort, or even than hygiene.

In the second half of the nineteenth century it did not seem so to the Chinese. All saw that the whole fabric of their culture was threatened by the innovations which the West either forced upon them at cannon's mouth or else spread through the alluring forces of commerce and education. Some thought that China must shut its doors and make a supreme effort to expel the germ of change. Others, recognizing the inevitable, hoped to adopt just so much innovation as was necessary to resist the onrush of the rest. A small but growing number came to think that Chinese culture stood condemned. This view came to prevail. It was believed by the early revolutionaries that China must be entirely reshaped to the Western pattern in order to be saved. It must cease to pretend to be a universal empire. It must industrialize and become a democracy. Indeed, this is what it tried to do.

The Confucian schools were closed. The examination system was terminated. Whatever direction the Chinese were going to be able to give China, it was clearly not within the Confucian framework. The sons of the intellectuals turned their minds towards the West; many of them studied there. The missionary schools increased their enrollment greatly. All were searching for new ways to order China. China was not only no longer the center of the universe. It was now but a weak member of it.

History had turned to revolution, the inevitable consequence of the West's physical and intellectual rape of the Middle Kingdom. And it is a revolution of which we, even in our lifetimes, will not see the full measure.

NOTES

1. C. P. Fitzgerald, *The Chinese View of Their Place in the World* (London: Oxford University Press, 1964), p. 4.
2. Anonymous, *The Sayings of Mencius,* trans. James Ware (New York: New American Library, 1960), p. 8.
3. J. K. Fairbank, ed., *Chinese Thought and Institutions* (Chicago: University of Chicago Press, 1957), p. 186.
4. K. Menhert, *Peking and Moscow* (New York: New American Library, 1963), p. 90.
5. Ibid.
6. Fairbank, *Chinese Thought,* p. 26.
7. Strictly speaking, there were several other classes and subclasses. I have used the two most important.
8. A. Wright, *Confucianism and Chinese Civilization* (New York: Atheneum Press, 1964), p. 300.
9. V. Simone, *China in Revolution* (Baltimore: Penguin Books, 1965), p. 59.
10. Ibid., p. 62.
11. Ibid., p. 70.
12. Raymond Aron, *The Industrial Society* (New York: Simon & Schuster, 1967), p. 1.
13. J. K. Fairbank, *The United States and China* (Cambridge, Mass.: Harvard University Press, 1967), p. 115.
14. Ibid., p. 118.
15. Albert Feuerwerker, ed., *Modern China* (Englewood Cliffs, N.J.: Prentice-Hall, 1964), pp. 158–160.
16. Ssu-yu Teng, *New Light on the History of the T'ai P'ing Rebellion* (Cambridge, Mass.: Harvard University Press, 1950), p. 20.
17. Fitzgerald, *The Chinese View,* p. 82.

MARCIA J. CARPENTER

Colorado College

Women: Old Ways and New Wants

Too often, social analysts interested in modernization examine the social systems—and such indicators as rising industrial output and more progressive laws—but fail to ask whether *people themselves* have accepted modernization, whether they have abandoned old life styles to meet the new demands. Unquestionably the social systems must be evaluated, but it is the people who make or break modernization by taking advantage or not of opportunities to develop themselves and their societies.

This relationship between people and modernization is emphatically illustrated in the case of women, traditionally regarded by nearly every culture as second-class citizens, ignorant instruments for bearing children, and hardly a progressive force in any sense. Yet women are, after all, "half the world's people," and the society

MARCIA J. CARPENTER *is a native of Golden, Colorado, and came to IHP from Colorado College, where she was a history major with a particular interest in Far East and Asian studies. She returned to Colorado College after IHP and graduated in 1971 summa cum laude with distinction in history, a member of Phi Beta Kappa and a Woodrow Wilson finalist. Marcia also received the Alpha Lambda Delta Award to a Senior Woman for Academic Achievement, and the Nethercot Prize for Excellence in Asian History. Marcia is presently enrolled in a doctoral program in Eastern European history at Yale University, where she is studying on a Yale Fellowship.*

which both allows them and inspires them to develop is one that has greatly increased its own potential. While most countries in recent years have increased the opportunities for women, the problem of inspiration remains more obstinate. Several experts now claim that as women are allowed more rights they retreat from their new-found opportunities, retiring into the home. And this retreat, they say, affects not only the woman herself but the society she deprives of her talents.

I decided to check the validity of this theory in the East and West. Japan, Hong Kong, India, Turkey, Yugoslavia, Sweden— these were the areas I selected as test centers. I measured the supposed trend in three ways. First, I analyzed the position of women in traditional society to determine the base of any subsequent progress. Second, I examined their rights and opportunities today to see if they were truly "modern." Third, I tried to determine whether contemporary women are indeed modern or whether they have started to slip back into traditional roles. For the sake of simplicity, all the women I examined were from the middle and upper classes. Thus, this essay will focus on these three areas, beginning with women in traditional society.

WOMEN IN TRADITIONAL SOCIETY

In most cultures, women were traditionally regarded as inferior and evil. The Indian sacred laws denounced women as "vile," "treacherous," and "degraded," while in Ecclesiastes they were termed "more bitter than death." Because women were thought to be so inferior in both East and West, it was held that they should be subordinate to men. Major religions of the world declared that women should be dominated by their male relatives, father, husband, and son particularly. A basic form of control exercised by the father was that of arranging marriage, sometimes without consulting his daughter. After her marriage, which often took place while she was very young, the wife left her own home to live with her husband and sometimes his entire family. Once ensconced in her husband's home, the wife's control over her fate was little improved. While a man could enjoy a good deal of respect in his family, as well as a vital say in decision making, a woman had no such grand prospect. One way she could earn a certain respect in the family was by producing large numbers of children, particularly males. Otherwise, her prestige remained minimal, while sometimes her security was in jeopardy. In China she could be divorced for failing to produce a male heir, while in India her husband was allowed to take another wife. Failure to bear a son in the West usually carried less serious consequences, though it was still important, as Matilda Gage points out:

Louis VII, referring to the number of girls born in his dominions, requested his subjects to pray unto God that He should accord them children of the better sex. Upon the birth of his first child, Margaret . . . his anger was so great that he would not look at her; he even refused to see his wife. He afterwards accorded an annual pension of three livres to the woman who first announced to him the birth of a son.[1]

Thus, a woman's status and security in the family often depended directly on her ability to produce one or more male heirs.

If women had little status in the family, they were also prevented from seeking it outside the home. In many cases, they were denied the education necessary for social or public achievement. Moreover, employment outside the home was strictly forbidden for middle- or upper-class women, while their participation in political affairs was almost unheard of. Activity in the home and family was the only major outlet for them: society was denied their efforts in a more public sense.

As her activity was restricted, so was her outlook. Since she was mostly unaware of affairs outside her own family, the effective limits of her world were, physically and psychologically, the walls of the home. Similarly, since her whole life was based on obedience to male authority, she had little sense of freedom. She made few creative decisions: her life was conducted in accord with traditional standards. Thus barred from exercising her own initiative, she was a nonachieving member of society, as is shown by Demetra Vaka in her description of Turkish harem women:

They were entirely natural and spontaneous. They did not pretend to be anything that they were not. They were as happy and merry as little brooks, whose usefulness was limited, but who at least had no aspiration to pass for rivers. . . . They never dreamed of setting the world aright; and when I talked cant to them to see how they would take it, they looked at me in bewilderment, then laughed and exclaimed: — "Why little blossom! Allah meant women to be beautiful and good. . . . Isn't that enough for a mere woman?"[2]

Demetra Vaka leaves little doubt that at least these women in traditional society were well satisfied with their lot. That they even reveled
in their role and had little thought of changing their lives was expressed by a member of another harem: "There is no happiness save
in a prison where the jailer is the lover and lifegiver."[3]

A MODEL FOR MODERNITY

If some women of yesterday claimed to be happy, others admitted
that they were not. Women's rights movements gained impetus, particularly in the twentieth century. By the end of World War II, many
countries had given, at least in a formal legal sense, equal rights to
women. Most governments of the countries I studied acknowledge
that women should be equal. In family law these countries stipu-
late that both parties in a marriage should have equal rights, and
that the consent of both is necessary for the marriage to take place
(except, in both cases, for Hong Kong). Legal age limits have been
set (except in Hong Kong) to ensure that women will not be married
until they are at least in their middle teens. For the most part,
women today also have equal divorce rights: they can no longer be
divorced for failing to produce a male heir (except, again, in Hong
Kong). In a further effort to free women from the burden of producing a large number of children, many governments and private
organizations have started intensive programs to promote family
planning. Moreover, many governments have made serious attempts
to equalize opportunities for women in education, employment, and
political participation. In general, then, there has been a move toward greater equality for women in most countries.

Since limited opportunities impeded the traditional woman's psychological development, we might expect modern woman to have an
expanded view of herself and the world. But what are the traits of
the contemporary female? Certainly, the concept of development
implies a concern with achievement: the woman who wishes to develop must be an achiever. Criteria for modernity, then, must ultimately be criteria for achievement.

Our basic task is to define the motive for achievement: what
makes a woman *want* to achieve? One answer is empathy, defined by
Daniel Lerner as "the capacity to see oneself in the other fellow's
situation."[4] By giving us an appreciation of a life style different from
our own, empathy instills aspiration. For a woman, empathy is of

particular importance: without it, she might always be content to follow her traditional role, secluded in her home and barred from achievement.

By aspiring to achieve something different from what is available in her own society, a woman has already broken with its values in an important way. If she is to achieve, the aspiring woman must be willing to question authority. She must, in other words, be free. For example, a woman in traditional society may wish to have a paying job, but unless she can free herself of the idea that she is inferior and incapable of achieving, she will never have the opportunity to satisfy her aspirations. Freedom permits achievement.

If a woman is to have freedom, and cease to depend on certain social values, she must also be able to think and act for herself. A woman may succeed in breaking away from her traditional role and find employment, yet if she is unable to solve the problems she faces in her job, she will fail to achieve just as much as she would have if she had retained her traditional role. Thus, creativity, the capacity to deal with problems, is another criterion of achievement.

These then are necessary for achievement: empathy, freedom, and creativity. Now it remains to define achievement itself. It is well known that we may have infinite ability and desire, but without action we accomplish nothing at all. Action is the functional criterion for achievement. But what is individual action worth in a mass society? The answer to this question is perhaps best illustrated in Kusum Nair's *Blossoms in the Dust,*[5] which contrasts the achievement of some Indian states and the stagnation of others. Nair attributes the great difference to the way in which individual peasants reacted to their circumstances. In Bihar, one of the most backward provinces, the peasants were content to let the government supply their needs, showing little initiative and creativity. The Punjabi peasants, living in perhaps the most advanced area in India, built up their state by recognizing certain needs (irrigation, for example) and then acting. Thus, achievement on a national level is often the result of achievement on a personal one.

If the social consequences of individual achievement seem obvious, the consequences for the woman herself are not. What does the modern woman achieve in terms of happiness? Or is modernization only a matter of social, political, and economic progress? No one can measure happiness, of course, but we may find some relationship between it and modernity in our comparative study of Eastern and Western women.

Before we discuss the study itself, however, two questions must be considered: (1) Are women in both East and West taking advantage of their increased opportunities and becoming modern? and (2) Is there any evidence that they have started to slip back into traditional roles? The problem was approached in two different ways. In the East the focus for the project was on family planning and women's reactions to it. Since the necessity for bearing children was felt most acutely by Eastern women, it was decided that if they supported family planning, they would be free of traditional demands. In the West the project was expanded to include all the criteria— empathy, freedom, creativity, and action—as well as happiness. Both in East and West, the subjects for the project were university students, most of them from the middle and upper classes. After we look at the data, we may be able to draw some conclusions.

THE PROJECT—EAST AND WEST

ATTITUDES IN THE EAST

To determine whether Eastern women have achieved relative modernity, I decided to compare the attitudes of men and women, young and old, toward family planning. I therefore designed questionnaires to be given to university students who were instructed to take copies to their parents. (In Japan, the girls took the questionnaires to their mothers, the boys to their fathers; in Hong Kong and India, students took them to both parents.) The total samples were as follows: Japan, 58; Hong Kong, 71; India, 80. Universities represented were Keio University, Tokyo; Baptist College, Hong Kong; and University of New Delhi, India.[6]

The students were predominantly social science majors; in India and Japan most had fathers in salaried professions, while in Hong Kong, more had fathers in commercial occupations.[7] Grandfathers showed the same pattern of occupational concentration, although many also worked in agriculture and the professions, particularly in Japan. The students' mothers in Japan and India were all housewives, while in Hong Kong 20 percent of them were engaged in commercial pursuits. In educational attainment of the students' parents, Japan was highest: 85 percent of both the mothers and fathers had finished ten or more years of school. In Hong Kong 55 percent of the fathers and mothers had finished at least tenth grade. In India, however, there were great contrasts between fathers and mothers, 77 percent of the men but only 39 percent of the women had finished ten or more years of school. In general, the students were social science majors coming from middle-class, comparatively small families, particularly in Japan. Parents came also from middle-class backgrounds but were less educated than their children and, save in the case of the Indian fathers, from larger families.

In both expected and actual age at marriage (see Table 1) women

TABLE 1
AVERAGE AGE AT MARRIAGE (ACTUAL OR EXPECTED)

	Sons	Fathers	Daughters	Mothers
Japan	27.2	28.6	24.5	21.3
Hong Kong	27.2	24.1	25.7	19.8
India	25.5	22.5	22.8	17.6

were younger than men. Moreover, parents had married younger than the students expected to, with the exception of the males in Japan. Trends for expected (or actual) age at the birth of the first child were similar, as seen in Table 2.[8]

TABLE 2
AVERAGE AGE AT BIRTH OF FIRST CHILD (ACTUAL OR EXPECTED)

	Sons	Fathers	Daughters	Mothers
Japan	29.1	28.7	25.8	23.3
Hong Kong	28.5	27.8	27.2	22.1
India	28.4	25.8	25.3	20.7

The double question regarding the number of children *expected* (or actual) and the number *desired* yielded the results shown in Figure 1. With some exceptions, men generally *expected* a greater number of children than did the women. Similarly, with a few exceptions, women generally *wanted* fewer children than did the men. Apart from the Japanese, young people both expected and wanted fewer children than had their parents. Women's expectations and desires were often closer than were men's.

Turning to the question "Do you support family planning?" it was found that the younger generation supported it more than did the older people in every country, as seen in Table 3. Among the students, support was virtually equal for males and females, while among parents men supported it more than did women (save in

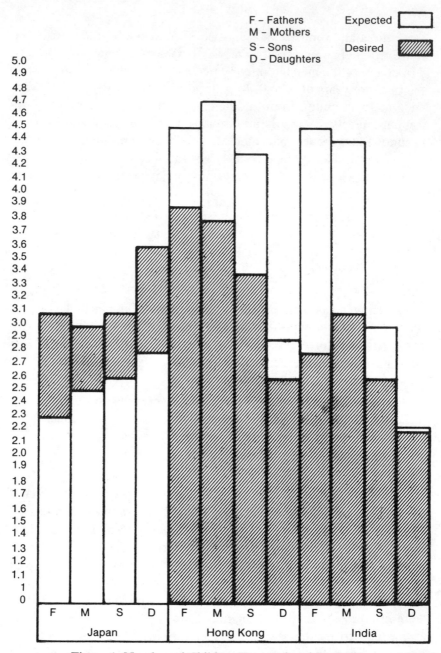

Figure 1. Number of Children Expected and Desired*

---

* The answers to the questions dealing with the ideal and actual numbers of children are averaged and, in order to express the differences clearly, are shown in
decimal form. The author realizes that "decimated children" do not in fact exist.

TABLE 3
PERCENTAGE IN SUPPORT OF FAMILY PLANNING

	Sons	Fathers	Daughters	Mothers
Japan	80	67	79	74
Hong Kong	85	76	86	69
India	85	82	86	77

Japan). People in Hong Kong and India supported family planning to a greater extent than did those in Japan, although the mothers in Hong Kong did not support it as much as did mothers in either Japan or India.

An Attempt At Interpretation. The results were generally as expected. Among members of the older generation, men married much later than did women, showing themselves to be free of the pressure to marry young. The daughters, by expecting to marry at an older age than had their mothers, also showed themselves to be freer. At the same time, the responses showed that sons and daughters were becoming more equal. The same result was found in the responses to the question on family planning. Fathers supported family planning more than did the mothers, while sons and daughters supported it equally, indicating that they were equally free of traditional values. In responses to the double question, it seems that women expected to have more control over their fate than did the men, at least on the question of family size.[9] Women wanted and expected fewer children than did their parents. Young people, in general, and women in particular, were considerably more advanced than their parents.

The only exception to a more progressive younger generation was found in Japan. This exception was surprising. According to what seems the most reliable indicator—the number of children borne by the parents—Japan was the most modern nation, followed by India, then Hong Kong. However, Japanese youth, particularly the women, both wanted and expected to have *more* children than did their parents, reversing the trend found in the other two areas. We may find an explanation for this if we analyze the older peoples' answers. In Hong Kong and India, the parents had had about four and five children, but perhaps regretted it, for they indicated they wanted fewer. Hong Kong and Indian youth were conservative in their expectations, but most still believed that they, like their parents, would have more children than they wanted. Accordingly, they strongly supported family planning. In both countries young women wanted and expected fewer children than their parents. The young Indian women in particular were so anxious to support family planning that they wanted and expected fewer children than did any group in any country. Hong Kong and Indian women were determined to be modern, unlike their parents, and were, even more than the young men, a force for progress, possibly in reaction to their traditional backgrounds.

In Japan, the family background of the young people was much different: the parents there were modern but still dissatisfied, for they wanted more children than they had. And their daughters wanted even more children. This is hardly a progressive reaction to a traditional background. In fact, young Japanese women appeared to be the least progressive and seemed to be slipping back into a traditional role, despite their support of family planning. This interpretation of the results is admittedly speculative, but it does seem clear that the relationship of women, modernity, and family planning warrants a great deal of further study.

Thus, while there is some evidence for the theory that women slip back into traditional roles once they have gained their rights, it is rather tenuous: the idea must be examined more thoroughly in terms of the five criteria in the West.

THE WESTERN APPROACH

To evaluate the modernity of women in the West, I conducted individual interviews. Twelve girls from Robert College, Istanbul, Turkey; seven girls from the University of Belgrade, Yugoslavia; and ten girls from the University of Stockholm, Sweden, were the subjects of my inquiry.[10]

In all three countries, the subjects were social science majors and were either freshmen or seniors at the university. As far as their parents' occupations were concerned, all of the fathers were members of the salaried, professional, or commercial groups, although none of the fathers in Yugoslavia had a professional occupation. The mothers in Turkey and Yugoslavia were housewives, but in Sweden over half were salaried workers. Altogether, the background of the subjects was similar: they were social science students at a university coming from small and apparently fairly prosperous families.

The evidence I obtained from the interviews indicated that these women were highly empathic. Not only were they educated but they also showed interest in current events of every type. With the exception of sports, many different topics were of interest to the subjects in each country, as is shown by Table 4.[11] Moreover, the subjects

TABLE 4
INTERESTS OF THE WOMEN INTERVIEWED (BY PERCENT)

	Turkey	Yugoslavia	Sweden
Foreign affairs	100	100	100
What the government is doing	83	100	100
What is going on in own community	92	100	100
Sports	33	43	10
Cultural affairs	100	100	90
Social affairs	83	100	90
Editorials	83	86	90

showed themselves capable of imagining themselves in different roles. When asked "If you were made a high official in the government what are some of the things you would do?" only two Yugoslavian girls said they "didn't know" or "couldn't imagine," the rest giving at least general answers. The subjects, then, were empathic: the *motive* for achievement was unquestionably present.

If the subjects were empathic, they also seemed free from traditional values. None desired, as did the traditional women, many children, wanting on the average two children in Turkey, and three in Yugoslavia and Sweden, while they expected to have even fewer. Although the Yugoslavs and Swedes wanted more children than they expected to have, no national group expected to have more children than did their mothers. All the subjects, then, were relatively free of traditional values.

Besides refusing to conform to traditional values, the subjects showed considerable independence from at least traditional authority. All of the Turks, 90 percent of the Swedes, and 86 percent of the Yugoslavs agreed that their parents, notably their fathers, would have no influence in their selection of a mate. Nor did they expect to be subservient to their husbands. They were asked "If you and your husband disagreed about family planning, who would be more likely to make the final decision, you or your husband? Is the same thing likely to happen in disputes over other matters?" Only 33 percent of the Turks and 14 percent of the Yugoslavs replied that their husbands would make the final decision, while none of the

Swedes believed that their husbands would do so. Most of these women, then, showed that they were free from traditional authority as well as traditional values.

If the subjects were free from the traditional authority of parents and prospective husbands, some were not free from authority as such, particularly the authority of public leaders. Some 86 percent of the Yugoslavs, 50 percent of the Turks, and 20 percent of the Swedes belonged to clubs of one sort or another. In both of the Swedish girls' clubs, leadership was rotated—a fact which, while it limited comparison with the Turks and the Yugoslavs, certainly indicated their independent attitude toward established authority. When asked about the leadership of their clubs, 50 percent of the Turks in clubs and 66 percent of the Yugoslavs answered that it was effective, while the remainder said that "it sometimes is," or "some of the leaders are." To the question "How could leadership be made better?" 66 percent of the Turks gave constructive suggestions to improve leadership, such as "they should give us more voice in club affairs," while one girl was not asked (as she was a club leader herself), and one girl offered no suggestions. Of the Yugoslavs, however, 66 percent said that they "didn't know" or that "it couldn't be better," while one girl avoided the question by saying that the club members should "work harder and take more responsibility," and another said "we can always change if they're not good." In general, the Swedes and the Turks who belonged to clubs had liberal attitudes toward authority, while the Yugoslavs seemed reluctant to question it in any constructive sense.

Interestingly enough, the ability to solve problems was closely related to freedom and autonomy. The subjects who were free from traditional values and authority were better able to solve their personal problems. All of the Turks, 90 percent of the Swedes, and 84 percent of the Yugoslavs declared themselves capable of solving their personal problems. And when asked what "individuals like yourself can do to help solve" national problems, all of the Turks and Swedes presented specific ideas on the subject, as is seen in the following examples:[12]

> Turkey: "The problem is education. I can teach in the village and help build schools there."
> Sweden: "Sweden needs to decide which bloc in the world she will affiliate with. I can be active in political life and try and convince people about what I think concerning this problem."

Of the Yugoslavs, however, 66 percent said they could do nothing, while the others answered only vaguely, one girl saying that people such as herself could "plan better and not be wasteful," the other saying that "they can work hard." Unlike the Yugoslav students, capable of solving only personal problems, the Turks and Swedes showed themselves to be more ambitious.

Concerning their participation, it seems striking that 86 percent of the Yugoslavian girls and 50 percent of the Turkish girls (but only 20 precent of the Swedish girls) belonged to organizations. The Swedish girls, however, seemed to be active participants. In the Turkish case, half of the girls were in the social science club, which built schools and visited villages to help with rural problems. They and the other club members were active in their organizations, emphasizing that women *should* participate in order to be equal and useful. As far as the Yugoslavs were concerned, 43 percent were members of the Communist Party and 43 percent were in the Student League, while 29 percent were also members of other clubs. Their participation seemed to take the form of "discussion, voting, working, and organizing." In view of their lack of public concern, however, one wonders just how effective their participation would be. My conclusion is "not very," which seemed to be supported by one member of the Communist Party who said that older members did most of the discussing; because she was younger, she did not participate. The subjects in Sweden and Turkey, then, seemed to participate more fully than the Yugoslav students.

The question of happiness remains. All of the Turks and Yugoslavs and almost all of the Swedes declared themselves to be happy (one Swedish girl declining to answer). Most based their happiness on the fact that they had what they wanted: a good university, good friends, good relations with parents, and in some cases a boyfriend.

Much more interesting were their ideas about trends in happiness from generation to generation. When asked, "On the whole, do you think you are more, or less, happy than your parents' generation?" the answers were distributed as seen in Table 5. When asked "Do you think your children will be more, or less, happy than you are?" they responded as in Table 6. The reasons for their answers were equally striking. The Yugoslavs cited lack of war and improving economic conditions as their reason for happiness. The Turks, who felt the same way, said they were "freer" than their parents; although they saw much that needed improving in Turkey, they felt their gen-

TABLE 5

DISTRIBUTION OF RESPONSES TO THE QUESTION "ON THE WHOLE, DO YOU THINK YOU ARE MORE, OR LESS, HAPPY THAN YOUR PARENTS' GENERATION?" (BY PERCENT)

	Turkey	Yugoslavia	Sweden
More	83	100	0
Less	8	0	10
The same	0	0	40
Can't compare	8	0	40
Don't know	0	0	10

TABLE 6

DISTRIBUTION OF RESPONSES TO THE QUESTION "DO YOU THINK YOUR CHILDREN WILL BE MORE, OR LESS, HAPPY THAN YOU ARE?" (BY PERCENT)

	Turkey	Yugoslavia	Sweden
More	83	86	10
Less	8	0	30
The same	0	0	20
Can't compare	8	0	30
Don't know	0	14	10

eration was more realistic and therefore better equipped to improve it. Of the Swedes, who failed to see any progress at all, several remarked that their generation was "confused" and "lost." One girl stated the case remarkably well:

Our parents had things to work for: they had difficulty with material things and also wanted freedom from strict social mores. Also, they had a calmer life than we have. Now everything is developing and moving, and, while we have good material conditions, we find ourselves a bit confused in this world. There are not so many mores to trust in and follow, not so many material things to work for. We, unlike our parents, have to find ourselves and our own direction.

As for the future, 30 percent of the Swedish girls felt their children would be less happy than they, not only because of the "terrible" world situation but also because "we are not taking care of human interests." On the whole, the Yugoslavs saw the most progress in human happiness, followed closely by the Turks and very reluctantly by the Swedes.

It seems clear that certain national patterns emerged from these students' replies. The Turks, who were generally empathic and free, were also creative and active. They seemed, in fact, to be determined to participate, feeling it was necessary for women to do so. They were working for Turkey, promising themselves to make it a better place. They saw increasing happiness, but emphasized that happiness depends on relevant activity in politics and social affairs.

The Yugoslavs, on the other hand, while empathic and free on a personal level, still respected public authority. Similarly, though creative in solving their personal problems, they "could do nothing" about larger ones. Nevertheless, they seemed happy, although their criterion for happiness was not shared by the Turks or Swedes.

The Swedes, although empathic, free, and creative, failed to participate. Although happy, they felt that happiness did not increase with succeeding generations, describing their own generation as lost and confused.

Ranking the countries according to my criteria, the Turks appear most modern, followed by the Swedes and the Yugoslavs. It seems, however, that some discussion of "meaningful participation" and "happiness" is in order, especially as these apply to the retreat into traditional roles.

SOME CONCLUSIONS

I now wish to return to the theory I mentioned at the beginning of my essay, the idea that as soon as women have gained their rights they surrender them again. Basically, the theory states that women, as they earn rights in society, turn their backs on their opportunities and return to the home and their families. They have more children which, in turn, keeps them more tied to the home. Their talents are lost to society, while they themselves feel dissatisfied. The assumption is, of course, that meaningful participation is *public* participation; that modern women must limit the size of their families in order to leave home, find jobs, be active politically: in short, to be equal to men. Only by doing so, the theory claims, can women be socially relevant, fulfilled, and happy.[13]

That some of the subjects seemed to agree with these contentions is clear. Women in Hong Kong and India wanted to limit the size of their families drastically compared with their more traditional parents. They were, then, modern to the extent that they were free to participate publicly. The Turks too were modern, and emphasized that happiness and fulfillment for women was to be found in social action to improve their country. They, like the Indian and Hong Kong students displayed no retreat into fecundity or complacence.

Similar to the Turks in their emphasis on activity were the Yugoslavs. Most of these girls participated in social and public affairs, yet they seemed to contribute little to the welfare of their organizations or to that of their country. The fact that they were happy contradicts the idea that happiness can only result from meaningful public participation.

Several other arguments against the theory of complacence and fecundity are brought to mind by the responses of the Japanese and the Swedes. That the young Japanese women wanted and expected to have more children than did their parents indicates a certain retreat into traditional ways. But they were modern in that they intended to marry late and did support family planning. It would thus be wrong to say that the Japanese were not as modern as the students from Hong Kong or India. Nor can we conclude that because the Yugoslavs or Turks participated, they were more valuable to society than were the Swedes, who were in fact just as modern in other ways.

Yet if they were modern, one might ask, why did the Japanese and Swedes choose the traditional paths of fecundity and nonparticipation? The answer may well be found in their societies. The Japanese parents had already demonstrated their modernity via family planning, and according to the Swedes their parents had succeeded in modernizing their country in many ways. The younger Swedish generation was thus faced with finding a new direction, for traditional social problems had already been overcome. Perhaps this is the reason for the Swedes' nonparticipation and the Japanese desire for more children: they had found a new place to achieve—in the home.

That this may be related to the conflict of career vs. home is easily seen. Traditionally, housekeeping and child-raising were regarded as menial because women were indeed inferior—unempathic, dependent, uncreative, having little to offer within or without the home. Now that women have more rights, however, they are in a position to expand their domestic role. And their influence in family decision making and economic planning, as well as their power over the psychological and material well-being of family members, is increasing. By making a significant contribution in these ways, women may have a significant contribution to society. To opt for the home and more children, then, is not necessarily a step backwards: in doing so, a woman may be both happy and vital to society.

It all depends on how she makes her choice. Whether she decides to be a career woman or a housewife, a woman must first be aware of the options open to her: she must be *empathic*. Secondly, she must be *free* of social pressures. Her choice of a life style will then be *creative*, depending only on a sense of herself and her relationship to the world. She will, as a result, be meaningfully *participant* in whatever occupation she chooses.

No one pattern is true for all the women in the modern world. Some seem truly modern, as the Turks. Some follow modern patterns but without creativity, as the Yugoslavs. Some seem traditional because they fail to participate and yet are modern in all other ways, as the Swedes. And some are classified as modern or traditional on the basis of one attitude alone, as the students from Hong Kong, India, and Japan.

But all this categorizing can be extremely dangerous. Few studies have presented reliable worldwide statistics to show that women are indeed returning to the home and bearing more children. Even fewer have considered the reasons behind such a move (if it ever in fact occurred). Too many studies examine systems but never people, statistical trends but never psychology. If women are returning to the home and having more children, how many of them are really regressing—and how many are discovering new direction?

NOTES

1. Matilda Joselyn Gage, *Women, Church, and State* (Chicago: Charles H. Kerr & Co., 1893), pp. 369–370.
2. Demetra Vaka, *Haremlik: Some Pages from the Lives of Turkish Women* (Boston: Houghton Mifflin Co., 1909), pp. 28–29.
3. Ibid., p. 233.
4. Daniel Lerner, *The Passing of Traditional Society* (New York: The Free Press, 1958), p. 50.
5. Kusum Nair, *Blossoms in the Dust* (London: Gerald Duckworth & Co., 1961), pp. 88–102.
6. Numerical distribution by generation and sex was as follows: Japan—15 sons, 15 fathers, 14 daughters, 14 mothers; Hong Kong—13 sons, 21 fathers, 14 daughters, 23 mothers; India—13 sons, 27 fathers, 14 daughters, 26 mothers.
7. The categories for occupational concentration used in my research were derived from *Summary of the Eighth National Survey on Family Planning* (Tokyo: Mainichi Shimbun, 1965).
8. All questions dealing with marriage, age at marriage, age at birth of first child, number of children expected and wanted were derived from Jean

Stoetzel, *Without the Chrysanthemum and the Sword* (New York: UNESCO, 1955), pp. 298–299.
9. Interpretations adapted from Stoetzel, p. 190.
10. In Yugoslavia and Sweden, samples were not large enough according to sample survey rules.
11. This and the following question are derived from Lerner, pp. 418 and 430.
12. Ibid.
13. For the best discussions of this theory see Jessie Bernard, "The Status of Women in Modern Patterns of Culture," *Annals of the American Academy of Political and Social Sciences* 375 (January 1968): 4–14; and Betty Friedan, *The Feminine Mystique* (New York: Dell Publishing Co., 1963).

BIBLIOGRAPHY

Afetinan, A. *The Emancipation of the Turkish Woman.* Paris: UNESCO, 1962.

Altekar, A. S. *The Position of Women in Hindu Civilization.* Delhi: Matilal Banarsidas, 1962.

Baber, Ray E. *Youth Looks at Marriage and the Family.* Tokyo: International Christian University, 1958.

Bernard, Jessie. "The Status of Women in Modern Patterns of Culture." *Annals of the American Academy of Political and Social Science* 375 (January 1968): 4–14.

Chiu, Vermier R. *Marriage Laws and Customs of China.* Hong Kong: New Asia College, 1966.

De Beauvoir, Simone. *The Second Sex.* New York: Alfred A. Knopf, 1952.

De Goncourt, Edmond, and Jules de Goncourt. *The Woman of the Eighteenth Century.* London: George Allen & Ursinus, 1928.

Friedan, Betty. *The Feminine Mystique.* New York: Dell Publishing Co., 1963.

Gage, Matilda Joselyn. *Woman, Church, and State.* Chicago: Charles H. Kerr & Co., 1893.

Ginzberg, Eli. *Life Styles of Educated Women.* New York: Columbia University Press, 1966.

Komarovsky, Mirra. *Women in the Modern World.* Boston: Little, Brown & Co., 1953.

La Mujer en la Sociedad y en la Economía. Beograd: Medunarodna Politika, 1965.

Leijon, Anna-Greta. *Swedish Women—Swedish Men.* Stockholm: The Swedish Institute, 1968.

Lerner, Daniel. *The Passing of Traditional Society.* New York: The Free Press, 1958.

Mead, Margaret. *Male and Female.* New York: William Morrow & Co., 1949.

Montagu, Ashley. *The Natural Superiority of Women.* New York: Lancer Books, 1952.

Nair, Kusum. *Blossoms in the Dust.* London: Gerald Duckworth & Co., 1961.

O'Hara, Albert Richard. *The Position of Women in Early China*. Baltimore: Archbishop of Baltimore-Washington, 1946.

Patai, Raphael, ed. *Women in the Modern World*. New York: The Free Press, 1967.

Pinkham, Mildred Worth. *Woman in the Sacred Scriptures of Hinduism*. New York: Columbia University Press, 1941.

Raymond, G. Alison. *Half the World's People*. New York: Appleton-Century-Crofts, 1965.

Rodriguez, Valentin. *Los Derechos de la Mujer en Yugoslavia*. Beograd: Publicisticko-Izdavacki Zavod "Jugoslaviya," n. d.

Shastri, Shakuntala Rao. *Women in "The Sacred Laws."* Bombay: Bharativa Vidya Bhavan, 1959.

Stoetzel, Jean. *Without the Chrysanthemum and the Sword*. New York: UNESCO, 1955.

Swedish Institute. *The Status of Women in Sweden*. Stockholm: Swedish Institute, 1967.

Vaka, Demetra. *Haremlik: Some Pages from the Lives of Turkish Women*. Boston: Houghton Mifflin Co., 1909.

Van Der Valk, M. H. *Conservatism in Modern Chinese Family Law*. Leiden: E. J. Brill, 1956.

Ward, Barbara E., ed. *Women in the New Asia*. Paris: UNESCO, 1963.

Winch, Robert F., Robert McGinnis, and Herbert R. Barringer. *Selected Studies in Marriage and the Family*. New York: Holt, Rinehart, & Winston, 1962.

LOUISE A. LERNER

Radcliffe College

Social Change Amidst a War of Words

When India gained its independence on 15 August 1947, English was the language of its administration, its courts, and its higher education. If it had been agreed at that time to maintain the status quo—if the idea of Hindi as a pan-Indian language had never materialized—India would not be facing many of the problems it faces today. However, strong nationalist sentiment dictated the expulsion of everything foreign, including the English language; and the constitution of India, on the basis of recommendations by the Official Language Commission, declared Hindi the new official national language of India, to replace English by 1965, while thirteen other languages were recognized for regional use. And in the twenty years since independence, the issue of Hindi versus English has become one of India's major political problems.

The reasoning behind the Official Language Commission's decision, and the ideas of the Hindi-supporters in general, have been the subject of serious disagreement and the basis for widespread dissent

LOUISE A. LERNER *grew up in Newton Center, Massachusetts, and was a linguistics major at Radcliffe College before she joined IHP. At Radcliffe, Louise was interested in languages and was active in the musical performances of the Harvard-Radcliffe orchestra. Upon her return to Radcliffe after IHP, Louise graduated in 1971* cum laude. *She is currently attending Boston College Law School.*

on the part of many of the non-Hindi-speaking linguistic groups of India, the majority of which are strongly in favor of the retention (or, at this point, reinstatement) of English as India's official language. Although both sides agree on the basic necessity of a pan-Indian language, they have very different opinions as to what this language should be, and why.

The English-supporters accept that a national language is necessary for cultural unity as well as for political unity and communication. However, they feel that "in the absence of a developed language of indigenous origin, a developed language of foreign origin, which was already known to all the educated people in the country, would have ideally suited us."[1] English is "already there"; it has been the official language of India since British colonization, and most books and documents are written in English. Besides, English is needed both as an international link and as a medium for development, being the language of science and technology, and, therefore, of modernization.

Hindi-supporters, on the other hand, feel that Hindi has the capacity for development. The Board of Scientific Terminology, constituted in 1950 for the purpose of preparing 350,000 new technical terms in Hindi, had already prepared 290,000 by 1963.[2] Other committees have been assigned the task of coining new terms for other fields. It is felt that by using an Indian language the masses of India will find it easier both to adapt to the new ideas and ways of life they will be experiencing in the course of India's development and to express their own ideas and feelings. Moreover, approximately 42 percent of India's population already knows Hindi, as opposed to 2.8 percent who know English,[3] and for those who know neither language, Hindi is much easier to learn than English, as it is closely related to many of the other regional languages of India.

Although these statistics seem to give Hindi a strong advantage over English, English-protagonists protest that "the claim that Hindi is spoken by 42 percent of the people is an obvious canard. A whole range of distinct languages . . . [was] included under Hindi to inflate the figures."[4] Many of the speakers of these languages would not understand the spoken language of others in this group. And what is more, one writer ventures to say that "not even one percent of the Hindi-speaking people understand what new passes as the new Hindi with its frenetic attempts to enlarge its vocabulary by all kinds of artificial monstrosities and resurrections from the dust-bin of dead words."[5]

This last attitude toward the "Sanskritization" of Hindi—the attempt to remove the foreign elements, both English and Persian, from the language and to make it more pan-Indian—is typical of pro-English sentiment. Writers on the subject stress the artificiality of the new Hindi and point out that a language cannot be developed to order. Although "to inject words into a language is not a difficult process, . . . the same cannot be done with concepts. Concepts cannot even be grafted; they have to grow out of the total ethos of a society."[6] Some feel that Hindi has not developed enough to express the concepts necessary for India's development and modernization. For this reason, too, English is considered to be essential for higher education: "A campaign against English in the field of higher education can only be a campaign against higher education itself."[7]

Hindi-protagonists, however, feel that although the use of English as official language might initially benefit a small elite group, a native language is necessary in order to reach the masses, for the "emotional integration" of the peoples of the country. It is not enough for the top layers of a society to share a language; there must be communication among all levels. There must also be communication among the various regions of the country on the mass level and not just among the elite. Hindi-supporters feel that only an Indian language has the power of uniting the masses through a feeling of common nationality despite their cultural differences.

However, this obviously has not worked, say the English-protagonists. On the contrary, the adoption of Hindi as the official language, rather than promoting Indian nationalism and the emotional integration of the people, has been the source both of a sort of *dis*-integration—a splitting into two factions, pro- and anti-Hindi—and of strong feelings of regional (as opposed to Indian) nationalism. Non-Hindi speakers claim that the adoption of Hindi is unfair in that it gives Hindi-speakers a natural advantage over them. Punya Sloka Ray's analogy explains this attitude beautifully:

One thing a wise mother never does is to give an only or a best prize in any contest to the biggest child. For she knows that even if the biggest one really deserves that prize, the smaller ones will not see it that way. They will feel that bigness has triumphed over merit and each will consider himself the victim of blatant injustice. The biggest child always has to make the biggest sacrifices, however exasperating to him it all is. The way to peace is to avoid contest between unequal brothers and, if it cannot any more be avoided, to give an equal prize to each, or, if there is only one prize, to give it to none, or if it must be given to one, to give it to a little one.[8]

It is obvious that the contest "cannot any more be avoided"—nor has it been. Hindi, Mother India's "biggest child," has been given the prize, and already the smaller children are complaining. Non-Hindi speakers deeply resent the imposition of Hindi as undemocratic; but along with this resentment "a fear has developed, a fear of another domination perhaps, a fear of unjust distribution of effort because those whose mother tongue and link language coincide have one less script and one less language to learn."[9]

It seems unjust that some people have to learn to communicate in a foreign tongue in order to advance while others can use their mother tongue. Yet, an "equal prize" cannot be given to each (the idea of fourteen official national languages was discarded long ago as impractical and inefficient). Nor would there be any advantage in "giving it to a little one" (the arguments of regional favoritism would only be revived). By analogy with Ray's reasoning, therefore, there is only one possible solution to the language problem: each region must give up its claims and accept a language equally foreign to all as national language.

However, the regional languages need not—in fact, must not—be given up entirely. Despite all the talk of educating the masses in the official language, it is highly unlikely that India will be able to achieve a wholesale integration of elite and masses, either via English or via Hindi, at any time in the near future, if ever. For India, "national integration [must be] of two types. The first is the integration between the intelligentsia and the masses in the same linguistic region and the second is the integration of the intelligentsia from the different linguistic regions."[10] The first of these must be achieved through the regional languages, and the second through the official national language. Thus, the logical solution, according to the English-protagonists, is "to give it to none" and adopt English as the official language of India.

At the same time, English-protagonists propose that there be two types of education available to the Indian student. "Education has two principal dimensions, its breadth and height, or quantity and quality. For ensuring its wide dissemination the regional language is the most suitable; but for its topmost reaches, in the arts as well as in science and technology,"[11] study in English is essential. While the regional languages must continue to fulfil their *intra*regional functions of communication, administration, and education, English must be reinstated as the official language of India, for *inter*-regional communication and integration, as well as for higher education and development.

The Hindi-protagonists, however, violently oppose the retention of English, as they consider it an unpleasant reminder of the British occupation of India, and wish to rid the country of this foreign element. English came in with the foreign invaders, and now it must go out with them. If India is to prove itself an independent nation capable of developing on its own, it must have an official language of its own, an indigenous language; and this language, continues the argument, must be Hindi. It is a question of national pride; for, as Gandhi said, "no country can become a nation by producing a race of imitators."[12] National pride has become such a strong emotional issue for many Indians that it has sometimes overridden any sort of reasoning.

"But we've got to have an *Indian* language!" Despite the emotional impact of this argument, the English-protagonists claim there is a basic fallacy in such an attitude. "A little thought would show that whereas a nation may have a language, a language has no nationality. Like any other acquisition in the field of knowledge, the English language belongs to those who know it and like it. Nationalist sentiment has blinded us to this simple truth."[13] Besides, why should language be more of an issue than anything else imported from the West? Should India give up its form of government, its judicial system, or its radios to avoid being branded a "nation of imitators"? "We have taken over the metric system in weights and measures, parliamentary life, our legal procedures, our political concepts like democracy, socialism and secularism, our economic ideas from abroad as instruments or tools to facilitate the life and progress of the country: should we now throw away the English language and not use it also as a similarly useful tool or instrument?"[14] The English language, claim its supporters, is as much a part of India as any of these. And "whatever importance we may give to a language, we must not forget that it is a means and not an end in itself. It must serve us in the tasks ahead. It is something we want to use for greater efficiency and progress."[15] If India is to develop and modernize, and if "our objective is to get all knowledge, created in any part of the world, and in any language . . . there can be no barriers to the import of knowledge."[16] Nationalist sentiment with regard to language must be overcome: nationalism must be realized through some medium other than language.

These are the main arguments of the pro-Hindi and pro-English factions. And at this point two questions seem to be of particular interest. First, do the actual language statistics for India support the claims of either faction? And second, how can their attitudes be explained?

Before we answer these questions, we ought to take a brief look at some facts and figures. The constitution of India recognizes fourteen official languages for use on the regional level. These languages —the "Schedule VIII" languages—include, in addition to Hindi, the following: Assamese, Bengali, Gujarati, Kannada, Kashmiri, Malayalam, Marathi, Oriya, Punjabi, Sanskrit, Tamil, Telugu, and Urdu. The principal language groups are distributed approximately as in Figure 1. Of these regional languages, all except four are Indo-Aryan; the other four—Kannada, Malayalam, Tamil, and Telugu —are Dravidian languages. It is worth noting in Figure 1 the location of the major populations of these speakers: the Dravidian speakers are located principally in the southern regions of India, the Indo-Aryan speakers in the north.

The Linguistic Census of 1961 (the most recent census) reveals important data about the relative numerical strengths of the various regional languages, as well as about the incidence of bilingualism throughout the country. Before looking into the results of this census, however, I want to mention a few of the problems involved in census-taking (especially in the taking of this census).

Any census which depends on spoken rather than written responses is subject to distortion. In the first place, different people may interpret the questions differently. For example, a respondent's "knowledge" of a given language might be anywhere on a scale from minimal ability to complete fluency. There is also the question of what one's "mother tongue" is. Is it the language he first learned and used? Or the language of his parents and their homeland? Or the language he uses at home, by preference, and in which he feels most comfortable? In some cases, these three languages are the

same, and then there is no problem. However, when these languages
are not all the same, respondents may interpret questions differently.

These responses may also be distorted by inconsistent labels for
caste and tribal dialects, geographical designations (for instance,
"Madrasi" for Tamil), or geographical labels which cover a number
of speech varieties (such as "Bihari").[17] This problem is especially

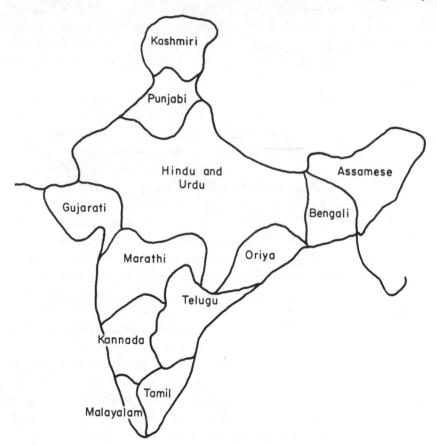

Figure 1. Distribution of Principal Language Groups

relevant in the case of Hindi and its related dialects, as the term
"Hindi" has been used for a wide range of social and geographical
varieties, some of which are quite different from each other. The
term "Hindi," as used in the 1961 census, probably includes a wide
variety of dialects, many of which are mutually unintelligible.

Another problem, equally serious, is the manipulation of figures by census officials. "A large number of difficulties result in one way or another from intentional distortions by the government taking the census, . . . in directions favorable to national policy."[18] Statistics can be inflated by combining figures for "closely related" or "mutually intelligible" dialects, or deflated by separating figures for varieties between which there are actually only minor distinctions. This has almost certainly occurred in the case of Hindi. In addition, the individual respondent himself may for patriotic reasons add to this "intentional distortion" of the figures.

Nevertheless, despite the probability of inaccuracies in the census data, we must proceed with the data available, bearing in mind their limitations. Table 1 is based on data from the 1961 Census of India. The language-related questions were: (1) What is your mother tongue? and (2) Do you know any other languages, Indian or foreign? Tabulations of second-language usage were based only on the first language recorded, provided that this language was a language other than the respondent's mother tongue or a dialect thereof. Also, in the census tables "bilingual data are presented only for [mother tongues with] at least 10,000 speakers for all India out of whom 5,000 speakers returned a subsidiary language. Further figures are given separately only for a subsidiary language, the strength of which is 5,000 or 10 percent of the total bilingual population. The remaining subsidiary languages have been clubbed together."[19]

The census also gives a detailed breakdown of bilingual data by state, area (urban or rural), and sex. However, for purposes of my analysis, I have adapted the tables on bilingualism to include only details on the Schedule VIII languages and English, omitting for the moment all statistics on regional and tribal languages and dialects.

Table 1 gives the number of mother-tongue (MT) speakers of each language; the number of speakers reporting its use as a second language (SL); the total number of persons speaking the language as a first or second language; and the percentage of the total population of India (about 500 million) speaking the language.

Table 1 certainly testifies as to the relative numerical strength of Hindi: the number of Hindi-speakers in India is more than three times the number of speakers of any other regional language—and more than ten times the number of English speakers. There is, however, an uneven distribution of knowledge of Hindi among the non-Hindi language groups.

TABLE 1
USE OF THE PRINCIPAL INDIAN LANGUAGES AS MOTHER TONGUES AND SECOND
LANGUAGES

Language	MT Speakers	SL Speakers	Total Speakers	Percentage of Population *
Hindi	133,435,360	9,363,068	142,798,428	28.56
Telugu	37,668,132	3,279,371	40,947,503	8.19
Marathi	33,286,771	2,723,727	36,010,498	7.20
Bengali	33,888,939	1,907,012	35,795,951	7.16
Tamil	30,562,706	3,659,400	34,222,106	6.84
Urdu	23,323,518	2,005,582	25,329,100	5.07
Kannada	17,415,827	3,550,642	20,966,469	4.19
Gujarati	20,304,464	558,066	20,862,530	4.17
Malayalam	17,015,782	217,884	17,233,666	3.45
Oriya	15,719,398	1,074,891	16,794,289	3.36
Punjabi	10,950,826	465,241	11,416,067	2.28
English	223,781	10,930,297 [20]	11,154,078	2.23
Assamese	6,803,465	1,648,638	8,452,103	1.69
Kashmiri	1,956,115	25,467	1,981.583	0.40

* The data in this column do not total 100 percent because only the principal Indian languages are included in the table.

Figure 2 shows the percentage of the total population of the language group that is bilingual in Hindi. These figures indicate that the use of Hindi is for the most part concentrated in the northwestern regions of India, with relatively little use in the southern regions and along the northeastern border. Census data not included here indicate that native speakers of Assamese, Bengali, Kannada, Malayalam, Tamil, and Telugu show a greater tendency to learn English than Hindi, while native speakers of Gujarati, Kashmiri, Marathi, Oriya, Punjabi, and Urdu show the opposite tendency. The areas showing a preference for English are precisely the areas of greatest protest against the adoption of Hindi as the official language of India. Which is cause and which is effect is, of course, debatable.

Our purpose in examining the 1961 Census was to determine, if we could, whether statistics supported the claims of either faction, pro-English or pro-Hindi. What have we really learned? First of all, that Hindi-speakers outnumber English-speakers ten to one. And yet, more Indians chose English as their second language than any other language, including Hindi. Surely this indicates the importance and usefulness of a knowledge of English.

In studying the conflict between Hindi and English, it is important to understand the social and psychological processes involved—the sociolinguistic attitudes of nationalism on the one hand, and language loyalty on the other.

To begin with, one thing at least seems clear: the artificial boundaries left behind by departing colonial administrations have created intense problems for the newly independent, developing

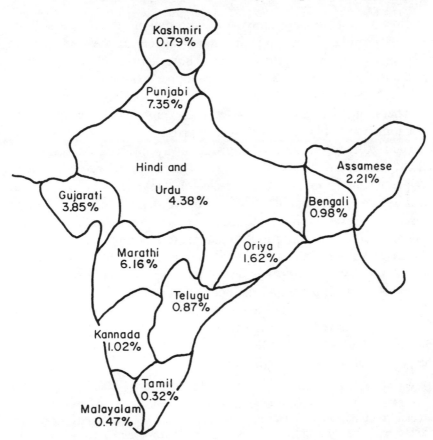

Figure 2. Percentage of People in Each of the Principal Language
Groups Speaking Hindi as a Second Language

countries of Asia and Africa, where new administrations now face the complicated task of "nation-building." And one way to create a national identity out of this cultural confusion is to invoke national language as a unifying force. Once a linguistic code is established, it can become a symbol of group identity.

In the past the language question was "solved" by the political authority, contact with this authority being limited to an elite group. The people in general were never consulted. With the democratization of the newly independent nations, however, came the ideas of a national community and participatory politics, and thus the need for a dialogue between the general population and the political authority.

However, attempts to unify or build a nation through the symbol of a national language can lead to bitter dissent on the part of other language groups within the country. Thus, there develops a conflict: at the national level, we have the development of nationalism; at the regional level, we have the development of a local consciousness.

The Indian linguist Jyotirindra Das Gupta describes the same phenomenon as the conflict between "primordial group loyalty" and "civic loyalty to the nation." A group always protects its own traditions, values, and loyalties, and any attempt to displace its language can result in an emotional resurgence of "language loyalty." This is precisely what has happened in India. Non-Hindi linguistic groups resent the elevation of another regional language, Hindi, to the national level, and have refused to submit to this injustice. As Gerald Kelley explains it, "the attempt to extend the domain of any variety of Hindi beyond its proper regional borders, even if it is done in the name of national pride and the need for a native language common to all the people, is seen as having the effect of promoting the regional interests of the Hindi-speaking people."[21]

According to Karl W. Deutsch's theory, this effect is not entirely coincidental. He defines a nationality as

an alignment of large numbers of individuals from the middle and lower classes linked to regional centers and leading social groups by channels of social communication and economic intercourse, both indirectly from link to link and directly with the center . . . [and] *pressing to acquire a measure of effective control over the behavior of its members. It is a people striving to equip itself with power,* with some machinery of compulsion strong enough to make the enforcement of its commands sufficiently probable to aid in the spread of habits of voluntary compliance with them. . . . Such power can be exercised through informal social arrangements, pressure of group opinion, and the prestige of national symbols. It can be exercised even more strongly through formal social or political organizations, through the administration of educational or economic institutions, or through the machinery of government. [Emphasis added.][22]

Thus the efforts of the Hindi-protagonists can be interpreted as an attempt to gain power through the use of the Hindi language as a national symbol and the adoption of this language by the educational system and government of India.

The strength of a nationalist process, however, depends on two factors: the extent to which the ruling class promotes the process, and the extent to which the masses have been mobilized. Although the Hindi nationalist movement has the support of the Indian government, it does not enjoy the full support of the masses. Anti-Hindi factions have recognized—or perhaps only felt intuitively—the thrust for power inherent in the nationalist movement, and they fear that the establishment of Hindi would mean more or less permanent second-class citizenship for all non-Hindi speakers. Therefore, they have violently resisted the adoption of Hindi as the official language of India and have instead reverted to their regional languages, refusing to place their absolute trust in a nation that is unjust to some of its peoples, and proclaiming English the only language capable of uniting India linguistically without dividing it politically, while leaving the regional languages separate and equal.

This "language loyalty" has seriously hindered the development of a sense of unity in India. Although language division does not necessarily lead to political crisis, its disruptive potential cannot be ignored. The reorganization of state boundaries along linguistic borders in the 1950s, although it greatly facilitated education and administration, also served to promote the development of language loyalties in various parts of the country, and thus has led to some degree of political danger. At very best, India can only hope to learn to compromise and unify; at worst, the language conflict could lead to another partition—a linguistic partition equivalent to the religious partition of India and Pakistan.

Is it not possible, however, to have political integration without national integration? According to Das Gupta, "a national political community does not require for its existence a precondition of sentimental solidarity. . . . In the multiethnic, multilingual, and multireligious new states the political development is likely to precede and is expected to promote national loyalty and cohesion."[23] There has been a tendency among writers to work on the assumptions that "social homogenization" is a prerequisite for national development, that systems like democracy are incapable of ensuring a stable development, and that social protest must be suppressed and the social cleavages between the groups eliminated through forcible amalgamation in order to make this development possible. Das Gupta, however, claims that

policies of imposition have mostly been of temporary value. Imposition in most cases has purchased political discipline at the cost of the alienation of social groups from the political authority. In doing this what is usually gained in point of temporary stability is generally lost in point of political integration.[24]

The existence of language divisions in a multilingual society cannot be denied; they must be considered reflections of legitimate group interests and settled through negotiation and compromise. Often, this will mean sacrificing regional interests to national ones. But what exactly are the national interests in the case of India? Joshua A. Fishman draws an important distinction between "nationalism" and "nationism": for the nationalist, the question is not one of language choice, as he is already committed in this respect, but rather one of reinforcement; for the nationist, "language choice is a matter of calculated effectiveness, of communicational ease, of operational efficiency. . . . Rival languages are considered in terms of what they can contribute to the functional strength of the nation."[25] It is a question of what is "best" for the country. This kind of movement is what is needed in India today—an objective appraisal of the linguistic situation and a rational decision as to the "proper" official language for India. By now, the language problem has become such an emotional issue that the solution is not at all clear.

Let us assume for the moment that, for better or for worse, India decides to stick by the constitution, and Hindi is to become the official language of India. We are then faced with the problem of codifying a language with no standard—or, rather, with several standards but no single standard. There are two schools of thought as to the direction the standardization of Hindi should take. There has been a concerted effort on the part of Hindi nationalists to purge the language of all English and Persian loan-words, thus "retaining its purity from the contamination of outside influences." This has resulted in the "Sanskritization," or "classicalization," of the language, which to a large extent defeats the purpose of standardization, since it tends to separate the speech of an elite from that of the masses, thus lessening rather than promoting mass comprehension and communication. Others, however, feel that "a common language for India should build on popular usage and convention and not on the literary injunctions of the Pandits and their political defenders." Emphasis, they say, should be on the common elements of popular speech, and the language should draw on all the languages of India to enrich itself. Technical terms should be drawn from wherever seems most appropriate, be it Persian, Sanskrit, or English.

In the meantime, we must recognize that the development of a language is a slow and difficult process. While planning for the long-range adoption of Hindi as the official language of India, there is nevertheless a need to fill the gap between a withdrawing English and a slowly advancing Hindi. At any rate, the crucial problem will be in engineering acceptance of the language.

As the struggle over language continues, language attitudes will have to be revised and relaxed. The necessity for compromise becomes increasingly apparent. One can only hope that through a careful and rational reappraisal of the linguistic situation, India will be able to reach a compromise suitable for its unity and its development within the near future.

NOTES

1. V. M. Tarkunde, Foreword to *The Great Debate: Language Controversy and University Education,* ed. A. B. Shah (Bombay: Lalvani Publishing House, 1968), p. vi.
2. Jyotirindra Das Gupta and John J. Gumperz, "Language, Communication and Control in North India," in *Language Problems of Developing Nations,* ed. Joshua A. Fishman, Charles A. Ferguson, and Jyotirindra Das Gupta (New York: John Wiley & Sons, 1968), p. 160.
3. Official Language Commission statistics, accepted and used by most pro-Hindi writers.
4. Frank Anthony, "English versus Hindi," in *The Great Debate,* p. 39.
5. Ibid., pp. 39–40.
6. Romila Thapar, "The Past," *Seminar 76,* New Delhi, December 1965, p. 16.
7. K. R. Srinivasa Iyengar, "Messing up the Medium," *The Great Debate,* p. 69.
8. Punya Sloka Ray, "A Single Script," *Seminar 68,* New Delhi, April 1965, p. 44.
9. "The Problem," *Seminar 76,* p. 11. Many Indian languages have their own scripts. This is an additional problem for communication and education,

and the question of a single script has provoked considerable controversy. For purposes of relative brevity, however, I have not discussed this aspect of the problem.

10. Triguna Sen, *The Great Debate,* p. 12.
11. K.C.S., "Education and Language," in *The Great Debate,* p. 49.
12. Mahatma Gandhi, in S. Mohan Kumaramangalam, *India's Language Crisis* (Madras: New Century Book House, 1965), p. 11.
13. V. M. Tarkunde, in the Foreword to *The Great Debate.*
14. K.C.S., *The Great Debate,* pp. 56–57.
15. Pravinchandra J. Ruparel, "Historical Survey," *Seminar 68,* New Delhi, April, 1965, p. 36.
16. Triguna Sen, *The Great Debate,* p. 13.
17. William Bright, review of *Census of India 1961, Language Tables* by A. Mitra, in *Language* 44, no. 3 (September 1968): 685.
18. Stanley Lieberson, "Language Questions in Censuses," *International Journal of American Linguistics* 33, no. 4 (October 1967): 139.
19. A. Mitra, *Census of India 1961,* vol. I, *India,* part II-C (ii), *Language Tables* (Union Publications, 1967), p. 437.
20. According to Bright, this figure is actually a bit higher, as his calculations are based only on reports of English as a second language for mother-tongue speakers of thirty-five major languages.
21. Gerald Kelley, "The Status of Hindi as a Lingua Franca," *Sociolinguistics,* ed. William Bright (The Hague: Mouton & Co., 1966), p. 300.
22. Karl W. Deutsch, *Nationalism and Social Communication: An Inquiry into the Foundations of Nationality* (Cambridge, Mass.: The MIT Press, 1966), pp. 101–104.
23. Das Gupta, *Language Problems,* p. 21.
24. Ibid., pp. 23–24.
25. Joshua A. Fishman, "Sociolinguistics and the Language Problems of Developing Countries," in *Language Problems,* p. 9.

BIBLIOGRAPHY

Bright, William, ed. *Sociolinguistics.* The Hague: Mouton & Co., 1966.
Bright, William. Review of *Census of India 1961, Language Tables,* by A. Mitra. *Language* 44, no. 3 (September 1968): 684–687.
Deutsch, Karl W. *Nationalism and Social Communication: An Inquiry into the Foundations of Nationality.* Cambridge, Mass.: The MIT Press, 1966.
Ferguson, Charles A., and John J. Gumperz, eds. *Linguistic Diversity in South Asia: Studies in Regional, Social, and Functional Variation.* Publication 13 of the Indiana University Center in Anthropology, Folklore, and Linguistics. *International Journal of American Linguistics* 26, no. 3 (July 1960): 92–118.
Fishman, Joshua A., Charles A. Ferguson, and Jyotirindra Das Gupta, eds. *Language Problems of Developing Nations.* New York: John Wiley & Sons, 1968.
Gumperz, John J. "Hindi-Punjabi Code-Switching in Delhi," *Proceedings of*

the Ninth International Congress of Linguistics, ed. Horace G. Lunt, The Hague: Mouton & Co., 1964.

Haugen, Einar. *Bilingualism in the Americas: A Bibliography and Research Guide.* Publication 26 of the American Dialect Society. University, Ala.: University of Alabama Press, 1956.

Kamath, V. B. *Linguistic Vivisection of India: Why Not Stop It Still?* Bombay: Bharatiya Vidya Bhavan, 1966.

Kumaramangalam, S. Mohan. *India's Language Crisis.* Madras: New Century Book House (P) Ltd., 1965.

"Language: A Symposium on the Issues Involved in the Language Controversy," *Seminar 68* (New Delhi, April 1965).

Lieberson, Stanley, ed. Introduction to *Explorations in Sociolinguistics.* Publication 44 of the Indiana University Research Center in Anthropology, Folklore, and Linguistics. *International Journal of American Linguistics* 33, no. 4 (October 1967): 134–151.

Mitra, A. *Census of India 1961.* Vol. I, *India,* Part II-C (ii), *Language Tables.* Union Publications.

"The Politics of Language: A Symposium on the Background to the War over Words," *Seminar 76* (New Delhi, December 1965).

Shah, A. B., ed. *The Great Debate: Language Controversy and University Education.* Bombay: Lalvani Publishing House, 1968.

Weinrich, Uriel. "Functional Aspects of Indian Bilingualism," *Word* 13, no. 2 (August 1957): 203–233.

———. *Language in Contact: Findings and Problems.* The Hague: Mouton & Co., 1967.

KATHY SUE WILLIAMS DONER

Stetson College

Traditional Versus Modern Medicine

The modernization of non-Western countries often involves changes the West itself did not experience, among them the abrupt updating of medicine. In Japan, China, and India, Western medicine did not simply fill a vacuum of medical knowledge; instead, it was superimposed upon the traditional lore. How did these two types of medicine interact? And what role does traditional medicine still play, years after the introduction of Western ideas? I want to explore these questions in an attempt to answer a larger one: Just what determines the role of ancient medical lore in a society?

I. THE EASTERN APPROACH

It is difficult to detect any coordinated system of traditional medicine in the history of Japan. In fact, my research has unearthed only a conglomeration of such disparate practices as the use of medicinal

KATHY SUE WILLIAMS DONER *left her home in Palm Bay, Florida, and her studies in biology at Stetson College, De Land, Florida, to join IHP. In addition to biology, Kathy Sue was also interested in literature, government, and religious affairs, and planned to become a doctor. After her year with IHP, Kathy Sue married and in 1970 completed her undergraduate work. She trained in public health and nutrition at the University of Michigan, and has done recent field work in Appalachia. She planned to enter medical school in the fall of 1972.*

teas, charred plants and animals, toad skin oil, and bear gall. These medications probably evolved as the result of superstition, or from experience by trial and error. When certain practices proved effective—for example, the massage and the steam bath—they were absorbed into the culture. Other practices, such as acupuncture and moxa-burning—the combustion of herbs directly on the skin or the tips of acupuncture needles—were adopted from China in the earliest centuries.

In contrast to the miscellaneous Japanese practices, Chinese traditional medicine is a distinct system based on philosophy, science, and practice. From its philosophical orientation, Chinese medicine developed its definition of health. The comprehensive concepts of Yin-Yang and the Five Elements, for example, depict man as a microcosm whose health reflects a harmony of these elements, both between man and his environment and within man himself. Diseases are diagnosed as imbalances in this structure. The ancients patiently observed the functioning of nature, deduced the functioning of man and his diseases, and then sought to restore health through cures compatible with nature's own laws. This worldview largely determined the extent of scientific investigation in Chinese medicine. Early theories which developed from the comprehensive principles were based partly on experimental results. When later experience accrued, however, the rigidity and scope of the previous body of theory and a reverence for ancient authority prevented any theoretical alterations despite the accumulation of new knowledge.

The result was a stagnant science in which the use of herbs and acupuncture for curing disease was limited by a well-defined theoretical framework. The science was partly fallacious. Since dissection was forbidden by Confucian teachings, and since the traditional attitude toward health was not one inclined toward examining the body in minute detail, anatomical drawings were incorrect. Nor was surgery an active field. Hence, the sum of early Chinese scientific knowledge is a large *materia medica* plus the practice of acupuncture, and these were passed on through the centuries.

It should be pointed out that its religious basis helped Chinese traditional medicine to survive for over two thousand years. Theory, practice, and the acceptance of authority held the system together among professionals, but the transformation of certain of its aspects into traditions yielded additional support. Examples of this can be found in the presentation of certain beliefs by gods or spirits and the reflection of theory in the diet lore.

In India there are at least four systems of medicine, but we can consider Ayurvedic as the traditional medicine since it is the oldest. Like early Chinese medicine it too seeks the attainment of a state higher than mere good health. For example, it defines the role of the soul in man. Furthermore, much of its understanding of man derives from its perception of the universe; indeed, "Ayurveda" literally means the "science of life." Traditional Indian medicine seeks to fit phenomena into simplistic patterns. Its definition of health is similar to that of the Chinese approach; the whole is not seen as the sum of the parts but as the principles which govern their inter-action. Disease is caused by an imbalance between organism and environment, not by bacteria, and a diseased mind is as harmful to health as is a diseased body.

Ayurvedic medicine is based not only on objective science but on subjective philosophy. The subjective and objective, or the phil-osophy and the science, are viewed in the Ayurvedic system as the concave and convex of the whole. Whereas philosophy determines the scope of concern and manner of presenting information, scien-tific investigation—not guesswork—furnishes the knowledge. For example, centuries of experience have yielded the present knowledge about herbs and various treatments; this is the knowledge that is now classified according to the three principles, the tastes, and the spe-cific effects. Two thousand years ago dissection of corpses was ad-vocated, and as a result Ayurvedic medicine claims to have reached a fair understanding of circulation and to have performed major operations with the aid of drugs and yoga. Even brain operations and a theory of germs have been mentioned; many of the details, however, have been lost with invasions of India throughout history. At one time there were eight specialized branches of Ayurvedic studies, including botany and veterinary medicine.

The practice of Ayurvedic medicine has retained certain qualities. First, great emphasis is put on the practitioner, whose skill was de-veloped through tutelage. His personality was likewise developed in his education, since Ayurvedic theory maintains that a powerful mind can help a diseased one. Since the practitioner treated everyone without charging fees, he was able to gain wide experience. The villagers provided for his physical needs in return for his services. Second, Ayurvedic medicine purports to be a "natural" application of knowledge. And, in that it uses many familiar herbs and it shares its philosophy with the people, it *is* natural. This bond with the culture ensures the same type of stability found in Chinese medicine. Third, Ayurvedic medicine does not promise quick solutions and instant relief; rather, it acknowledges that recovery is often a slow process. In fact, it claims that its patience can offer permanent relief from chronic disease which Western medicine can only suppress.

Ayurvedic medicine prides itself on these three aspects of its practice. They contribute to the superiority which Ayurvedic medicine feels able to demonstrate in its practice: its drugs supposedly have controlled side effects and show little danger of overdosage; nervous cases are treated without habit-forming drugs; and gastrointestinal problems are not further aggravated by antibiotics which destroy helpful intestinal bacteria.

We have seen how the traditional medicines of China, Japan, and India differ, but now one might ask what they share in common. In contrast to Western medicine, traditional medicines

- emphasized the importance of philosophy,
- sought cures through other than physical means,
- relied on personal observation rather than on standard tests,
- sought to prevent illness by emphasizing the need for a balanced life,
- reflected on agricultural society, and
- developed slowly because it was difficult to test the efficacy of treatments.

II. THE WESTERN APPROACH

With this description of traditional medicines in mind, let us consider Western medicine and its three components of philosophy, science, and practice. Western medicine acknowledges that its scope of concern is smaller than that of the traditional approach; no knowledge of metaphysics is necessary to understand human disease, nor are spiritual goals. Instead, it focuses on problems with an intense specialization and trusts in dissection and surgery. One observes in Western medicine a drive for constant innovation as this modern system rebels against comprehensive explanations. The approach is systematic, since Western medicine increases knowledge stepwise by forming and often disproving hypotheses and since it does not deduce facts from general classifications. Hence, "philosophy" as it appears in Chinese and Ayurvedic medicines has no apparent role in Western medicine. Indeed, Western medicine's compulsion to acquire knowledge and solve problems—its "philosophy" —closely parallels that of Western science. For Western medicine is above all scientific, and the physician's art has been replaced by laboratory tests. This medical practice reflects industrialization (just as traditional medicines were expressions of agricultural systems), and has achieved greatest progress through mass action. For example, public health measures and mass immunization have drastically reduced infectious diseases. Moreover, many of its treatments are standard. Perhaps Western doctors see health more in terms of populations and lab tests than in terms of individuals. This attitude is as "unnatural" as is industrialization; drugs and machines are created and used in treatments. The urgency of the Western approach also contradicts the patience shared by practitioners of traditional medicines. Applying new treatments without decades of testing reflects the contemporary compulsion to alter the environment.

These two types of systems, traditional and Western, express the cultures in which they developed. But what can one expect in an entirely new situation—when a developing nation retains some traditional characteristics while acquiring modern ones?

III. THE IMPACT OF WEST AND EAST

It appears that Western medicine was early embraced by the Japanese. Indeed, it is said that medicine was the principal avenue for the introduction of Western knowledge into Japan. As early as 1641 the Dutch established a trading post at Dejima and taught medicine to Japanese representatives. Also, the first book to be translated and published in Japan was a Western anatomical text. Since Japanese medicine was already a conglomeration of native and borrowed practices, Western ideas were smoothly absorbed.

Why, then, has the advent of modern medicine caused such conflict in China and India? One significant difference is this: in China and India medicine was not simply a collection of treatments and theory, as in Japan, but an integrated system of philosophy, scientific heritage, and practice. Above all, the systems were stable, and could not so easily accommodate themselves to the new ideas from the West. In fact, the survival of traditional medicine itself was at stake when Western medicine claimed to have greater knowledge or better cures.

When science was embraced as a means to modernize China, it appeared as a threat to Chinese culture. Naturally, medical practitioners concerned with their own survival and that of their heritage reacted defensively by pointing out the inherent differences between the two systems. For instance, the ancient medical heritage of the East claims to have been already advanced when Europeans were still living in caves. Slogans differentiate the systems; traditional medicine calls itself the "Way of Virtue" or the "Way of the True King," while Western medicine is called the "Way of Force" or the "Way of the Tyrant." Furthermore, Western medicine is frequently criticized for lacking a comprehensive view of life and for de-emphasizing the art of intuitive diagnosis.

For their part, Western doctors in China react in different ways. Some find it easy to consider traditional medicine only in terms of the aspects they see in their practice. For example, orthopedic surgeons are angered by the traditional bone-setters whose treatment sometimes necessitates later amputation. And surveys show a higher mortality rate from measles for children treated by a traditional herbalist than those treated by a modern doctor.[1] Any viewpoints based on this type of experience are likely to be prejudiced. Not all Western doctors, however, are exposed only to the traditional practices, and those who consider the entire system often declare it to be obsolete. More generous observers acknowledge that the accumulated lore might contain some useful information on the uses of herbs.

In India, Ayurvedic medicine has also reacted against the Western intrusion. While Chinese traditionalists feared their government might threaten their survival, in India the Ayurvedic schools are more concerned with the intellectual challenge to their validity. Ayurvedic science claims to be on at least an equal footing with Western science. Moreover, it attacks the philosophy of Western medicine and cannot condone, for example, the use of aspirin in relieving symptoms when the cause of the pain has not been ascertained. Other aspects of Western medicine which might not challenge Ayurvedic medicine directly are still viewed with skepticism: Western techniques mean nothing until translated into Ayurveda's comprehensive scheme.

Ayurvedic philosophy and its influence on Ayurvedic science have hindered the West's understanding of this traditional system. In addition, misunderstanding of the philosophy has been accentuated by what the Ayurvedic schools claim to be a gross mistranslation of its terminology by the West. When viewed by the West in this distorted form, the central concepts of Ayurvedic medicine can easily be rejected. Although it is easy for Western doctors to disregard Ayurvedic medical lore as mere myth, some of them have managed to ignore the philosophy and focus on the science.

What about the impact of Western medicine on the cultures of Japan, China, and India? In Japan, acupuncture, moxa-burning, and some herbal preparations are still used, and such traditions as hot baths and massages have remained part of the culture. The Japanese borrowed what they considered the superior skills of Western medicine—training techniques from Germany and America, health insurance plans from Germany, and health center designs from WHO. In short, Japan relies heavily on Western medicine.

The Chinese, on the other hand, have attempted to integrate the two systems into a uniquely Chinese product:

Unite all medical workers, young and old, of the traditional school and modern school, and organize a solid united front to strive for the development of the people's health work.[2]

But why use traditional lore to attain national health? Would it not be more expedient for China to rely on Western medicine, as did Japan, regardless of protests from the traditional school? Evidently, China has had a certain success with traditional medicine and wants to take advantage of the herbs, the acupuncture, and the bone-setting techniques. Moreover, there is a large manpower pool of traditional practitioners, and traditional medicine with its link to the culture of the people is more likely to be accepted than a new foreign approach.[3]

Examples of the use of Chinese traditional medicine demonstrate its role in this modernizing country. Village doctors trained in both medicines might use Western techniques for diagnosing and treating acute diseases while relying on traditional medicine for treating chronic ailments. A doctor might practice acupuncture because the people ask for it, whether or not he believes it to be theoretically sound. Another example is a Western home-nursing program in Hong Kong which employs an acupuncturist for patients who request him or who cannot be helped by Western medicine. Traditional practitioners of Chinese medicine are also employed in the Chinese public health centers. And at research institutes the useful aspects of traditional knowledge are investigated; the effective techniques are then combined with modern ones, and the syntheses appear in scattered reports in Chinese medical journals.

Besides the synthesis forced by national policy, there is a natural integration of traditional and Western medicine which takes place when the Chinese people themselves select parts of each medical system and use both to maintain their health. In Hong Kong even many of the educated use the traditional bone-setters. Others believe that traditional medicine is especially effective for nervous, digestive, or gynecological problems. Also, a small survey of hospital wards shows that some patients patronize traditional medicine because they fail to respond to Western treatment.[4] People in Hong Kong use traditional medicine as much for its intimate approach as for its physical benefits: practitioners are more than likely to be family doctors and will spend more time with the patient than would doctors of Western medicine. One would also expect to find cultural ties with traditional medicine a reason for patronage; this is probably more the case in China than in Hong Kong, where herbs are expensive and in short supply while Western medicine is cheap.

This natural integration would surely have been slow had not the strong and persuasive communist government officially blessed traditional medicine. Other Chinese customs have declined with modernization, and it is not unreasonable to assume that had the government willed it, traditional medicine might have met a similar fate. In summary, then, we can see that the role of traditional medicine in China has been largely determined by national policy.

India is unique in its continuing ability to accommodate potentially conflicting medical systems. In this pluralistic country there seems to be little of the Chinese urgency to integrate different systems into a single national scheme. No political ideology is necessary in India to justify the retention of Ayurvedic medicine, and the body of Ayurvedic medicine is not fragmented nor is its role colored with ideology. As a result, Ayurvedic medicine has maintained more of its identity than has traditional Chinese medicine. This does not mean that Ayurvedic and Western medical systems ignore each other. Conflict generated from the philosophical impact of the two systems has been partly offset by their progressive scientific natures; they have avoided contradiction by exchanging the best of each other and ignoring each other's philosophical bases. Thus, Ayurvedic medicine is quite distinct from, but nevertheless coexists with, Western medicine.

It is worth noting here how Ayurvedic medicine adapts certain techniques of Western medicine. In one Ayurvedic hospital certain eye operations are performed by the Western method with Ayurvedic pre- and postoperative care. This hospital has also introduced female nurses into its organization, a wholly modern practice. It is evident that Western medicine is not seen as a threat to the validity of the ancient system but as an aid and a challenge. For instance, Ayurvedic medicine welcomes the Western knowledge of anatomy and physiology with the attitude that this new knowledge will fill in the details that Ayurvedic medicine has lost over the years. The Western X-ray machine and experimental techniques are used for confirming that which Ayurvedic medicine has already predicted. Thus, the progressive scientific nature of Ayurvedic medicine will ensure its relevance and durability.[5]

Our original question was: If traditional medicine plays different roles in different countries today, what has determined these roles? The major factors seem to be these: the stability of the ancient system; its ability to absorb new knowledge; the existence of forces which demand integration; the political ideology; and the degree of support for Western medicine. Anyone who seeks to influence medicine in a developing country must take all these factors into consideration.

To approach these nations with scorn for their traditional lore will render our assistance ineffective, and even counterproductive. Perhaps even more important, such a narrow response to their heritage would blind us to ancient remedies and concepts which might shed light on modern medical research. We do have much to give traditional medicine, this we know. But perhaps we also have much to learn.

NOTES

1. J. D. F. Lockhard and G. I. Forbes, "Some Aspects of Measles Mortality in Hong Kong," *Far Eastern Medical Journal* 4, no. 3 (March 1968), 99–101.
2. Mao Tse-tung, *China's Medicine*, September 1967, p. 690.
3. American scientists Arthur Galston of Yale and Ethan Signer of MIT recently returned from the People's Republic of China where they observed a middle-aged woman undergo a major operation—the removal of an ovarian cyst—with acupuncture as the only anesthetic. In this instance, the surgeons inserted a number of brass-handled needles in the woman's wrists, and the patient remained fully conscious throughout the operation, showing no signs whatever of distress. (For a full account see *Newsweek*, June 6, 1971, p. 78.)
4. Gerald Choa, "Chinese Traditional Medicine and Contemporary Hong Kong," in *Some Traditional Chinese Ideas and Conceptions in Hong Kong Social Life Today* (Hong Kong: The Hong Kong Branch of the Royal Asiatic Society, 1967), p. 32.
5. I obtained all my information about Ayurvedic medicine from interviews with students and professors of Ayurvedic medicine in Lucknow. I also interviewed a Western-trained doctor in Lucknow, and a doctor trained in both systems in New Delhi.

BIBLIOGRAPHY

Bowers, John Z. *Medical Education in Japan*. New York: Harper & Row, 1965.

Crozier, Ralph C. *Traditional Medicine in Modern China*. Cambridge, Mass.: Harvard University Press, 1968.

Huard, Pierre, and Ming Wong. *Chinese Medicine*. London: World University Library, 1968.

Joya, Mock. *Things Japanese*. Tokyo: Tokyo News Service, 1958.

Needham, Joseph. "The Pattern of Nature-Mysticism and Empiricism in the Philosophy of Science," in *Science, Medicine, and History*, vol. 2, ed. E. A. Underwood. London and New York: Oxford University Press, 1953.

Siu, R. G. H. *The Tao of Science*. Cambridge, Mass.: MIT Press, 1957.

Wong, K. C., and Wu Lien-teh. History of Chinese Medicine. Tientsin: Tientsin Press, 1932.

Chapter Three | Changing Economies

Economic development is predicated on human and social change. The transition from a traditional economy to one characterized by sustained growth requires a transformation of individual lifeways and values. Too often, development is presented as an evolution of governmental perspective rather than a revolution of human wants. The essays in this chapter convey well the sense of individual impatience and dissatisfaction so familiar to those who live in modernizing societies.

As we progressed around the globe on our journey, it became increasingly clear to us that, whether we liked it or not, many developing countries were using the United States as a model for constructing their own economy of high mass consumption. Many students we talked with seemed less interested in ideology than in automobiles, stereos, and air conditioners. In societies where up to three-fourths of the people live in rural areas and are engaged in agricultural occupations, many covet transistor radios and TV sets.

The impacts of these changes in human wants are profound. Changing wants, as the next five essays document, require changes in the entire society. The essay "Urbanization, Industrialization, Modernization," makes clear why men move to cities in developing countries, and demonstrates that urban and industrial growth are inextricably entwined with economic development. The cities of modernizing societies are as old as they are new; the urban milieu is one characterized by a juxtaposition of old traditions and new ambitions; of oxcarts and autos. "Who Gets Ahead," the essay by David J. H. Dean, seeks to determine why entrepreneurs are among the most empathic individuals in developing societies, and explains why the merchants are more eager to discard family customs and embrace change in a developing society than are the peasants, workers, or governmental officials.

Yet cities and merchants, although they unwittingly consolidate a society as they look out for themselves, are insufficient to fire the engines of change and propel a country to economic self-sufficiency. Science and technology are also needed, as Michael S. Siegal points out in his essay, if a developing country is to succeed in the Global Science Game. A scientific establishment is of critical importance to a nation concerned with expediting economic change, Siegal insists. Young scientists and technicians need to be trained to help chart the future course of the nation and to disseminate the information on new techniques vital to every dynamic economy.

Even when a developing country has the scientists, and the merchants, and the cities, the going may be inexorably slow. John H. Zammito discusses the importance of the balanced development of the agricultural and industrial sectors in India, and explores the impediments in India's path to modernity and economic stability in "Why Doesn't India Make It?" His essay pinpoints the difficulties presently plaguing the Indian economy. Though patience is a crucial ingredient for ordered progress in lesser developed countries like India, patience breeds frustration as factions argue about economic priorities. In the final paper comprising this chapter, John A. Almstrom examines the limited role of one such segment—the military—in speeding economic development when political contention among civilians slows modernization.

Economic change is the most critical aspect of the developmental process. With their limited resources, high illiteracy rates, low investment, and snowballing urban growth, developing countries are under a great strain to appease their citizens' aspirations adequately. The race is not only against time. In societies where burgeoning populations compound the difficulty of achieving sustained economic growth, the race is with life itself.

THOMAS A. HIATT

Wabash College

Change is that which marks our era
faster now than e'er before.
Man revises, god despises
the waves that washed faith ashore.

With each day comes more revision
improving man's exacting vision,
Until, by man, he knows it's he
that manipulates his destiny.

Urbanization, Industrialization, Modernization

I. URBANIZATION AND MAN

There's a city there, Adana, all of clear glass. It sparkles day and night, just like the sun. You walk in the alleys between the houses, they call them streets, and it's all glass. It's as clean as can be. Trains come and go. On the sea, ships as big as villages go to the other end of the world. Everything shines like the sun, bathed in light. If you look at it just once, you can't take your eyes away. If it's money you want, it pours like a flood in the Chukurova. All you've got to do is work.—DURSUN TO OSMAN in *Mehmed, My Hawk*

THOMAS A. HIATT *is from Indianapolis, Indiana, and joined IHP from Wabash College in Crawfordsville, Indiana, where he was studying political science, German, and Russian. After IHP, Tom did independent research at the United Nations, and graduated from Wabash magna cum laude, a member of Phi Beta Kappa and recipient of the Phi Beta Kappa Prize. Having completed studies in international business and economic development at the Sloan School at MIT where he edited the Sloan Management Review, Tom is now working for the Ford Foundation in Islamabad, Pakistan.*

Developing nations around the globe are presently experiencing one of the most traumatic crises of their histories. This common experience is an internal one—and is not only a source of concern to all emerging nations but to the superpowers as well. This repercussive and dynamic process is the flood of humanity to the cities. It is called rapid urbanization.

Rapid urbanization is both universal and inevitable. And it is more rapid now than ever before.[1] Many people find objectionable man's urban destiny, yet they are often unaware of urbanization's close ties with human advancement. I contend that urbanization is a vital and necessary element of development. It is a process entwined with technological progress, and as a vital influence on the pace of this progress, it should command a high priority from those charting their nations' courses.

Many aesthetes indict urbanization as the debasement of man, the corruption of virtue, the end of happiness. They claim it distorts values and destroys morality. They speak of "commitment," "participation," "full living," "morality," and "values" like commodities that can be reaped with the crops in rural areas; they condemn "alienation," "frustration," "boredom," and "unhappiness" as natural concomitants of city life. Such critics, however, are themselves usually disgruntled urbanites who know little of rural living's rigors. With nostalgia they picture their forefathers happily tilling the land and deriving enormous satisfaction from working sixteen hours a day. They forget that rural life in much of the world is a life of poverty and misery.

Let me make one thing perfectly clear. I view urbanization as a good thing. If people are a little more comfortable or have a little more to eat in a city, then they should go there, regardless of the trouble caused for urban planners and government officials and regardless of the macroeconomic consequences. The worst urban poverty in emerging countries is still better than most rural conditions, and people should not be kept from seeking comfort.[2] The freedom to get up and *move,* to search for a better job and greater comfort—this is perhaps man's most important privilege. Whether or not all men have this privilege can make a tremendous difference in development.

The city has lured man for a long time. It has beckoned him with its opportunities for work, education, love, and wealth, and with its distinctive aura of excitement.[3] The city has not only affected man's decision concerning where to live; it has also determined how he shall live and whom he shall live with. Social scientists generally prefer to distinguish between the factors motivating man to accept an urban way of life by separating them into two categories: "pull" and "push." Pull factors include steadier and less arduous labor, higher wages, better homes, greater convenience, the desire for an education, the search for a spouse, and simple urban magnetism. Push factors commonly involve a high man/land ratio: a surplus of population in the rural areas, coupled with limited agricultural resources, forces a man to look beyond farming for a better way to support himself and his family.

How the motivation is labeled is, in the last analysis, unimportant. Clearly the main reason a man comes to the city is to work there, regardless of whether he is spurred by lack of employment in the country or attracted by the promise of more money in town. What is important is that men everywhere are finding the city a more attractive and convenient place to live. This trend toward an urban world has important consequences for both the men that choose to live in the city and for the city itself as a social unit.

For a man it means adapting to a new way of life. It means finding a job, seeking shelter, and rearing a family in an unnatural environment. It means higher literacy rates, increased chances for obtaining an education, and more exposure to the mass media. It means greater communication between the governing and the governed, and a resulting rise in individual political participation.[4] In short, it brings a man closer to the mechanisms of change, closer to trends in social reform and technological innovation. Economist Bert Hoselitz, who has been involved in much of the contemporary theorizing on economic growth, writes that "the rapidity with which a country modernizes, or at least with which psychological attitudes favorable to modernization are created, is dependent upon the growth of its cities."[5] It is in its capacity to mediate and facilitate change that the city most affects the lives of the men who comprise it.

As a unit of social organization, the city increases in importance directly in proportion to its size. As a collective unit of men the city enjoys a special legitimacy because it stands as the transitional unit between household and state. It derives this legitimacy from its role in three spheres: the economic, the political, and the social. Economically, the city is responsible for developing a domestic economy into a state or national economy. As a constellation of small enterprises the city is an arena of regional exchange for the surrounding district. Economically, then, the city acts as the catalytic agent for the national economy. Politically, the city is a natural center for supervisory, governmental, and legal institutions because the localized population base and the improved communication and transportation facilities enhance political effectiveness. Socially, the city is important because it is with its emergence and growth that men first band together and take action to safeguard their welfare. Such social organizations as labor unions confirm that the rise of cities coincides with a new awareness among men that public action is the most effective method of obtaining services for the individual while at the same time preserving his autonomy.

Modernization has increased the significance of the city's roles. As cities grow so do their responsibilities and their potential. They become loci of power, knowledge, and wealth. The rural and uneducated in the developing countries look to the cities with a new and sometimes naïve hope for an easier and more comfortable way of living. Simultaneously the world looks to the same burgeoning cities with the hope that they will relay change to those who need it most.

II. THE FIELD

Show us not the aim without the way,
For ends and means on earth are so entangled
That changing one, you change the other too;
Each different path brings other ends in view.
        —FERDINAND LASSALLE
        Franz von Sickingen

JAPAN

In few countries in recent years has urbanization been more dramatic than in Japan. The deluge of people into the cities has been concentrated and continuous. The Japanese city, once a quiet center of religion, culture, and feudal life, is today a noisy, pulsing, sprawling, industrial metropolis. Though Japanese cities have been in existence many centuries, this rapid growth is a contemporary phenomenon.

With an area smaller than the state of California and a population half that of the United States, Japan is the world's seventh most populous nation and ranks fourth in population density with 653 people per square mile. In density of population per square mile of arable land, however, Japan ranks first.[6] Given so many people, a dearth of farmland, and a paucity of natural resources to boot, one might contend that the urbanization of Japan was inevitable. Such a simplistic explanation, however, does not sufficiently explain the speed with which the process has occurred. Urbanist Takeo Yasaki notes that between 1920 and 1960 the nation's urban population swelled from 18 to 63.5 percent.[7] What are the reasons for this phenomenal growth?

The first three columns in Table 1 present the facts. They show

TABLE 1
POPULATION OF JAPAN [8] (UNITS: 1,000)

A Year	B Population	C % Urb.	D U/R Coef.	E % Pri. Ind.	F % Sec-Tert Ind.	G I/P Coef.
1920	55,391	18	0.22	53.5	23.3	0.44
1930	63,873	24	0.32	49.4	25.3	0.51
1940	72,541	38	0.61	— *	—	—
1945	71,998	28	0.39	—	—	—
1950	83,199	38	0.60	48.3	25.9	0.54
1955	89,276	56	1.28	—	—	—
1960	—	—	—	32.9	33.6	1.0
1965	98,275	68	2.13	25.8	37.1	1.4
1968	100,000	70	2.3	20	40	2.0

* These figures are not available.

the increase in and distribution of the population in Japan from 1920 to the present. Column B shows the increase in the total population while Column C indicates what percentage of the growing population is urban. Column D, which will be referred to as the urban/rural coefficient throughout this essay, is the urban population as a fraction of the rural.

To gain further insight into the factors behind the urban growth outlined in Table 1, I interviewed and circulated a questionnaire among twelve Japanese urbanists. Most of them suggested that the industrialization of their country was the primary factor behind its urbanization. This hypothesis explains that cities, as centers of high capital concentration, attract workers because of the higher wages they are able to offer. Not only is it advantageous for the wage-earners who get paid more in these production centers, but urbanization is also good for the factories which, with more workers, can produce more, make more profit, and eventually expand, creating more jobs which attract more men. This cyclical growth pattern suggests why urbanization speeds up when it occurs along with industrialization and why there exists such a wage discrepancy between urban and rural areas.

To test this theory I sought out data on the structure of the Japanese industrial population. According to the hypothesis, a move to the city would involve a corresponding change in occupation. Noting that the primary occupations (agriculture, fishing, lumber) seem to be the characteristically nonurban ones, I defined industrialization as the growth of the secondary (manufacturing and construction) and tertiary (trade, commerce, transport, storage, communications, and other services) sectors at the expense of the primary. The figures I collected on the population's industrial activities are presented in Columns E, F, and G in Table 1. Column E shows the percentage of the labor force involved in the primary industrial sector from 1920 to 1968; while Column F, in keeping with my definition, shows the *average* of the percentages of the labor force working in the secondary and tertiary industrial sectors for the same years. (For example, in 1920 20.8 percent of the industrial labor force was engaged in secondary types of industry and 25.7 percent was employed in the tertiary industrial sector; hence, the entry for "secondary-tertiary industries" for 1920 is 23.3 percent.) Note that the steady decline (except for the war years) of the portion of the labor force involved in the primary industrial sector is offset by a relatively even growth in the secondary and tertiary industrial sectors. Column G presents what we can call the industrial/primary coefficient. It is the industrial (secondary and tertiary) population as a fraction of the primary, and was obtained by dividing Column F by Column E.

These figures imply that since secondary and tertiary industries are found in towns and cities—not rural locales—a trend toward growing participation in urban types of labor is manifested. The striking degree to which these trends of urbanization and indus-

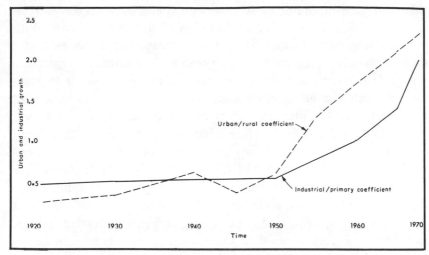

Figure 1. Urbanization and Industrialization in Japan

trialization correlate is readily visible in Figure 1. In this figure I have plotted the urban/rural and the industrial/primary coefficients against time. From the intimate numerical relationship it can be readily concluded that Japanese urbanization and industrialization have been inseparably related. To a large extent they appear to be complementary phenomena, each nourishing the other. Though urbanization outpaces industrialization, industrialization fired the rapid growth of the former; man's migration to the cities in search of employment, and industry's response by hiring him, clearly boosted industrial expansion and ever greater city-ward migration.

In addition to industrialization, one can cite other reasons for Japan's speedy urban growth. Anthropologist Takeo Sofue of Meiji University in Tokyo states that 95 percent of all Japanese households owned television sets in 1967 (against 89 percent in 1965 and only 26 percent in 1957). This flow of urban culture via the media into rural homes has undoubtedly contributed to the impressive rate of urban growth. Economist Tokue Shibata of Tokyo Metropolitan University feels that a major portion of the urbanizing population is youthful. Young Japanese, he contends, come to the cities after graduation looking for a job and a more exciting life. The young see urban life as colorful and free; the daring long to escape familial obligations and take part in such fads as the "peacock revolution"— the Japanese expression for colorful mod garb. Besides this factor of urban magnetism, Shibata also places great emphasis on the agricultural revolution as a major explanation of urban migration. With the wealthier farmers increasing their acreage (up to three acres, maintains Shibata, a large farm by Japanese standards) and purchasing modern farm machinery, the small farmer is finding it increasingly difficult to make a subsistence living by farming his small plot and marketing his produce. Competition forces his prices down, pushes him off the farm, and heads him toward the city. Other, more elaborate explanations for the urbanization of Japan are discussed by Takeo Yazaki in his *Social Change and the City in Japan.* He prefers to describe the city and its growth in organic terms, maintaining that people come to cities to be near institutions, that businesses collect there to be nearer other businesses and administrative centers, and that employers locate their enterprises in the city to gain access to a more qualified labor force.

Industrialization, however, clearly stands above the others as the main factor speeding the urban development of Japan. Since the Tokugawa Era of post-Meiji Japan, the emergence of modern Nippon has been swift and progressive. It is not reckless to suggest that the mutual rise of the city and industry has been instrumental in spurring a rate of development unparalleled in all Asia. Japan today has the world's third largest economy, generating some one hundred billion dollars a year. This amazing achievement is itself a witness to wise policies pursued in the past—and points to a path worth following.

Despite its incredible progress, however, Japan can ill afford to rest on its economic laurels. Even with one of the largest and fastest growing economies Japan remains twenty-first in rank of per capita income. This economic gap is reflected not only in the distribution of wealth among individuals—which may well be challenged in the near future—but in inadequate social spending as well. Japan's rapid modernization has not left it without wounds that need dressing. What Japan now needs is a shift in economic orientation; especially in the area of urban services does more social revenue need to be directed. I would urge sacrificing a portion of the world's highest growth rate for more immediate and much needed investment in human comfort and well-being. Lewis Mumford, in *The City in History,* writes that "democracies are often too stingy in spending money for public purposes, for its citizens feel the money is theirs."[9]

Let Japan heed his admonition. It is time to match the rapid private growth with generous spending in the public sector.

INDIA

It is hard to talk about India without discussing essentials. The Indians themselves are so confused about priorities and paths that it is more than a little presumptuous for an outsider to offer comment. Nobody has ever modernized an India before, but nearly everybody stands ready to give advice.

It seems to me that perhaps the biggest barrier to India's modernization is the present distribution of land, for land ownership in parts of contemporary India approaches feudalism. Entrepreneurs residing in New Delhi may own a thousand acres in the Punjab and another seven hundred in Hyderabad and not visit the holdings once a year. If these large tracts were broken up and given to the peasants to till and cultivate as their own, a farmer might feel he finally had something to work for and strive to improve his lot. And once he had some cash in his pocket, he would be bound to consider urban life more attractive and thus make his way to the city. In an urban community he, or at least his children, would be more likely to become literate and more economically productive; and both would become more sensitive to such issues as birth control. Perhaps most significant of all, land reform would mean urban migration as a result of ambition rather than destitution.

Enacting such a land reform would work no immediate miracles; but it would encourage the shift from rural to urban and in the long run stimulate the country toward a more acceptable rate of industrialization. With 18 percent of the country urban and an average of 14 percent of the population employed in the secondary and tertiary sectors (1961 figures), the present state of India's development is indeed pathetic. Table 2 substantiates this by presenting the population figures with their urban/rural breakdown and India's industrial structure.

Further discussion, beyond noting the extremely low coefficients in the table, seems superfluous. More insight, however, is gained by considering Figure 2, which depicts the rate of India's urban and industrial growth since 1900. The reader is cautioned not to be misled by the inflated scale of urban/industrial development used here: the apex of both lines is around 0.2 for India; but in the graph for Japan (Figure 1) it was above 2.0.

TABLE 2
POPULATION OF INDIA [10] (UNITS: 1,000)

A Year	B Population	C % Urb.	D U/R Coef.	E % Pri. Ind.	F Sec-Tert Ind.	G I/P Coef.
1901	238,340	10.9	0.12	71.8	14.1	0.20
1911	252,010	10.6	0.12	74.9	12.6	0.17
1921	251,240	11.4	0.13	76.0	12.0	0.16
1931	278,870	12.1	0.14	74.8	12.6	0.17
1941	318,540	13.9	0.16	— *	—	—
1951	360,950	17.3	0.21	72.1	13.9	0.19
1961	439,070	18.3	0.22	72.3	13.8	0.19
1968	527,340	—	—	—	—	—

* These figures are not available.

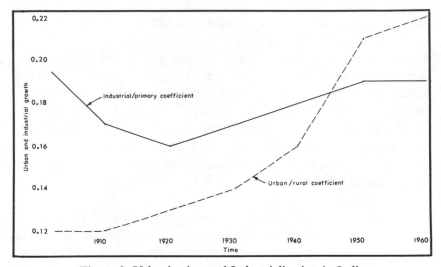

Figure 2. Urbanization and Industrialization in India

Urbanist Ashish Bose, whom I interviewed at the University of New Delhi, contended that one strong deterrent against increased urban migration is the backlog of unemployed and underemployed in the urban areas.[11] He maintained that unless the surplus labor force in the nonagricultural sector is accommodated, there can be no shift from the agricultural to the nonagricultural sector—and hence no large-scale urbanization. I disagree, however. I think the Indian peasants who come to cities do so in virtual ignorance of the employment situation there. Bert Hoselitz has a more acceptable explanation for the backward demographic and economic situation. He contends that certain characteristics of the Indian economy—

underdeveloped urban industry, a generally unskilled urban labor force, and a noncompetitive urban labor market—impede the optimum allocation of resources. These factors also prevent upward social mobility and sustain unemployment in Indian cities.[12]

But these impediments to urban and economic growth are not the only obstacles to India's development. A strong philosophical tradition which discourages action, a stifling bureaucracy, and a confusion of national priorities also thwart change. In Indian society the Hindu ethic inhibits the spatial and social mobility upon which the modern industrial community is predicated. The Hindu denunciation of the accumulation of wealth and political power as neither worthy nor respectable,[13] coupled with the ultimate belief that all life is illusory, creates in many peasants the fixation that ambition goes unrewarded. The peasant invests back-breaking labor and scarcely alters his existence. He has neither the mechanism for self-improvement (ambition), nor the goal (unfulfilled desires).

The nepotism of the Indian bureaucracy also stifles action by placing weak men in positions of authority. There was a consensus among the fifteen Indian urbanists I interviewed that "good leadership" was essential to the effective solution of urban problems. It is not easy for an administrator hemmed in by bureaucrats to make sweeping reforms.

Finally, a confusion over national priorities precludes action. While in New Delhi, the members of the IHP group heard Mr. Sondhi, a leader of a major opposition party in India (Jan Sangh), contend that the only way India could achieve international dignity was through the possession of nuclear armaments. We also heard Mr. Thapar, a member of Mrs. Gandhi's "Kitchen Cabinet," speak with contempt of the "Japanese path":

What India doesn't want [is] a few families controlling her economy. We want better things than unadulterated economic growth and worker exploitation. The Japanese path means an abandonment of a planned economy. We don't want foreign capital in here marketing cheap records and TV's which we know will be purchased. We need to discourage this and direct our capital into the heavy industry we require.

This demonstrates what I mean about confusion over ends and means. No thoughtful person deeply concerned with India's welfare would advocate spending already limited funds on the development of a nuclear capacity. And no thoughtful person would scorn the approach which gave rise to Asia's richest and technologically most advanced nation. The barriers of parochialism need to be dropped; and the Indian government needs to reappraise its goals with detached calculation. The leaders must for a moment forget about centralized economic planning, and encourage industrialization and agrarian development for their entire worth. India cannot afford to be choosy, and if cheap records and television sets mean more jobs, more money, and a speedier development, then India should put away its dignity and accept them. Dignity and nuclear weapons do not put food in the mouths of the poor.

It is time for India's leaders to realize that no path to development is easy. Admittedly, urbanization and industrialization bring problems—brutal problems like urban unemployment, urban poverty, and urban slums—but no one guarantees that the transition to development will be smooth. Industrialization in England was one of the hardest eras the people of that country had to suffer through, and the "stockyard" period in American history was just as bleak. Development is often a country's most formidable obstacle, and most developed countries can attest to the blood the process exacts. Nevertheless, most modern nations would agree that the ultimate omelet is worth the broken eggs.

India should continue its efforts toward birth control and literacy —speed them up if possible. It should also turn its attention to rural productivity and reform and urban industrialization of all sorts. There are thousands of things to be done, but these seem the priorities now facing the nation.

CHINA AND THE SOVIET UNION

A discussion of two authoritarian governments without data is somehow symbolic. Facts would allow us to evaluate the communist path of development; but, after skimming through piles of translations of the Mainland Chinese Press and hearing the ambiguities voiced by a Soviet economist at the Marx-Engels Institute in Moscow, one gets the distinct impression that quantitative evaluation of progress is not encouraged under communism.

Perhaps the most noteworthy aspect of urbanization and industrial development in China and the Soviet Union is the degree to which these processes are centrally controlled. Control over internal population migration and the structure of the industrial labor force is strictly exercised. In fact, these two controls are often implemented as one—a person may not move from a rural area unless he can show proof to the authorities of a job offer from urban industry. Such controls were cited by the Soviet economist of the Marx-Engels Institute as instrumental in preventing both urban unemployment and urban overpopulation. The Chinese also employ such methods and seem to use demography as a political as well as an economic tool. Several excerpts from recent Peking press articles substantiate this:

Displaying boundless loyalty to our great leader Chairman Mao, middle school graduates from Changsha, Hunan Province, have recently gone to the countryside to help build new Socialist villages. To date more than 200,000 college and middle school graduates in the province have gone to the forefront of agriculture.[14]

Today 70,000 revolutionary young intellectuals and revolutionary parents in Canton are gathered here at this massive oath-taking rally to express loyalty in going to mountains and rural areas, pledging with unbounded revolutionary lofty spirit to go to mountains and rural areas and firmly take the revolutionary path of integrating with the worker and peasant masses in accordance with great leader Chairman Mao's teachings. All intellectuals who can work in the countryside should go there happily.[15]

Today's *People's Daily* frontpages a report on how large numbers of cadres in Feni County, Kiangsi Province, East China, have gone to settle in the rural areas. The poor and lower-middle peasants have put it aptly: "City folk have come down to work as peasants in the villages. The wind has changed!"
Since last July, the Feni County revolutionary committee has sent more than 1,900 cadres . . . to the rural areas.[16]

I can only label such restraints on urban development provincial and economically deleterious. Mao's prejudices against city life—nearly as intense as Gandhi's—are doing far more to hold back economic progress than to generate it.

All controls, both the indirect kind employed by the Soviets and the more direct human-freighting tactics used by the Chinese, do much to thwart economic growth. History has demonstrated that the most rapid growth occurs when people are allowed to live where they obtain the greatest benefits. Centralized controls on mobility often prevent fully productive employment, thereby stifling the economy and its growth rather than aiding it.

The Chinese and Soviets may have less urban unemployment and fewer urban headaches as a result of these policies, but they also have more rural poverty. For all the Soviets' pride about their absence of urban slums, the living conditions we saw as we passed through the villages on the way to Zagorsk were exceedingly primitive.

With their controls the Soviets and the Chinese have admittedly avoided the chaos that faces India's urban planners. It remains to be seen, however, what repercussions these actions will have on national economic development in the future.

TURKEY

Turkey presents a case remarkably similar to that of India—so similar that I was tempted at first to group them together. There is, however, an essential difference which sets them apart—for Turkey there is more hope.

As in India, I consider Turkey's chief impediment to speedier development the archaic distribution of land. In parts of eastern Anatolia there exist yet today *aghas* who extract from their serfs as much as one-third of what they produce as rent for the land they occupy. That such restraints—restraints which tie the peasant to the land and prohibit agricultural mechanization as well as rural mobility—are allowed to exist in a land purportedly democratic is inexcusable. Kemal's *Mehmed, My Hawk,* written only a decade ago, provides a valuable insight into life in an isolated Turkish village. Repeatedly stressed in his account are the ignorance and docility of the peasants, the rigors of rural living, and the drabness of life in the small village community. Turkish peasants today are virtually cut off from the world by ancient practices of land ownership still in existence. Not only is it nearly impossible for them to accumulate enough wealth to leave the village, but the limited number of roads inhibits mobility and prohibits contact with travelers as well.

Unfortunately, this is not the only obstacle blocking the path of Turkey's progress. While the figures in Table 3 demonstrate that the urban population is increasing and now approaches 35–40 percent of the total population, the portion of the population employed in the secondary and tertiary industries has been extremely low, and this has acted as a great drag on the country's industrial emergence. Though the most recent data available at the time of writing indicate a slight rise in the speed of the country's industrialization, the present level of development is near that of India. Columns E, F, and G in

TABLE 3
POPULATION OF TURKEY [17] (UNITS: 1,000)

A Year	B Population	C % Urb.	D U/R Coef.	E % Pri. Ind.	F Sec-Tert Ind.	G I/P Coef.
1927	13,648	24.2	0.32	— *	—	—
1935	16,158	23.5	0.31	82.0	9.0	0.11
1940	17,821	24.4	0.32	—	—	—
1945	18,790	24.9	0.33	80.2	9.9	0.12
1950	20,947	21.9	0.28	—	—	—
1955	20,065	28.8	0.40	78.0‡	9.0‡	0.12‡
1960	27,755	26.3	0.36	75.0‡	10.0‡	0.13‡
1965	31,391	34.4†	0.52†	—	—	—

* Missing data are not available.
† Approximate figures.
‡ These figures are affected slightly by the deletion from the total labor force of those workers whose occupations were unknown.

Table 3 present the data I was able to collect on the structure of the Turkish labor force, and Figure 3 plots the urban/rural and industrial/primary coefficients against time for a more complete understanding of the problem plaguing the nation's development. The striking rise in urbanization from 1960 to 1965 could quite possibly have fostered a corresponding increase in industrialization which may make present conditions less bleak than they appear. At this point, however, we must examine the facts and avoid speculation. From Figure 3 it is clear that the growth of Turkey's urban and industrial population could be greatly speeded up, and that any

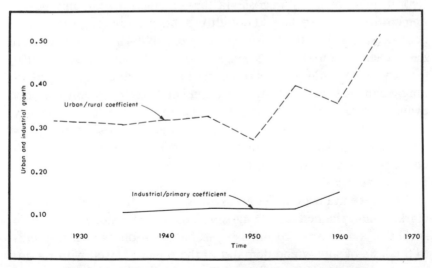

Figure 3. Urbanization and Industrialization in Turkey

barrier which prohibits this and thus bars the nation's swifter progress should be removed.

Additional light on Turkey's demographic development is shed by a close inspection of the location of the country's most rapidly growing cities.[18] The most significant urban growth in the last two decades has occurred in western Turkey, and *big* cities have come to this region in only the last ten years. To me, these developments are signs of hope—it is this area of Turkey which has seen the slowest growth. The promising sign of more and larger cities in this area means more loci of industrial progress and seems to portend more rapid modernization.

YUGOSLAVIA

Contemporary Yugoslavia, the wayward member of the Eastern European bloc, is distinguished from its communist neighbors by more than just its annual absence from their trade conferences. Perhaps the most obvious characteristic that has marked the nation's deviant path since it was ousted from the Cominform in 1948 is the near-total decentralization of government authority. Following the failures of state agricultural collectivization and national economic centralization in the early postwar years, Yugoslavia discarded the centrist values of the Soviet Union and slowly began to inaugurate reforms of its own.

It is precisely this decentralization, coupled with a judicious land reform, that has given Yugoslavia the impetus for economic development its neighbors lack. Though urbanization in Yugoslavia has been occurring at a fairly even pace (see Table 4), industrialization has picked up rapidly since 1953, and I feel this can be credited directly to the country's departure from traditional communist planning techniques. The last three columns in Table 4 present the only available data on the structure of the Yugoslav labor force, but they suffice to make clear my point. In 1953, the industrial/primary coefficient was about 0.19—India's level! In 1961, the index was well above 0.3—a good sign that industrial progress is occurring, and at a fairly rapid rate.

With decentralization, Yugoslavia is more characterized by free markets than planned ones. Yugoslav Finance Minister Janko Smole speaks of a decentralized market mechanism—one which responds to the laws of supply and demand at the regional level, with the intervention of the federal government to help the underdeveloped

TABLE 4
POPULATION OF YUGOSLAVIA [19] (UNITS: 1,000)

A Year	B Population	C % Urb.	D U/R Coef.	E % Pri. Ind.	F Sec-Tert Ind.	G I/P Coef.
1921	12,529	16.5	0.20	—	—	—
1931	14,517	17.4	0.21	—	—	—
1948	15,772	19.7	0.25	—	—	—
1953	16,937	21.8	0.28	72.4	13.8	0.19
1960	18,667	28.0	0.39	—	—	—
1961	—	—	—	60.9	19.6	0.32
1965	19,821	31.0	0.45	—	—	—
1968	20,186	33.0	0.49	—	—	—

areas—as characterizing the Yugoslav economy.[20] This abandonment of a planned economy and the injection of free competition into the industrial arena has generated the wealth which will drive Yugoslavia to a still more rapid rate of development, as is also suggested in the mutual growth of urbanization and industrialization shown in Figure 4.

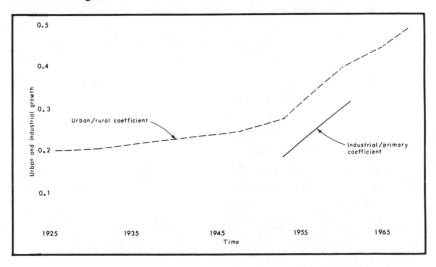

Figure 4. Urbanization and Industrialization in Yugoslavia

Yugoslavia still has a low level of urbanization.[21] With 28 percent of the population urban in 1961, the country was categorized as "insufficiently urban" by the United Nations.[22] With 33 percent urban in 1969, it probably still belongs to the same class. But tomorrow's prospects are brighter. With more closely integrated urbanization and industrialization should come a more rapid and stable economic development which will provide more jobs and ultimately increase the urbanization level. On the whole, the Yugoslav outlook looks healthy. More rapid modernization appears imminent.

SWEDEN

Quiet Sweden has led a peaceful, prosperous, and unassuming existence since Karl Jon Bernadotte smote Napoleon in Sweden's last war, in 1814. Neutrality abroad and stability at home appear to have given Sweden a special license for ordered development. Unhampered by overpopulation or land limitations (Sweden, like Japan, is the size of California, but has only eight million people) and singularly blessed with rich resources and a planning-oriented people, Sweden's path to progress has not been beset with the usual obstacles, nor has it been cushioned by outside aid. Indeed, what is extraordinary about the Swedish model of development is its very ordinariness; it is the way every economy should be able to develop —and the way few do.

The Swedish pattern has been that of democracy plus free enterprise. There have been no restrictions on urbanization,[23] no planned markets, no structured labor force, and no revolutions. Today, Sweden has the world's second highest per capita income and has obliterated urban poverty and rural unemployment. How can one explain this most astounding development?

As I have hinted earlier, I believe the key to smooth progress lies in a sound integration of urban and industrial growth. If this hypothesis is to be borne out, the Swedish configuration should substantiate the pattern by exhibiting a close interrelationship of urbanization and industrialization and, since there has been no external interference, a relatively smooth rate of progress.

Let us turn to the data to see if this is the case. The first three columns of Table 5 give the breakdown of Sweden's population by residence from 1870 to 1965. Columns E, F, and G, which give the percentage structure of Sweden's industrial population, require a special note of explanation. The figures from the years 1870 to 1950a are taken from a Swedish Census Bureau volume called *Historical Statistics* and are computed using the *total* Swedish population of each year as a base figure. After 1950 this method of enumeration was stopped; thus, the data for 1950b through 1965 differ slightly because they are computed using only the *economically active* population as a base. Though the percentages show the im-

TABLE 5
POPULATION OF SWEDEN [24] (UNITS: 1,000)

A Year	B Population	C % Urb.	D U/R Coef.	E % Pri. Ind.	F Sec-Tert Ind.	G I/P Coef.
1870	4,169	13.2	0.15	72.4	13.8	0.19
1880	4,566	15.4	0.18	67.9	16.1	0.19
1890	4,785	19.1	0.24	62.1	18.9	0.30
1900	5,136	25.1	0.34	55.1	22.5	0.41
1910	5,522	30.0	0.43	48.8	25.6	0.52
1920	5,904	45.2	0.82	44.0	28.0	0.64
1930	6,142	48.5	0.94	39.4	30.3	0.77
1940	6,371	56.2	1.3	34.1	32.9	0.96
1950a	7,042	67.9	2.1	24.6	37.7	1.5 ⎫ 1.7
1950b	7,042	67.9	2.1	20.2	38.6	1.9 ⎭
1960	7,498	72.8	2.7	13.6	43.2	3.2
1965	7,766	77.4	3.4	10.5*	45.7*	4.4*

* Approximate figures.

pact of the change, the coefficients do not seem to be greatly affected. For the year 1950 data were available for both methods of calculation; they are included to show the difference. The only consequence is that the industrial/primary coefficient might be a little inflated.

If we translate the data in Table 5 into a graph (Figure 5), the correlation is nearly perfect: the urban and industrial sectors have engaged in a commensurate rise since 1870. Growth in one area has

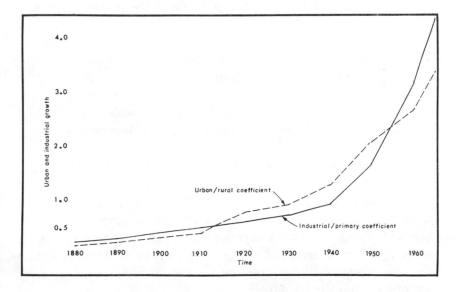

Figure 5. Urbanization and Industrialization in Sweden

nurtured growth in the other and shaped a model of modernization that is even more dramatic than Japan's. Sweden's rise to progress —the result of a democratic social order and freely competing market forces allowing unhindered mobility—has been a flawless one and is certainly worthy of closer inspection. The next section of my essay will thus examine the planning attitudes which facilitated this unparalleled growth.

III. PLANNING

We have somehow become responsible for evolution . . . a reality is to be constructed and not events awaited.   —GASTON BARGER

If urbanization is the most significant development of the contemporary world, then its spatial implications are the phenomenon's most arresting feature. Along with the natural population increase which in itself is steadily accentuating the limitations of finite living space, the growth of cities not only represents a reordering of the existing spatial arrangement but also dictates the rational use of space for the advancement of human society. Progress has rendered space a social resource which must be allocated carefully for optimal development. Careful allocation means careful planning.

In the course of this study, I have interviewed some sixty-five urbanists in six different countries. I have discussed with each the urban problems he feels are plaguing his community and his nation. I have listened as each has described his country's planning organizations for coping with these problems, and each has explained its faults to me and made his personal suggestions for its improvement. These talks have convinced me that planning's main thrust should be curative; it should never be employed in a manner which will endanger development (and it often is), nor should it be a course embarked on merely for its own sake. I am further convinced that the smoothest route to development calls for a minimum of interference rather than a maximum. Planning, when used as a delicate instrument to guide development—in such fields as birth control and literacy—can have an advantageous effect, but when applied to such areas as the organization of markets, the control of production, and the structuring of demography and labor forces, its consequences are often extremely harmful.

The IHP trip has shown me there are many different ways of achieving planning's objectives. Comparing the efficacy of these planning systems is not so easy, however; for the goals of these systems are often quite different. Nevertheless, I feel that brief recognition is due those countries whose special efforts and priorities set them apart. I have chosen to recognize these systems by distributing among them special awards.

The 1969 Award for the Most Effective Control of Demography and Prevention of Urban Problems goes to the authoritarian regimes, the Soviet Union and China. These nations have aimed at controlling the urban population and in this they have succeeded well. All other nations wishing to check internal migration are advised to consider the installment of a strongly centralized government as perhaps the most straightforward method of achieving this aim.

The 1969 Award for the Most Effective Planning System in Executing Urban Planner's Desires goes to Yugoslavia. A concentration of authority localized at the metropolitan level has enabled the urban planners of Yugoslavia to design and finance such ambitious schemes as Novi Beograd—a modern, multi-million-dollar comprehensive living area only recently completed. Due to this inverted distribution of power, officials at the city level are virtually unrestrained in deciding the scope of the projects they wish to execute. Yugoslavia was the first country I polled where most urban planners were satisfied with their system as it existed.

The 1969 Award for the Greatest Planning Effort goes to Hong Kong. In the wake of an overwhelming population increase over which it has little control, the Hong Kong colonial administration has made admirable headway in achieving its aims. Now the government is the landlord for over one-quarter of the colony's population. Though the housing provided is sometimes substandard and not always in the best location, the administrators have put forth an enormous effort to tackle a herculean task. Their successes have been continually dimmed by the Chinese who daily stream across the border and who have no shelter. Noteworthy is the fact that Hong Kong has financed its endeavors through the taxation of free enterprise.

Conspicuously absent from the list of award recipients are Japan, India, and Turkey. The urbanists of Japan felt more strongly than those of any other country that their planning system was cramped by an outmoded distribution of authority (nine of twelve advocated

a shift of power to the prefecture) and that their country and especially Tokyo was enjoying limited or no success in attaining their
planning goals. Japan has the capabilities of achieving the same
degree of success as any other nation; she lacks as yet the governmental organization. India and Turkey at this point simply do not
have the capital that modern urban planning requires.

The country I believe to have the most developed and judicious
planning system is Sweden. This is evident not only in the visually
pleasing results that can be seen throughout Stockholm, but also in
the sheer number of related planning organizations in existence.
Pragmatic Sweden places a high priority on planning, and has the
needed revenue (from the highest taxes in all Europe) and governmental structure to ensure good planning results.

Financially, Swedish planning is facilitated by a distribution of
governmental revenue which keeps approximately half of the total
tax money at the local level. With adequate revenue at the local
level Sweden, like Yugoslavia, avoids not only the problems of peti-
tioning higher governmental levels for funds but also the possibilities
of having such requests denied—problems which were so great in
Japan. Structurally, Sweden's coordinated planning system is especially effective because it entails the review of planning schemes at
two, and sometimes more, governmental levels before they can be
approved. All plans, except regional ones, originate and are funded
by the local commune, and all urban planning in Sweden falls under
the jurisdiction of the *Kommunikationsdepart,* a national body which
coordinates county and commune work. The Swedish planning
mechanism, with its long-range orientation and its comprehensive
and regional approaches to urban problem solution, is a polished
planning organization with advantages which demand attention.

IV. MODERNIZATION

To be prepared for the modern world is first of all an exercise of the mind
and temper. We must first be modern in outlook, be modern in our choices
and decisions, be modern in our investment priorities, be scientific and modern in planning and structure of the country's education.

—Editorial, *Ceylon Daily News,* 7 February 1971

After suggesting the roles of urbanization, industrialization, and
planning in development, I have particularly stressed urbanization

as a determinant of the pace of industrialization and consequently of economic growth. I shall now take one presumptuous step further by prescribing what I feel to be the most acceptable method of charting modernization and recommending a path for achieving it. Before, I only hinted at my prejudices; now I shall delineate them.

Figure 6 is a compilation of the five preceding graphs. It presents, for direct comparison, the path of development each nation has pursued. Note that the urban/rural and industrial/primary coefficients for each nation are largely congruent. Where urbanization has increased, so has industrial growth, and vice versa.

This graph leads me to suggest a combined urban/rural-industrial/primary index for both charting and predicting development. The index—which for simplicity will be called the urban/industrial index—is obtained by averaging the urban/rural coefficient with the industrial/primary coefficient. By noting the rate of increase of the index between two or more periods of time, we can obtain some idea of future trends.

First, consider Figure 6 again. Of the countries represented, Sweden and Japan are clearly the most advanced in urban and industrial development. Note that these countries' paths began to accelerate as soon as the urban/rural and industrial/primary coefficients reached about 0.6 on the scale—that is, when 38–40 percent of the population lived in cities and about 55–60 percent were engaged in secondary and tertiary industries. This point of the urban/industrial index was reached in about 1915 in Sweden and 1950 in Japan. From the available evidence it seems we could justifiably call this point the "acceleration" point, for in both cases development has visibly speeded, if not taken on startling proportions, when the coefficients have reached this level.

If this point is important—as I feel it is—then our urban/industrial index takes on new dimensions. With it we can calculate when development in the emerging nations will become a generative and dynamic process. Let us take Yugoslavia as an example. If we average the urban/rural and industrial/primary coefficients for 1953 and 1965 we get an urban/industrial index of 0.24 and 0.36. By simple extrapolation we can obtain 0.54 as the approximate industrial/primary coefficient for 1969, which gives us an urban/industrial index of 0.53 for the year. By the following method of extrapolation, based on a projected increase of the same magnitude between the two base points, we have calculated that the value of the Yugo-

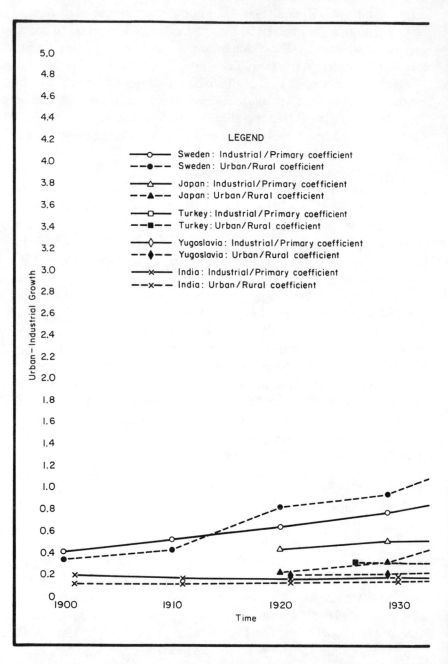

Figure 6. The Field: Urban and Industrial Growth against Time

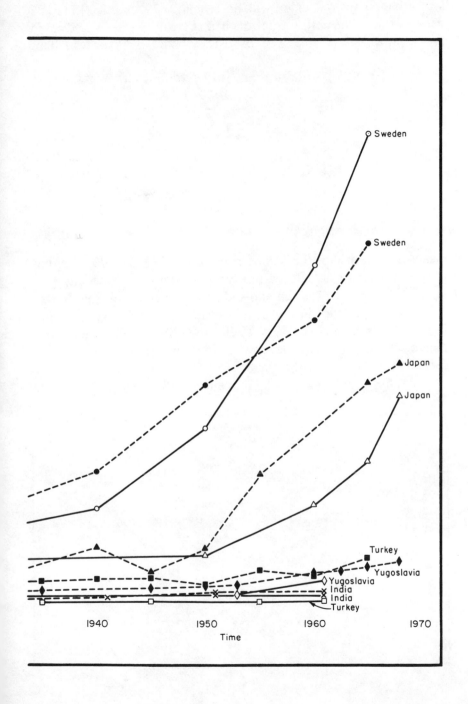

Sweden

Sweden

Japan

Japan

Turkey

Yugoslavia

Yugoslavia

India

India

Turkey

1940   1950   1960   1970

Time

slav urban/industrial index will be around 0.79 or 0.8. (Figure 6
demonstrates that until 0.6 is reached, growth is often steady and
predictable. Hence, this type of extrapolation is in order.) This

$$0.53 - 0.36 = 0.17 \quad \text{(difference between} \\ 1969 \text{ and } 1960)$$

$$\frac{X \cdot 0.36}{100} = 0.17$$

$$X = 47\% \quad \text{(magnitude of 1960} \\ \text{to 1969 increase)}$$

$$(0.53 \cdot 0.47) + 0.53 = 1978 \text{ value}$$

$$1978 \text{ value} = 0.79 \text{ or } 0.8$$

means that the critical 0.6 will be reached in 1972 or 1973, and that
progress thereafter should be more rapid. Figure 7 shows my prediction for the rate of urban and industrial development that Yugoslavia will experience in the next decade. If the acceleration point
is actually attained in the early 1970s, then the growth in the latter
half of the decade may be even swifter than that which is dia-
grammed.

The same calculations can be made for Turkey and India, but the

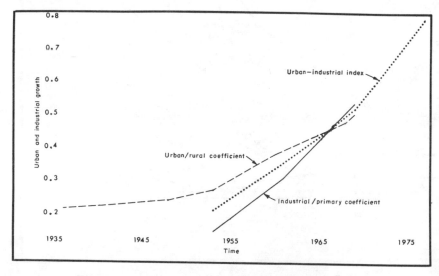

Figure 7. Modernizing Yugoslavia: A Prediction

results are not as encouraging. Turkey, according to my computations, will reach the acceleration point sometime in the late 1980s—either 1988 or 1989. The outlook for India is more bleak. If it continues to crawl along at the bottom of the graph as in the past, it will not reach 0.6 for another thirty-eight decades, or sometime during the twenty-fourth century.

I feel I must caution again that these figures mirror only trends and do not claim to program the future. They should be examined with due skepticism and not be regarded as absolute. The enactment of a new law in India may cut the time I predict in half; a revolution in Turkey or Yugoslavia may radically lengthen my predicted time in those countries. With this as a reminder, let us push only one step further.

Defining "modernity" as that stage when two-thirds of a country's population is urban and when the average of those employed in the secondary and tertiary industries is twice the number employed in the primary (that is, an urban/industrial index of exactly 2.0), we observe that Sweden reached this point in 1951 and Japan in 1967. It therefore took Sweden forty-six years to climb from the acceleration point to modernity and Japan only seventeen. What does this mean for Yugoslavia, Turkey, and India?

It is almost impossible to say. I personally feel that Yugoslavia's development will be unparalleled in Eastern Europe. I believe that Yugoslavia can, in the course of another twenty-five to thirty years, achieve an urban/industrial index of 2.0 and will in the process outstrip its neighbors by a wide margin. Turkey, possibly, can reach the same point at the end of the first or second decade in the next century. On India I feel too modest to comment.

What, ultimately, do all these figures imply? All the data presented here (and summed up visually in Figure 6) clearly demonstrated that there exists a direct correlation between mobility and economic growth. The close interrelationship of the urbanization and industrialization lines in the graph suggest that neither process can be restrained without restraining the other. Thus, the communist path of development, which holds back urbanization or ships people to the countryside, is clearly poor economic planning. Also intimated in the figures is that restrictive land policies which tie rural workers to the soil and inhibit mobility also greatly impede the urban/industrial transition.

The signs point to a path which facilitates the smoothest yet swiftest shift from rural to urban and from agricultural to industrial. It seems to me that this can only be the path of democracy and free enterprise. The highest level of progress in the field has been achieved in the shortest time by the two democratic nations, and decentralized Yugoslavia is beginning to follow suit. To take any other avenue to modernity seems provincial and, in the light of the data, more than a little indulgent. Those who regard this as ethnocentric are advised to look again at Figure 6.

V. ENDNOTE

Myopia is a malady which often affects those who deal with a single issue for a great length of time. I think, however, that the IHP trip has immunized me adequately against at least this disease.

It would be naïve to suggest—and throughout this essay I have not—that the processes of urbanization and industrialization should become man's paramount priorities. Our world today is marked by war, overpopulation, hunger, ignorance, disease, and the threat of nuclear destruction. It is in these areas that man should first focus his energy.

In this essay I have merely attempted to outline how I feel our world can get a little better a little quicker. Change is in itself certainly no virtue; but as long as the nations who do not have it regard economic development as a goal worthy of pursuit, then change is underwritten.

NOTES

1. For more detailed comment on the rise of the level of world urbanization, see the first chapter in Gerald Breese's *Urbanization in the Newly Developing Countries* (Englewood Cliffs, N.J.: Prentice-Hall, 1966).
2. Marshall Clinard in *India's Urban Future* notes that the poverty of Indian urban slums is not as great as it first appears. In his article "Urban Community Development: Delhi," he writes that due to factors like proportionately smaller rents and multiple incomes within families, *total* family income is much greater than one would initially suspect. Clinard's article is co-authored by Chatterjee and appears in Roy Turner's edition of *India's Urban Future* (Berkeley: University of California Press, 1960).
3. In Belgrade, urbanist Dr. Ljubinka Pjanic, professor of spatial economy and authority on metropolitan housing, contends that a major factor

contributing to Yugoslav urbanization is the number of immigrants who come to the cities looking for a mate.

4. See Daniel Lerner's *Passing of the Traditional Society* (New York: Free Press, 1958) for the background behind this statement. His paradigm in Chapter 2 is especially relevant.

5. Bert Hoselitz, "Role of Urbanization in Economic Development: Some International Comparisons," in Roy Turner's *India's Urban Future,* p. 164.

6. Richard K. Beardsley and John W. Hall, *Twelve Doors to Japan* (New York: McGraw-Hill, 1965), p. 35.

7. In Japan, urban municipalities (*shi* and *ku* of Tokyo-to) are usually those having 30,000 or more inhabitants. They may include some rural areas as well as urban clusters.

8. Columns B, C, and D are based on data from Dr. Tokue Shibata's report to the United Nations in November 1968. His source was the *Japanese Statistical Yearbook* (Tokyo, 1968). Column E is also from Shibata's report; F and G are my own calculations.

9. Lewis Mumford, *The City in History* (New York: Harcourt, Brace & World, 1961), p. 197.

10. Column B: *India 1967* (Research and Reference Division, Ministry of Information and Broadcasting, Government of India), p. 6. Column C: Ashish Bose, *Studies in India's Urbanization* (University of New Delhi, 1966), p. 3. Column E: *1961 Census of India.* (Government of India), 1962. Columns D, F, and G are my own figures.

11. In India, those places classified as urban are *towns* (places with municipal corporations, municipal area committees, notified area committee, or cantonment board); and also all places having 5,000 or more inhabitants, a density of not less than 1,000 persons per square mile, and at least three-fourths of the adult males employed in pursuits other than agriculture.

12. Hoselitz, "Role of Urbanization," p. 168 (n.)

13. Karl W. Kapp, *Hindu Culture, Economic Development and Economic Planning in India* (New York: Asia Publishing House, 1965).

14. "Educated Chinese Young People Go to Countryside" (New China News Agency—English; Peking, 19 November 1968), *Survey of the China Mainland Press* no. 4305, 25 November 1968, p. 22.

15. This exhortation is from a speech by Hung Jung Hai, chairman of the Canton Municipal Revolutionary Committee and also vice-chairman of the Kwangtung Provincial Revolutionary Committee and Commander of Kwangtung Military District. It was made to youths who were about to leave for mountain and rural areas. Text from Canton *Chung-hsüeh Hung-tai-hui* (Middle School Red Guard Congress) of 30 October 1968, reprinted in *Survey of the China Mainland Press* no. 4306, 26 November 1968, p. 18.

16. "Cadres Settle in Countryside in East China Province" (New China News Agency—English; Peking, 29 October 1968) no. 4292, 5 November 1968, p. 18.

17. Columns B and C: 1927 to 1960 figures are from *United Nations' Demographic Yearbook.* The 1965 figures are from the *Turkish Population Census of 1965.* Columns E and F; 1935 and 1945 figures from Walter

Galenson, *Labor in Developing Economies* (Berkeley: University of California Press, 1962), p. 259; 1960 figures from *Report on Scientific and Technical Information Requirements of Turkish Industry,* by Appleton, 1964, pp. 18–19. Columns D and G are my own figures.

18. The 1955 definition of an urban area was an administrative center of a province or district. The 1960 definition included all localities of more than 10,000 inhabitants.

19. Columns B and C are based on data from *Housing Development in Jugoslavia,* (Federal Institute for Urbanism), p. 5. The 1968 data for these two columns are from an unpublished manuscript given to me by Z. Kovacevic, Director of the Standing Conference of Towns, Belgrade. Columns E and F: 1953 data are from *Statistical Pocketbook of Jugoslavia* (1960), p. 25; 1961 data are from the *Statistical Yearbook of SFRY* (1968). Both were published by the Federal Institute for Statistics, Belgrade. Columns D and G are my own figures.

20. Harry B. Ellis, "Jugoslavia—Fresh Surprises in Store for Eastern Bloc?" *Christian Science Monitor* (26 November 1968).

21. In Yugoslavia, the following places are considered urban: localities of 15,000 or more inhabitants; localities of 5,000 to 14,999 inhabitants of which at least 30 percent are not engaged in agriculture; localities of 3,000 to 4,999 inhabitants of which at least 70 percent are not engaged in agriculture; and localities of 2,000 to 2,999 inhabitants of which 80 percent are not engaged in agriculture.

22. Pjanic, Stefanovic, and Duranovic, *Urban Development—Its Implications for Social Welfare* (Belgrade: 1966), p. 9.

23. Sweden considers urban those built-up areas with at least 200 inhabitants having usually not more than 200 meters between houses.

24. Columns B and C: 1870 to 1950a figures are from *Historical Statistics of Sweden* (Stockholm: Statistiska Centralbyrän, 1955), p. 29. Figures for 1950b to 1965 are from *Population and Housing Census in 1965,* Vol. 2 (Stockholm: National Statistical Bureau, 1968), p. 25. Columns E and F: 1870 to 1950 figures are from *Historical Statistics*; 1960 figures are from Rune Tryggveson's *Urbanization in Sweden* (Stockholm: National Bureau of Statistics, 1967), p. 58. Tryggveson talks about "densely" and "sparsely" populated areas rather than urban and rural ones.

DAVID J. H. DEAN
Austin College

Who Gets Ahead?

To have what we have without being what we are: This is a problem many new nations encounter in their drive for modernization.
In fact, some leaders seem to think they can achieve their economic
goals with next to no human or social change.

Can the developing world really achieve economic prosperity
without disturbing traditional values and customs? And if some social change is inevitable, how much? These are questions only time
can answer, but we can at least sharpen our focus on this problem
by considering the entrepreneur in developing societies, for the businessman who initiates new enterprises and renovates older ones is the
human factor which determines the future of economic development.
Managing the ubiquitous government project or seizing upon an
opportunity in his village, the able and ambitious entrepreneur is a
crucial component in economic growth.

Traditional traders, merchants, and moneylenders, however,

DAVID J. H. DEAN *is from Pecos, Texas, and left Austin College in Sherman, Texas,
to become a member of IHP. At Austin College, David was interested in economics
and government as well as the Australian stock market and photography. David
returned from the IHP journey to Austin College, and graduated in 1971 with an
interdisciplinary major in the social sciences. He has recently married and plans to
enter graduate school after he finishes his duty with a Navy OCS military intelligence
unit.*

seem to lack the characteristics of the innovative entrepreneur. The ideal modern entrepreneur is a rational, self-reliant, mobile opportunity-seeker who plans long-range goals and seldom gives up. But the traditional businessman, often the holder of an inherited position and thus immobilized by social ties, carries on his traditional business emphasizing high profits and low reinvestment. Few people would fit either role perfectly, of course, but the traits of each can often be observed.

The fact that traditional enterprise in the developing world was unable or unwilling to keep pace with the West is obvious. And almost as certain is that with so much catching-up to do, traditional enterprise alone will not suffice. Thus, there appears to be a great need for a "corps of entrepreneurs" if a new nation is to develop.[1] Surely there exist at least a few modern entrepreneurs in many developing countries. The Koç industrial empire in Turkey and the Tata group in India are two examples of conglomerations manned by well-educated, modern entrepreneurs. Such examples are few, however.

What explains such a dearth of entrepreneurial activity in the developing world? This is a matter upon which we can only speculate, but it might be worth our while to examine a generalization based on the few studies which have been made in the new nations. This generalization explains the evident lack of entrepreneurs among literate and illiterate, modern and traditional, socialist and capitalist, as well as among various regions and groups within a country. This generalization, although oversimplified and of value only as a theoretical device, explains not only economic development itself but the social and political relationships as well. This generalization is called "the rules of the game." The rules of the game decide who can become an entrepreneur, and also determine his effect upon society.

In the course of the International Honors Program, it became apparent to us that each country has its own rules of the game. Fixed by its own history, culture, and institutions, each country's rules for success are unique. While in one country a racial group may supply the major entrepreneurs, in another that same group may be ostracized. Indeed, the rules of the game often allow several diverse types to become successful, while excluding others.

These rules, this game, are key issues relating to the entrepreneur, and directly affect the ability of a developing country to retain traditional values while seeking economic development. If unable to have their cake and eat it too, the developing nations may find these issues useful in determining how much of their tradition they must give up to reach the desired level of economic growth.

I am not saying that the rules of the game have always been unsuitable: yet it must be evident that for the game of economic development they are far from adequate. Nor am I saying that new nations, if they are to achieve economic development, must be mirror images of the West: yet it must be evident that adopting certain characteristics of the West would facilitate development. In theory, any country could develop rules for supplying enough entrepreneurs to ensure a desired level of economic growth, rules quite different from those in the West. The important thing is that the rules account for possible economic, social, and political effects when the game is played. And certainly it must be stated that few, if any, rules for the game, in the West or elsewhere, provide a perfect breeding ground for the entrepreneur.

Such generalizations are meaningless unless applied to actual situations. However, the problem of choosing an example is by no means a simple task. Ideas of what the rules are in various countries range from infrastructure, market size, capital availability, and technology to the numbers of college graduates, psychological need for achievement, degree of exposure to the outside world, and marriage customs. While all these ideas may well be part of the rules, there are two general topics—social ties and institutional regulations—which, if not as striking as those above, may be more important.

Social ties are personal relations strengthened or denied by membership in a commercial network, by patterns of kinship, by residence in a village, by birth in a caste, by belief in a religion, or by any of a number of other predominatly extralegal relationships. As rules of the game, these ties can be extremely powerful influences on entrepreneurship.

Village relationships in Turkey and caste ties in India illustrate the dual capacity of social ties to promote and to restrict entrepreneurship. However, because of the isolated nature of the first and the cultural heritage of the second, social ties, let alone village or caste, should not be counted as an important rule in every country.

As a nation which opted for economic development forty-five

years ago, Turkey has had a spectacular, if not a successful, history. When Mustafa Kemal Atatürk founded the modern nation in 1924 on the ruins of the Ottoman Empire, numerous Ottoman traditions remained. Since Ottoman debts had brought in a system of capitulations by which outsiders owned most businesses in the empire, and since there was an apparent desire by the Ottomans themselves to retain power over the population by preventing the rise of a business elite, Atatürk's Turkey was at first without an entrepreneurial class.

In other ways Turkey was ill equipped for the goal of westernization. Few people were literate. Few were city-dwellers. The country to all appearances was shackled by the doctrines of Islam. Atatürk began many ambitious projects to reform the country single-handedly but died in 1938, before their fruition. With a new government in the 1950s, in fact, many of the projects were shelved, and a carefree government spending program took priority. Even after a military coup in 1960, and the subsequent return of the government to the people, the country's economic policy leaves much to be desired. The Turkish government fails to back exporters by refusing to devalue the currency; the bureaucracy plays favorites with assistance.

This helter-skelter view of the Turkish environment shows at once a few of the problems that face the entrepreneurs in their quest for economic development. Despite all these problems, social ties seem to have stimulated the supply of entrepreneurs from at least one group: the people who were raised along the Black Sea coast of Turkey and who have emigrated to Istanbul have somehow become major entrepreneurs. Commonly referred to as Laz, these people live in densely populated villages on the coast and, because of population pressures, are forced to leave their homes and traditional occupation as fishermen. Lacking both pedigree and capital, two assets characteristic of success in Istanbul, the Laz have nevertheless become dominant in the construction, fishing, and transportation industries. And village connections seem to be an important factor in their success. The story circulated is that a few of these people were involved in transporting goods by sea to Istanbul, and prospered. As word of their good fortune spread, and as population pressures forced others to leave their villages, more Laz came to Istanbul. Through the established villager in the city the newcomers found a job, raised some money, and set out in their own businesses, which were generally related to their traditional maritime trade. The process has continued to the point where the Laz now dominate a few industries.[2]

Without these village connections it is highly unlikely that the Laz would control these industries in Istanbul, and improbable that entrepreneurs in these industries would have developed so quickly otherwise. The shoddiness which is said to characterize Laz construction may be caused by the same rules of the game which allow such a village group to reach prominence.

Not so encouraging is the caste system in India which, by birth, ascribes the likelihood of poverty or plenty. India's interest in economic development and modernization began when it became independent in 1947. At first, its leaders had great faith in state planning as the key to development. Borrowing their federal structure, their bureaucratic framework, and their state plans from the developed nations, the Indians achieved remarkable successes at first, but the tempo quickly slowed. Instead of uniting, social groups polarized and became more restless.

The farmer in India, a country where approximately 70 percent of the population is engaged in agriculture, is now widely believed to be the new key to development. Five-year plans are made to assist him, and the Ford Foundation envisions market towns with service facilities and foresees the development of agro-based industry.

However, caste groups appear to be quite an obstacle to such development—especially for those traditionally engaged in agriculture. Though the government has outlawed caste discrimination and has attempted to provide opportunities for oppressed castes, one Indian authority has noted that "caste is so tacitly and so completely accepted by all, including those who are most vocal in condemning it, that it is everywhere the unit of social action."[3]

As a social tie, the influence of caste seems to vary from caste to caste and from region to region. Where there is no immediate need for innovation and where business is not lucrative enough to attract outsiders, such castes as barbers and washermen are bound to their traditional occupations. Between peasants and untouchables—two castes that are often engaged in agriculture—one vivid example of caste as an impediment to entrepreneurship was presented by Scarlett Epstein:

One Dalena Untouchable wanted to act as building contractor. He started
by building a fine house for himself of the type usually inhabited by wealthier
Peasants. Dalena Peasants regarded this as upstart behavior . . . they made
sure that none of Dalena's Peasants would use the services of this Untouchable contractor . . . even though Dalena Peasants were very keen to build
new and better houses and the Untouchable was underbidding his Peasant
competitor.[4]

In nonagricultural occupations, a more modern and much smaller
section of the economy, caste seems to act in a different way. According to D. R. Gadgil, in these industries "caste taboos or prohibi-
tions did not count for much . . . backwardness in education, lack
of capital accumulation and, above all, lack of . . . connections
seemed to determine the position of the different communities."[5]
But even these factors are not unrelated to caste status. Industrial
success in a study by a UNESCO team was found to depend upon
"the ascriptive criterion of caste, with its characteristics of education and economic standing."[6] Though these few findings may not be
representative of the whole of India, they do seem to indicate that
caste is a social tie which has strongly affected entrepreneurship.

In contrast to social ties, which usually affect potential entrepreneurs on an informal, personal basis, institutional regulations are more
often legal enticements or restrictions which influence the creation
of the "corps of entrepreneurs" in a larger sense. Often concerned
with such economic considerations as import quotas, interest rates,
and investment priorities, institutions become preoccupied with details and overlook the larger task. To illustrate, lack of capital is
one reason the "man with the bright idea" fails to become an entrepreneur in Turkey. Robert W. Kerwin, Ford Foundation consultant
in Turkey, attributed this lack of capital partly to the banking industry's preoccupation with outdated import-export transactions
rather than with lending.[7] Thus, the entrepreneur is limited to non-
institutional sources of credit—often the family—which, though
easy to come by, are often insufficient.

Other institutions have become so mired in corruption that their
services are often diverted to those who can pay the biggest bribe.
India is an oft-quoted example where black market money is said to
purchase success, and the political payoff to secure it. If true, the
effects on the supply of entrepreneurs are clear.

Far more complex and less certain is the effect on entrepreneurs of a noncapitalistic institutional system. In Yugoslavia, which is it-self atypical of Eastern Europe, the government permits only limited ownership of the means of production, and no large private industry. Therefore, the story is told (as proof that ideology stifles entrepre-neurship) of the peasant who migrates to a developed region, works steadily in a factory for several years, earns some money, and re-turns to his backward village—where, because he is denied the op-tion of capitalism, he fails to become an entrepreneur and settles down to a life of conspicuous consumption.

While the institutional rules of the game in Yugoslavia clearly preclude the development of the private entrepreneur, the rules af-fecting the entrepreneur in the public sector are more subtle.

Yugoslavia can be said to have begun serious efforts toward eco-nomic development as late as the end of World War II. The country has always been culturally divided. From 1389, when Muslim in-vaders took control from the Byzantines of an area of what is now Yugoslavia, until the end of World War I, non-Western culture dominated parts of the country. In other regions, the Austro-Hun-garian Empire dominated the scene with purely Western culture. At the outbreak of World War I, then, the republics of Slovenia and Croatia were firmly in Austro-Hungarian hands with Bosnia and Herzegovina precariously annexed; Macedonia was under Ottoman control, with Serbia and Montenegro not long divorced of its influ-ence. After the war the six republics were tenuously joined in a kingdom which amounted to a Greater Serbia.

In 1941, civil war as well as world war engulfed the country, even-tually decimating the population and destroying 40 percent of all industrial plants. Tito, as leader of an underground movement, gained control of the country and effected a rapid reconstruction of key industries. Discarding the Russian pattern with which he began to govern Yugoslavia, Tito soon embarked on his own course.

Choosing a self-management system, Tito created an institution, in theory independent of government, for the operation of industries and service facilities to be controlled by the workers. In practice, the workers elect representatives to a workers' council to decide basic goals of the enterprise, and to select a manager to carry on day-to-day business.

It is at this point that the institutional rules have failed to account for social and political history and have instead perpetuated the economic diversity between regions. Politics until recently played an important role in determining the managers of enterprises in some regions. Since the manager of an enterprise is nominated by representatives of the local commune, as well as by representatives of the workers' council, a local politician could use his power and prestige to get himself appointed manager, and workers could try to get favors in Belgrade through the politician. Underdeveloped regions, those previously under Ottoman control, were evidently quick to utilize this "loophole" to choose a politician instead of a businessman to run their enterprise. In the developed regions the system was working quite well, however. In fact, workers' councils in Croatia and Slovenia are said to choose well-educated and highly trained managers and to give them free rein to operate much as the ideal entrepreneur. It is clear from what has been said that, despite the disincentive of public ownership, at least certain regions of Yugoslavia have been successful in their attempts at economic development.

As a postscript, in December 1968 the law governing the nomination of the enterprise manager was amended to provide only the workers with nominating power. Such an amendment was enacted, perhaps, in recognition of the failure of existing institutional rules to check entrepreneurial weakness in lesser-developed regions.

Social ties affect entrepreneurship in Turkey and India, and institutional regulations affect entrepreneurship in Yugoslavia. This much is fairly certain. Whether these factors act as rules of the game in other countries cannot here be proved. But, given the crucial role of entrepreneurs in a developing economy, and assuming the need for "rules" to supply them, the concept of the rules of the game is a handy tool for measuring economic progress. The extent to which the society fails to meet its goals will likely indicate the need to adjust the rules and abandon such traditional values as caste discrimination.

Changing the rules of the game—discarding some of the traditional values and adjusting policies—is another, even more perplexing, matter. Nevertheless, we know that rules have changed over and over again throughout history. In *On the Theory of Social Change,* Everett Hagen explains that social change is most likely to come about when a group loses its place in society: when its members no longer value the work they have traditionally done, and when others no longer respect that occupation. Termed "withdrawal of status respect," this process is followed by a stage of retreat during which the group passively accepts the vagaries of life, and then by an innovative stage which begins a chain reaction of change throughout the society.[8] The only discouraging part of the theory is that such a series of events has occurred only over several decades.

If it is the decision of the new nations to seek economic development which has brought about the "revolution of rising expectations," and if it is the haphazard rules of the game mixing traditional values and modern methods which have brought about the "revolution of rising frustrations," then it is doubtful that social change can be peacefully delayed for generations.

NOTES

1. The term "corps of entrepreneurs" comes from W. W. Rostow, *The Stages of Economic Growth* (Cambridge, England: Cambridge University Press, 1962), p. 140.
2. I first heard this story in an interview with Demir Demirgil, professor of economics at Robert College on 10 March 1969. It was corroborated on 17 March 1969 in an interview with Bay Fahir Ozsoy of the Turkish management consultancy organization.
3. M. N. Srinivas, "Caste in Modern India," *Journal of Asian Studies* 16 (August 1957): 548.
4. Scarlett Epstein, "Social Structure and Entrepreneurship," *International Journal of Comparative Sociology,* 5 (1964): 163.
5. D. R. Gadgil, *Sholapur City: Socio-Economic Studies* (New York: Asia Publishing House, 1965), p. 252.
6. UNESCO Research Center, *Small Industries and Social Change*; *Four Studies in India* (Bombay: Allied Publishers, 1966), p. 30.
7. From an interview with Mr. Kerwin on 14 March 1969.
8. Everett E. Hagen, *On the Theory of Social Change* (Homewood, Ill.: Dorsey Press, 1962), pp. 185–220.

MICHAEL S. SIEGAL

Harvard University

The Global
Science Game

Most developing nations accept the importance and the prestige of a science establishment. Yet few agree on the steps which must be taken to develop one. The particular legacy of history—often including extended colonial occupation—places each country at a unique starting point; and with the strengths and handicaps of a given tradition and a given set of current political ties, the speed and direction of development is often difficult to predict. Nevertheless, our investigations into the organization and pursuit of science in eight countries have suggested certain vital relationships. The links between science planning organizations, independent research laboratories, educational institutions, government, and industry contribute to what has been called the "climate of combination" within

MICHAEL S. SIEGAL *is from Bayside, New York, and was studying chemistry and physics at Harvard University before he came to IHP. While at Harvard, Mike expected to continue in the physical sciences through graduate or medical school, but was also very interested in the humanities, particularly French literature, music, and social work. After his year with IHP, Mike resumed his studies at Harvard and graduated in 1970* magna cum laude. *He has since entered the medical scientist training program leading to M.D. and Ph.D degrees at Columbia University's College of Physicians and Surgeons. Mike is currently in his third year of graduate work at Columbia, and has spent a recent summer doing biological research at Woods Hole, Massachusetts.*

which a country's science effort must operate. This essay aims to describe the "scientific process," and then to examine in some detail the apparent motivations and difficulties of four developing nations now attempting to make science work.

In formulating a "science policy," government may be seen as subject to at least three constraints: the economic situation, the ideology, and the military needs. A country's degree of industrialization, its wealth, its balance of payments prospects, and its economic planning provide the economic context for the growth of science. Ideology provides a language for articulating and justifying goals and the means envisaged to attain them. And military needs as perceived by government decision-makers (and perhaps influenced by the defense industries) effect the formation of a "military-industrial complex" and the priority funding of certain research areas.

All of today's Big Science countries are now, or have been in the recent past, subject to compelling military concerns. In each, the need was felt at some point to develop an independent military/industrial infrastructure in which Big Science would necessarily play a pivotal role. An ideology, whether traditional or contemporary, seems to lubricate the process of scientific development and, in a sense, gives it meaning. This is not to say that Japanese laboratories are not at times distressingly inefficient as they act out the traditional ideology of interpersonal hierarchy; or that China might not well be risking a whole generation of scientific quality in sending her physicists to shovel manure; or that Russia was not obliged to compromise an advanced school of geneticists on behalf of Lysenko's Ninchurinism. In balancing its ideology and its military needs, a country is constantly weighing means against ends, and running the risk of confusing the two.

And what is the government's role? After analyzing these military, economic, and ideological factors, it determines priorities and transmits them to the planning organization; it supplies funds indirectly to the planning organization or directly to research units; and it formulates rules (generally imposed on industry) in the form of currency controls, programs of import substitution, regulations on foreign investment within the country, and preestablished royalty rates for imported technology.

Money is obviously a major tool for shaping development. Yet the percentage of overall funding for scientific education and research provided by the government is in itself an unreliable indicator of the sophistication of a country's science. A country at an early stage (for example, Turkey or India) might conduct research only in educational or independent research institutions (if at all), funded nearly entirely by the government. The existence of a mature industrial research complex generating its own research and development investment capital might be reflected in a lower figure for government participation (Japan), whereas considerable military investment might cause the figure for government participation to rise again (as in America, Sweden, the Soviet Union, and perhaps China).

Allocating funds is an essential and difficult task for any country interested in harnessing science for development: a science planning organization must be sensitive to each sector of the science infrastructure.

Thus, the government supplies the money and the priorities—the latter perhaps in the form of specific project needs or general production goals set by economic planners. The breadth, quality, even the workability of these priorities will depend on the efficiency and intelligence of government economic planning, on the amount of economic information available, on the reaction time of planners to new economic developments—in short, on a formidable number of nonscientific factors. The science planning organization must in addition be sensitive to the research needs and capabilities of the industrial sector and be able to inform industry of the nature of contemporary technology available both within the country and abroad. It must be staffed at least in part with scientifically trained personnel. Finally, it must distribute research funds to scientific education facilities, independent research organizations, and industrial laboratories. Virtually no country has developed a science planning organization with which it is wholly satisfied, and the case studies that follow describe some of the enormous difficulties associated with planning.

To develop its science a country needs scientists and institutions in which to train them. It is most often in these same institutions that the bulk of a country's basic research is carried out. Such research may be funded either directly by a government (national or foreign) through its science planning organization, or by industry, banking, and private capital. Reciprocally, scientific institutions must furnish research results, teachers, and planners.

Developing countries without a strong Western scientific tradition often import their scientists at first, or at least train them abroad. Japan, China, Israel, and Turkey have followed this pattern. To maintain a steady supply of scientists, developing countries must deal with the challenges of insufficient local job opportunities, and the lure of more lucrative positions and sophisticated research facilities in more advanced countries. Turkey, for example, has chosen training institutions as a starting point for the development of science, and by establishing science high schools, and research laboratories at the Middle Eastern Technical University (METU), has actually succeeded in drawing back to Turkey native scientists who had been working abroad. India has yet to accomplish as much.

Science is perhaps most important to the modernizing nation as a tool for developing an indigenous industrial base, capable of realizing self-sustaining economic growth. The "military-industrial complex" is only one of several links which connect industry to science and the economic outside world.

Government controls are most often directed at industry. To buy foreign technology, industry needs foreign exchange, and it is the government's currency control and licensing regulations which will monitor these transactions in view of the country's balance of payments prospects. Joint ventures with foreign firms must ordinarily be reconciled with sensitivity to economic imperialism, cooperation among native industries, and ideological aversion to monopolies. Even Japan, traditional example of the successful importer of foreign techniques, has of late insisted that once a Japanese firm pays for a technique, it must itself have the right to pass the same know-how on to other Japanese firms via licensing arrangements. The vast range of success and failure experienced by different countries that import technology suggests that a country's effective use of available knowledge may be more important than its initially sophisticated research capabilities.

Even a successful program of development requires access to research results. If industry cannot conduct its own research it must turn to outside organizations and indigenous educational facilities. Industry needs information on know-how available within and without the country. It must be aware of possibilities within the country and react to consumer needs and preferences. There must be competent managers, there must be a threat of competition both domestic and foreign, there must be access to investment capital. Only 10 percent of the cost of successful product innovation is devoted to research and invention; the rest of the expense is most often in development, in machine tooling, and in initiation of production. Without these subsequent steps, the initial 10 percent is economically useless.

The development of effective science within a country is the development of a series of institutional links which, in its ideal form, might be represented by Figure 1. This network can vary from country to country. In a given country many of these links might not yet exist, but in all they are constantly undergoing modification and reevaluation.

We turn now to an examination of some specific difficulties encountered by four developing nations—India, Israel, Yugoslavia, and China—in order to analyze and compare their recent attempts to survive, or even to excel, in the global science game.

I. INDIA: THE MAZE OF MINISTRIES

Once considered the brightest jewel in the British Imperial Crown, the ancient subcontinent of India sees itself today as a vast young nation struggling to recover from two centuries of colonial occupation. The fabled land of silks and maharajahs now faces staggering problems of competitive regionalism, widespread illiteracy, population explosion, and external military threats; moreover, it attempts to reconcile an international course of Third World neutralism with continued aid from both the United States and the Soviet Union. In its search for a workable science policy India must coordinate the unevenly developed sectors of its present science infrastructure. Faced with the dismaying inertia of a sluggish bureaucracy, India seeks to create a working "climate of combination."

It would not be at all unusual for an atomic scientist to arrive late at a top-level nuclear planning session and give as his legitimate excuse a traffic jam occasioned by the breakdown of an oxcart in downtown Delhi. India is even today a country of outrageous contrasts. At the same time that it receives scientific aid, India sends engineering consultants to Iran, Kenya, Ceylon, Malaysia; and although some Indians will admit that "for a large country with such a huge population the Indian contribution to science has been insignificant,"[1] India has produced such great scientists as R. S. Krishnan, C. V. Raman, and J. C. Bose.

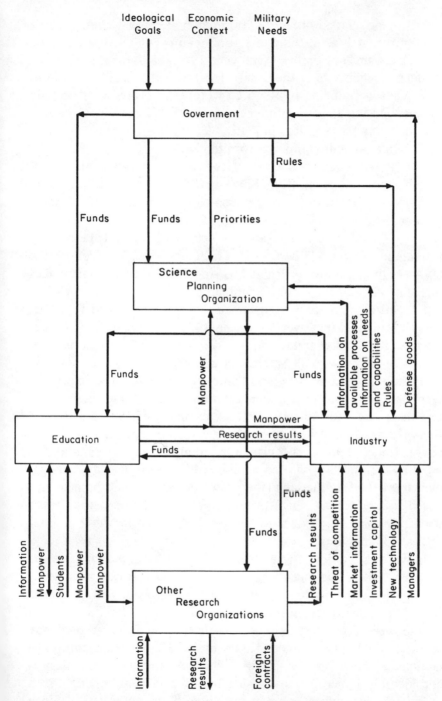

Figure 1. An Ideal Science Infrastructure

With a population of nearly 500 million and a per capita income of approximately $75, India is a poor country with severely limited capital resources. For the fiscal year 1967–68 India's balance of payments deficit was of the order of Rs. 860 crores ($1.12 billion) with loans outstanding of Rs. 5,654 crores (1 crore = 10 million rupees). During 1966–67 India received $1,472 million in foreign aid, including $896 million in loans, $97 million in grants, and $4.8 million in commodity imports from the USA.

Clearly, large-scale resource allocations are not available for research and development (R and D)—in fact, the portion of the Gross National Product for R and D (research ratio) is expected to *reach* 0.35 percent by the end of the Fourth Five-Year Plan. This is to be compared with a research ratio of approximately 1.1 percent in Communist China, 1.5 percent in Japan, and over 3 percent in the USA (including military R and D). And India's small GNP makes this allocation all the more inadequate.

Education is compulsory between the ages of six and fourteen; yet it is estimated that over 60 percent of the population is illiterate. Technical education and the supply of manpower face a number of serious problems as well. Salaries in industry lure potential teachers away from the universities, and "without adequate screening in the secondary schools, a greater and greater number of inferior students find their way into India's expanding technical education system."[2] Regional political strife has resulted in the demand that local languages (there are at least fourteen different languages in India, and hundreds of dialects) be used at universities, and that "the change-over from English, the language presently used, should be accomplished in five years."[3] Such provincialism is a tragic detour for a country hoping to produce active participants in the international scientific community.

India faces a serious Brain Drain. The number of Indian scientists working abroad has been estimated at 25,000. In an attempt to remedy this situation the Indian Council of Scientific and Industrial Research under the Ministry of Education and Sciences set up a "manpower pool." A young scientist returning from abroad may join the pool at a guaranteed salary of Rs. 300–700 a month until he finds scientific employment in India; unfortunately, this salary is considerably higher than that which an Indian student, having stayed in India for his studies, could hope to obtain upon graduating. Since the demand for scientists in industry is discouragingly low, and university lectureships in India start at a salary of Rs. 400 a month, the returning scientist is often better off remaining officially unemployed and moonlighting at some second nonscientific job. Many do just that.

Furthermore, the effectiveness of scientific education is hampered by bureaucratic sluggishness and poor planning, as evidenced, for example, by the recent glut of trained engineers. This situation led finally to a demand that a ten-year ban be imposed on the establishment of new engineering colleges.

What sort of demand does Indian industry furnish for native manpower and the results of native research? Unfortunately, a rather limited one:

There is as yet no way of associating professors with industrial problems since independent consulting work among faculty members is rarely encouraged. (The Indian Institutes of Technology are the exception.)[4]

The general economic picture is such that

so many industrialists in India are preoccupied with problems such as shortage of raw materials, shortages of foreign exchange, etc., that they have too little time for the problems involved in improving their operations through the use of research. Furthermore, the fact that demand outruns supply in India hardly provides an incentive to the improvement of the quality of the products: in the absence of any mutual competition there is little desire to utilise research even to outpace the rivals in the field.[5]

When innovation is desired

Indian industry is disinclined to use indigenous know-how when it is in competition with foreign know-how, especially when the latter is accompanied by technical and economic guarantees and financial participation.[6]

Any attempt at industrial cooperation is frowned upon due to India's hypersensitivity to monopolies. Furthermore,

in India the role of cooperative research associations is obstructed by the fact that many industries are very widely spread over larger areas of the country and often have local or state loyalties. Foreign owned companies have not been so keen to join research associations because this might mean pooling some of their imported specialized knowledge.[7]

The obvious alternative is to depend on imported technology.

Foreign know-how reaches India either through direct sale or through collaboration agreements. The government's guidelines here are simple—nondiscrimination, freedom to remit profits, compensation in the event of compulsory acquisition, majority ownership by Indian nationals. Preference is given to single-process purchase in areas where future development is likely to be slow (such as mechanical engineering). Royalty is the rule, certain rates being set by the ministries, with a five-year limit on the period of know-how payment and inflow of technology. To extend this limit a special request must be submitted along with proof that such extension would be of benefit to the country.

In March 1968 the Foreign Investment Board was established in India to license certain collaboration agreements and assign the licensing of large-scale technological ventures to a cabinet committee. Despite claims of greater efficiency, it is likely that the principal aim of this reorganization is the political practicality of diffusing among cabinet members the responsibility for major policy decisions.

What level of technology should a developing nation purchase?

Emphasis should . . . be placed on restricting import of marginally recent or marginally superior technology since, very often, the trend of research and development in the more advanced countries is toward sophistication of a type that may not yet be necessary in India.[8]

There is a view that intermediate know-how is far more suitable for use in a developing country than the most advanced and sophisticated know-how available in the world. . . . [But] such a policy would lead not only to stagnation but also to the widening of the technology gap . . . it would be more economical to borrow and pay for technology rather than waste resources and time on re-invention.[9]

There is as yet in India no discernible policy with regard to this fundamental issue. Some Indians are also irked by the fact that different Indian firms will often pay high royalty rates for the same process. There is now a new rule, inspired by the Japanese, that all collaboration agreements must delete a secrecy clause; the Indian company purchasing the technology would then have the right to sell the process to other Indian producers at a lower rate than that originally paid. From this same problem

the idea of having a single central organization to purchase the know-how outright has emerged. . . . [But it] can be of no practical value, as a single agency cannot get the best know-how in a continuous manner. If this proposal is pushed ahead it would create in our country a big technology gap.[10]

The underlying reservation that this statement conveys—hesitation to consign a continuous competitive process to the responsibility of a centralized bureaucracy—must resonate through many of Delhi's administrative buildings.

Since the Chinese invasion in the early 1960s, and the later war with Pakistan over Kashmir, India's defense needs have led it into the middle of an intense international arms competition. The thirty laboratories of India's defense R and D organization are developing their own radar, microwave, and computer technologies.

India's atomic energy program was designed largely by the late Homi Jehangir Bhabha, a leader of the Tata Institute of Fundamental Research and of the Atomic Energy Establishment at Trombay. Although expenditures for atomic energy seem less liberal than during the Bhabha era, there are in India three nuclear power stations (Tanapur, Rana Pratap Sagar, and Madras) in various stages of completion. The station at Madras will be entirely Indian-built, and subsequent Indian reactors will use domestic reactor-grade uranium instead of the imported enriched type necessary for the earlier installations.

There is no doubt that India is capable of producing an atom bomb; it has not signed the nuclear nonproliferation treaty, in part because of the threat of Chinese nuclear blackmail. Yet the cost of a military atomic program is prohibitive and is seen by many as a ludicrous expenditure for a country with India's economic difficulties. Nevertheless, recent developments indicate that the Indian nuclear program may take a significant turn.

Nearly the entire bill for scientific research in India is paid by the government—private industry contributes less than 1 percent of the total. Laboratories are able to get some royalties on processes developed, but so far this source has proved insignificant. Tight money and even tighter foreign exchange, coupled with nearly complete centralization of the funding apparatus, make acquisition of even the simplest item a bureaucratic calvary.

Basic research, carried out in university and technical school laboratories in India, is funded by the central government. There exist as well twenty-nine research laboratories and institutes affiliated with the Council of Scientific and Industrial Research (CSIR) also funded by the central government. The CSIR was established in 1942 to guide all of India's scientific research. Theoretically, the CSIR directs the entire science effort through centralized coordination; decisions about what research work is to be done and at which point it is to be attempted are clearly of pivotal importance:

Emphasis must shift from fundamental research to practical research. Also, the National Laboratories should themselves take the responsibility to ensure that the processes developed by them are sold for commercial use.[11]

But the base requires to be broadened and every major industrial unit should establish and develop its own research design and engineering personnel in addition to design and engineering devices. . . .[12]

The private sector is on its own—naturally one doesn't expect the government to subsidize it.[13]

These three ideas are at what might be called positions of paralytic equilibrium—they are not quite mutually exclusive, nor are they contradictory—and in the context of severely limited resources, giving each its due consideration makes effective action impossible.

The obvious problem here is the use of a series of centralized ministries linked by a sluggish bureaucracy, for the establishment of a climate of cooperation among the universities, the private sector, and the public sector of the economy. Due to monetary and foreign exchange limitations this economy is protected by high tariffs, and is thus largely immune to the constraints of international economic competition which could be expected to shape the climate under ordinary circumstances.

It became clear that Indian industry was not profiting suitably from the results of domestic scientific research as early as 1954. The National Research and Development Corporation was thus established to exploit the technical know-how developed by the CSIR laboratories and other government research institutes or industries. Even so, as late as 1964 it was acknowledged that "there is a missing link between the pilot plant stage and production over a very wide field of the activities of the CSIR."[14]

The meager showing is understandable because domestically developed processes are furnished without the necessary design data, and because pilot plant facilities are grossly inadequate. Moreover, besides a lack of commercial guarantees there is also hesitation on the part of both government and industry to risk large sums. Finally, full details of processes are not available to entrepreneurs before a contract is signed, despite the distinct possibility that the process may prove unsuitable in a given industrial setting.

Under the Industrial Development Regulation Act of 1951, the establishment of any new undertaking (or its expansion) requires an industrial license, if the value of the plant and equipment is greater than 25 lakhs (1 lakh = Rs. 100,000). No industrial license is necessary, however, if (1) the increase is not greater than 25 percent of originally licensed capacity; (2) no additional plant machinery is installed, other than minor balancing equipment procured domestically; (3) no additional expenditure of foreign exchange is involved; and (4) no additional demand for scarce raw materials is imposed. It is clear, then, that any sort of meaningful technological improvement is subject to industrial licensing. After an application is received, the Ministry of Industrial Development and Company Affairs distributes copies of the application to the relevant ministry and to the other agencies concerned, obtaining their comments and preparing a summary note which is formally considered by the Licensing Committee. This committee—consisting of the representatives of the concerned ministry, the Ministry of Finance, the Planning Commission, and the state government—makes recommendations based on projections of expected demands and anticipated capacity. From 10 to 15 percent more new licensing capacity is granted than called for in the demand projections to provide a cushion. The CSIR is also consulted to point out which materials and processes are already available in India. Domestic goods must be purchased—often at considerably higher prices than the imported equivalent—if the undertaking is to be licensed.

Of the four conditions under which an industrial license is not necessary, the restriction on imported raw materials may be waived in the case of a "priority industry." Suffice it to say that any firm with influence can qualify as a "priority industry"—from fertilizers to "scientific instruments," to preserved fish. When everybody has priority, nobody does. Technological development lacks direction.

In addition to the "priority industries" there exist the "key industries" and the "banned industries." Key industries are considered important for self-sustaining industrial growth, and a special internal procedure ensures prompt disposal of their applications.

"Banned industries" are those in which sufficient capacity has already been established and for which an application for license may ordinarily be rejected without reference to the Licensing Committee. In some "banned industries" expansion and diversification are, however, allowed. It is nonetheless dismaying to find that pig iron, alloy steel, ferrochromics, other ferroalloys, automobile ancillaries, rubber chemicals, and sulphuric acid appear on both lists.

As a final example of the inconsistencies of Indian planning, consider the problem of mechanical engineering, clearly a discipline of great importance to a country weak in design planning and dependent on foreign know-how. Dr. M. Suri, Director of the Central Mechanical Engineering Research Institute, noted at the Symposium on Import Substitution (1968) that 47 percent of the technology borrowed by India during the period 1957–66 depended directly or indirectly upon mechanical engineering. During the Third Five-Year Plan the largest imports dealt with mechanical engineering for equipment and plants. Yet during that same period only 1.16 percent of the total research expenditure was devoted to mechanical engineering.

We have seen, then, that India lacks a clear-cut policy of priorities for technological development and is hindered in solving immediate problems by a lumbering bureaucracy and an inadequate system for gathering information. Concentration on agricultural inputs such as fertilizer and seeds should soon permit India to become agriculturally self-sufficient, and even provide cash crops and thus sorely needed foreign exchange reserves.

Equally important, the country must remedy the labor, industrial, and educational shortcomings that have made the progress of Indian science so inexorably slow.

II. ISRAEL: SCIENCE FOR SURVIVAL

Israel's continued success in developing technology will be essential to its survival during the coming decade. Like India, Israel suffers a serious balance of trade deficit—whereas India's is about $1.2 billion, the figure for Israel has been above $400 million for a number of years. In fact, in 1969 it was above $835 million. Because of the vast disparity in their populations, Israel's problem would seem more acute—but Israel is able to thrive, in part, because its yearly deficit is covered almost in full by unilateral capital transfers (mainly through German war reparations and the world-wide United Jewish Appeal), loans, and the sale of development bonds.

Between 1950 and 1967 Israel maintained a 9 percent average yearly increase in GNP—the phenomenal and consistent postwar growth of Japan comes to mind—yet Israel is scarcely one-fortieth the size of Japan and at the moment lacks anything comparable to Japan's sophisticated commercial technology. Israel resembles a developed Western European country, yet at the same time it faces the distinctly non-European problem of assimiliating large numbers of untrained and often illiterate North African immigrants. And, of course, Israel has been at war intermittently with all of its neighbors since 1948.

In manpower, and even in the basic scientific awareness so often lacking in underdeveloped nations, Israel was well past the "take-off" point even before independence. Chaim Weizmann, first president of Israel, was himself a distinguished chemist who had done military R and D work for the British during World War I; the state was in fact born with an elementary infrastructure of academic science institutions, European-trained scientists, agricultural research stations, and mineral-extracting plants. Many of these had attained a certain measure of autonomy before statehood, and are to this day somewhat resistant to rigorous central science planning. Israel's Weizmann Institute boasts, with unique distinction, a reverse Brain Drain: more scientists have come to Israel from America to join the institute than have left it to emigrate to America. (Dr. Albert Sabin, the American researcher famed for the development of an oral polio vaccine, has recently become the institute's director.) Clearly, then, science in Israel operates in a context of special problems and special advantages. What concerns us here is Israeli manpower and education, industrial and military R and D, and, finally, the critical climate of combination to which these contribute.

Secondary education is not yet compulsory and free in Israel, and only 13 percent of 18 year olds graduate from an academic secondary school. Unique among developing countries, Israel has had until recently the benefit of a scientist immigration about equal to the yearly number of graduates of institutes of higher learning in Israel. By 1964, only half of Israel's scientists and technicians had been trained in the country.

There exists in Israeli industry only a weak market for research results. The government is the major shareholder in Israel's basic extracting industries—the potash and phosphoric acid plants located at the Dead Sea, and the petrochemical industry based on the distillation products of the Haifa refineries. In 1964, the government attempted to encourage more use of research by establishing the Israel Mining Institute (IMI), an independent R and D organization funded half by the government and half by the sale of research know-how.

Yet Israeli industry has until recently preferred to buy rather than produce industrial technology. In 1965 Israel received $300,000 in industrial royalties but paid out over $2,000,000, an unfavorable ratio of nearly 8:1 as compared with approximately 2.5:1 in either France or Germany.[15] The fact is that Israel's graduating scientists turn not to industry but to the greater material rewards and prestige of academia. Moreover,

. . . in Industry, the sophisticated research infrastructure is virtually non-existent. With one or two notable exceptions (chemical mining, water prospecting and utilization) there is no Research and Development activity in Industry and a good basic idea in scientific development in an institution may never reach industrialization.[16]

The Western pattern of industry conducting its own research or sponsoring research within the university, rarely holds in Israel—industry simply lacks the capital. The difference is reflected in Table 1.

TABLE 1
COMPARATIVE INDUSTRIAL/SCIENTIFIC MANPOWER (BY PERCENT)

	Scientists and Technologists in R and D (industrial, government, university)	Scientists and Technologists in Industry	
Israel	16	18	(1961)
USA	33	56	(1959)
UK	36	41	(1959)

In fact, it is often the university that attempts to interest industry in the results of research projects. The Yissum ("Application") R and D Company of the Hebrew University (1964), and the Yeda ("Know-How") R and D Company of the Weizmann Institute (1959) are two university organizations engaged in such activity. In addition, the National Council for Research and Development maintains a Research Initiation Fund which "provides support for any proposal whether from a private individual, a scientific institution, or a commercial company—which the Directors of the Fund consider likely to advance applied research and the industrial development of the country. In the latter case the Fund's support is usually given on a 50-50 basis with the Industry concerned."[17] Yet one must still interest the corporations; and this is a problem, for the industries prefer to buy finished know-how from abroad.

Israel's defense forces have also purchased heavily abroad. It is estimated that 80 percent of the trade deficit can be attributed to defense needs, and the Israelis' hope is that by 1973 heavy investment in the defense industry will have diminished the need for imports in this sector. In fact, the Ministry of Defense already owns or is associated with the more sophisticated sectors of the optics, electronics, and metallurgical industries. It is felt in Israel that some of the best men are doing some of the most exciting research in some of the country's best-equipped laboratories in the Science Department of the Ministry of Defense (although few details of this activity are available). As I have mentioned, the first president of Israel did military R and D work for the British during World War I. It is therefore no surprise that the current Ministry of Defense Science Department grew out of the Army Research Unit, established by David Ben Gurion on the eve of the war of independence—even before there was an organized army—to fight the war of improvisation.

Ta'as, the Israeli military defense industry, was the weapons production unit of the Hagannah—the underground Israeli resistance army—and was secret for many years after independence. Ta'as has some twenty plants throughout Israel, and a capital turnover of about $100 million, of which some $15 million is in exports. In fact, Yitzhak Ironi, Director of Military Industries, has boasted that Israel can produce its own armaments if necessary:

We have doubled manpower and tripled production since the Six Day War. We were not surprised by the extension of the embargo. . . . What we cannot buy in other markets we will make. I repeat: there is nothing that we cannot produce in the way of arms, ammunition and accessories in the next 8 to 12 months. . . . We have learned a lot of technology from France and are grateful for that. . . . The French are a good customer of ours. . . . If Israel decides to make its own jet it will have the technology and industrial capacity to do so within the next 2 to 3 years.[18]

Ernst D. Bergmann, for many years the director of defense science efforts, notes that the Army Research Unit introduced electronics into Israel and contributed to the computer effort as well as to the study of solid-fuel rocket propellants; he thus stresses the value of a military/science establishment to a developing nation through spin-off—the process by which many new unexpected products and industries are created through scientific research. It is also because of eventual spinoff to industry and agriculture that Bergmann justifies Israel's investment in such "glamour areas" as atomic energy.

Besides the growing military sector, research in Israel is carried out in the institutes of higher learning—principally the Israel Institute of Technology in Haifa (Technicon), the Hebrew University of Jerusalem, and the Weizmann Institute of Science in Rehovot—the government research institutes, and the industrial research units. Universities account for over half of the research done in Israel, the Weizmann Institute specializing in biological and medical research, the Technicon in testing materials and products and advising companies in Israel and abroad. By 1965 the government's contribution to such academic institutions was approximately 52 percent. Private donations, research grants, and international foundations are other sources of research capital.

Over half of the funds for medical research conducted in Israel come from abroad, and in 1965 about one-quarter of Israel's total research bill was paid by the United States. Israeli government expenditures for scientific research have increased steadily since 1961, and the country maintains a research ratio of approximately 1.3 percent of GNP. This does *not* include the apparently substantial expenditures on research in the Ministry of Defense, and thus compares quite favorably with the figure for the advanced Western European countries. The academic researcher has considerable social status in Israel, and the university professor is encouraged to devote time to pure research. Such positions are thus attractive alternatives to graduating scientists.

Government research institutes conduct from 35 to 40 percent of Israel's applied research and are almost entirely government-funded. The applied research conducted by private industry constitutes an exceedingly small percentage of the total national effort in terms both of manpower (10 percent) and of expenditure (5–7 percent).

As early as 1949 concern for this national effort led to the formation of the Research Council for Israel (twelve scientists, the prime minister, and, later, representatives from the three major universities), which is responsible for advising on science policy. By 1959 the RCI was enlarged to twenty-five members and renamed the National Council of Research and Development (again enlarged in 1967 to thirty-six members) now including senior civil servants from the Treasury and ministries concerned with scientific and research activities. The National Council distributes research grants but relies on "good will" for execution of recommendations, acknowledging the autonomy of research institutions. Other government ministries have research facilities under their jurisdiction for which policy is decided by a joint committee of ministry and National Council members. The Ministry of Agriculture, for example, operates the Volcani Institute for Agricultural Research, the largest government laboratory in the country.

Although approval for a foreign exchange expenditure must be obtained from the Ministry of Commerce and Industry and from the Treasury, this is in practice easy. The contrast with India's tight foreign exchange reserves and lumbering bureaucratic licensing procedure is striking. Tax allowances are also used in Israel to encourage foreign investment, particularly in the Negev and other areas designated for development. Yet is is clear that there is no central policy regarding the importation of technology. The difficulty in introducing truly effective central planning is attributed, by the Israelis, to an early experience with excessive political and institutional pluralism:

. . . the new State of Israel started its existence with a strong scientific and technological background in agriculture, medicine, physical sciences and engineering. In addition it had numerous well-founded socio-political bodies. All this would appear to bode well for a strong policy of science, but the negative aspects of the same background cannot be underestimated: the new State started with well established scientific and educational institutions highly jealous of their hard-won autonomous status, and with many well established economic and political groupings.[19]

There is a great deal of speculation on the future of Israel's science effort. As we have seen, neglect of industrial R and D is dangerous for a large power interested in competing with other giants on the world market. And in view of the challenge posed by certain developing nations having at their disposal extremely cheap labor, "the more enlightened Israeli industries—drugs and . . . chemicals among them—have adopted the attitude that the only possible economic viability for Israel lies in developing products which are not being made elsewhere."[20] Such special products constitute the industrial "cash crops" to be sought by science-developing nations. In Japan, these products were in the fields of optics and electronics. In Israel these fields are investigated largely in the military research sector. The computer software industry, which prepares and evaluates the data going into and coming out of computers, could be a new and lucrative field for Israeli brainpower. There are now the beginnings of an Israeli machine-tool industry as well as attempts at the world air transport market in the government-assisted production of the Arava, a 22-passenger twin-engine Israeli aircraft.

Perhaps the greatest question mark hovering over the Israeli science effort concerns the production of atomic weaponry. Israel has requested that the Phantom aircraft purchased from the USA be equipped to deliver atomic bombs, but so far both France and America have declined to provide such specifications. Of the Israeli Dimona nuclear reactor Neville Brown writes: "Dimona may rank as a small reactor, but Israel is accumulating enough nuclear material there to make a Nagasaki bomb every year."[21] And the late Prime Minister Eshkol often argued, "Why should Israel rush into signing the convention on the non-proliferation of nuclear weapons, so long as the Arab states and the Soviet Union are represented on the supervisory body, while Israel is not?"[22] Yet the official Israeli position remains that "Israel is not a nuclear state and, as in the past, the attitude of the Israel Government is that Israel will not be the first to introduce nuclear weapons into the Middle East."[23]

Israel's scientific organization, manpower, and funding thrive, then, in a unique environment. The consolidation of the chemical extraction industry for more effective R and D, and the already extensive military R and D, seem to parallel, at a somewhat later stage of development, the Japanese experience with technology via *zaibatsu* (large monopolies) and heavy investment in armaments. In Israel, the familiar pattern of development—that of a significant military role in the growth of Big Science—operates in the unusual context of advanced education and research. The hope in Israel is that the present heavy weighting in favor of basic research will eventually make up for the lack of adequate industrial R and D, and prepare Israeli industry for a competitive position in certain special world markets. Because of the understandable secrecy in which some of the best research in Israel—electronic, optical, nuclear—is shrouded, it is difficult at this time to speculate further.

III. YUGOSLAVIA: A SOCIALIST WAY

As a developing socialist country Yugoslavia ostensibly suggests a Different Way to observant young nations. As a self-proclaimed (and oft-condemned) breakaway from the postwar Stalinist field, Yugoslavia is by no stretch of the imagination a Soviet satellite following one Soviet path. What then is to be learned from Yugoslavia's search for a practical policy of technological development?

Yugoslavia entered the postwar era with the ruins of what had been a backward, predominantly agricultural economy. By the end of the war nearly one-ninth of its population had been destroyed—and it faced a grisly civil war at home and the menace of the Red Army at its borders. Before the planners, moreover, lay the task of switching over to an economy with a major industrial sector.

Prewar Yugoslavia had only three universities within its borders; and the amount of scientific research conducted there was minuscule: during the period 1935–1940 only nine Ph.D.'s were granted in the entire country. There was clearly a need for reform of poor facilities and archaic structure, as well as for tremendous expansion, if the country was to begin fulfilling its manpower needs. Such expansion was given top priority. By 1960 there were four times as many entire faculties in mathematics, the physical sciences, and engineering as in 1939; a greater proportion of students was involved in technical studies; and there had been a seven-fold increase in the number of university students.

The initial drive toward establishing an industrial base involved a great deal of technological transfer. In 1954, the Federal Fund for the Advancement of Industrial Production was established; technological institutes were separated from the science academies and made partly responsible for their own funding through industrial research contracts. Universities could draw on this fund for the support of technological research and could also accept research contracts from industry. Yet the lack of research persisted; industry contracted predominantly for routine work on production problems and quality control; universities complained that industry was uninterested in supporting longterm research.

In 1960, a number of independent industrial research laboratories were established to carry out longterm projects of major national interest and to conduct basic research. At the same time tax deductions were announced for all research expenditures by industry for work performed either within the enterprise or contracted for elsewhere. The research institutes themselves were tax-exempt if they devoted the amount that would have gone to taxes, along with 50 percent of their annual income, to the establishment of their *own* research funds to be used either for basic research or for staff training. In an interesting variation on the theme of technological purchase, the Yugoslavs hope to use restricted access to research results to foster R and D competition:

In order to give further impetus to the use of research by industrial enterprises, and especially by smaller and medium sized firms, the Federal Fund has offered to defray a part of the cost of quite a number of research or development projects on the understanding that the research results will not be disclosed to anyone but the sponsoring firm for several years.[24]

In the area of technology importation Yugoslavia has, since 1968, attempted to encourage foreign investment, but has so far met with difficulties due to the Western fear of nationalization and of workers' councils. Although there are no specific currency restrictions on buying technology, a firm must secure the financial backing of another enterprise or a bank. Banks thus have a great deal of say in this matter. And although there is no central policy on importing technology, importation is restricted to enterprises with research facilities that would permit development of the purchased process or machinery.

There is precious little information available concerning the Yugoslav military science effort. Nevertheless, an article in *Ekonomika Politika* treating the reorganization of science funding revealed that

. . . disproportionately high funds (more than 50% of the Federation money for science) have been reserved for years for the operation of nuclear institutes out of the budget, usually under the cover of nuclear secrets which, in fact, were reduced to the ambition of working over nuclear reactors to produce nuclear arms. When these ambitions proved to be unrealistic, there was a basic reorganization.[25]

What are the principal research organizations in Yugoslavia? And how have they evolved since the creation of the republic? Directly after the war the universities had difficulty in obtaining research funds, as they were in competition with the Federal Nuclear Energy Commission and the academies of science. For at least the first ten years of independence these academies were seen as the focal points of Yugoslav research. Nuclear energy was also funded heavily. The Yugoslav Academy of Science and Art in Zagreb (founded in 1866), the Serbian Academy of Science in Belgrade (1886), and the Slovene Academy of Science in Ljubljana (1938) had all been more or less honorific institutes before the war; yet after independence they were entrusted with the organization and administration of the country's research institutes. It was later realized, however, that such preference—in neglect of university research—was a serious error. Thus, along with independent research institutes, another sort of laboratory is now beginning to appear—one established jointly by the government, the universities, and a number of industrial enterprises. In such efforts the government provides the building and research equipment costs; member enterprises pay subscription rates; and the institute generates income from subscription rates, contract work done for member enterprises, and public funds. University professors serve as part-time researchers, and graduate students can be trained using institute facilities.

The search for an effective policy of funding scientific research has been closely linked in Yugoslavia with an effort to create an effective climate of combination. From the end of the war until 1957 science was funded directly out of the federal budget. Institutions received funds according to the number of "research units" they comprised, and determined their own programs. Universities, however, were funded by the separate state or people's republic governments.

The economy neither invested funds in science institutions, nor participated in their formation, development or orientation. Science institutes were not concerned with better "results" of their work, but with the number of research units, even if they had nothing to do.[26]

Furthermore, "this system of financing caused many difficulties for the institute and fostered a rather injurious administrative interference."[27] The inherent centralization in the system of funding caused research institutes to become isolated from industry. The result was a general neglect of applied R and D. For these reasons, the budgetary form of financing was eliminated in 1957 and a system of "funds" at the federal and republic level was established; now individual application is made by project.

Specifically, federal money is put into the Federal Fund for Financing Scientific Research, from which it is distributed by the Federal Council for the Coordination of Scientific Research. (According to a 1965 resolution, 0.2 percent of the national income was to be channeled into the fund for research during the middle plan period.) The 250-member council, composed of scientists and prominent scholars (half nominated by the Federal Assembly, half by research institutions designated by the assembly), considers the targets and tasks of the federal plan and sets the guidelines, by field, for the funding of basic research and related areas. Allocation is by contract, with application made to the managing board of the council, consisting of ten university professors and five industrial leaders. Council funds are crucial to basic research in Yugoslavia—they constitute about 20 percent of the total science expenditure. Roughly 20 percent is provided by the republics (educational institutes, for example, are funded by the individual republics) and 60 percent by industry.

We see then that Yugoslavia has attempted to use economic persuasion—in the form of tax deductions, secrecy provisions, and directed funds—to encourage organizational cooperation and the development of a climate of combination. Yet there are problems. Inadequate information on contemporary research methods—and even results—causes needless repetition of research already conducted elsewhere: "Nearly 13,000 experts in our country are engaged in discovering America."[28]

Moreover, bureaucratic bottlenecks delay the realization of funding goals, and the post-1957 piecemeal funding approach raises the problem of disparate research efforts:

Even today, like so many times in the past, we can see a number of very small and split up scientific units. . . . The activities of many of them are directed towards earning more money rather than towards serious research. . . . Just of late many of these institutes have been orienting themselves towards conclusion of business contracts with foreign countries, whereby they are insuring . . . decent earning for their personnel.[29]

By the end of June 1968, the allocations for the federal fund for 1969 were announced. The expenditure of 120 million dinars was broken down into five categories: elemental natural sciences, 35 percent; technology, 25 percent; agriculture, forestry, and veterinary medicine, 19 percent; social sciences, 16 percent; and medicine, 5 percent. It was also noted that science organizations interested in projects in technology (applied R and D), agriculture, forestry, and veterinary medicine which expect resources from the fund, should secure half of the funds "on their own." Researchers in the other fields were expected to secure 20 percent of the funds through contract work.

In December 1963 it was clearly stated that private organizations should finance applied and developmental research; whereas only fundamental research in the exact science) would remain in the sphere of socio-political communities:

The participation of the economy in the cost of research should continually increase, while that of the socio-political community should gradually decrease. In 1965 funds secured from work organizations covered 56.5% of the income of scientific institutions. This figure is expected to rise to 69% by 1970.[30]

Reservations are also expressed concerning the feasibility of making institutions responsible for funding their own work. *Ekonomika Politika* observed that "for the moment, there are still many difficulties in engaging economic and other organizations. . . . Banks have not shown a major interest in investment in scientific projects."[31] Even with the final compromise of cost-sharing, Yugoslavia is likely to face the same problems of unavailable risk capital which have paralyzed much of the nascent R and D effort in India.

On the question of clear science priorities Yugoslavia is very much at a loss. Electronics and superconductors, chemicals, metallurgy, and machine engineering are most often singled out, but always with the qualification that these are not yet part of a conscious program. With respect to organization the feeling now is that individual project funding has resulted in a plethora of small uncoordinated tasks, and the newest idea is the creation of a council for Macro Projects. Yet how should proportionate funding, presumably at the federal level, be determined among the republics? *Ekonomika Politika*'s reply was that "no matter how attractive the new concept may be it is neither perfect nor absolutely feasible."[32]

We see, then, that the "Yugoslav experiment" is still very much that. It is something to be watched. If the Yugoslavs are able, with the onus of fiscal bankruptcy and the prospect of concrete material reward, to generate a working system of technological development, they will have accomplished a feat of great interest to most young nations. The crucial question is whether they will be able to rally faith in science among banks and enterprises sufficient to get the country started on a path of sustained economic growth, and at the same time prevent both their investors and their laboratories from turning abroad for proven processes and more lucrative contracts.

IV. COMMUNIST CHINA: IDEOLOGY INTRUDES

Paging through speech texts, official editorials, and news agency releases from Communist China, one is overwhelmed by the mass of rhetoric and appalled at the paucity of facts. No government statistics have been released by the Chinese since 1960; publication, or at least foreign dissemination, of the *Journal of the Chinese Academy of Sciences* ceased in early 1966. Thus, a detailed assessment of the current organization, planning, and execution of scientific R and D in Communist China seems difficult if not impossible.

What the reams of official jargon do indicate is the "background noise" of ideology in which scientific research must operate. Scientists have been among the most distrusted members of Communist Chinese society, representing a potential "autonomous interest group" and perhaps even a significant source of leaders down the "road to technocratic bureaucratization" and downright "revisionism." Although scientists were rather insulated for some time because of their obvious utility to the regime, recent reports from the mainland seem to suggest that even the science machine directly linked to the People's Liberation Army is now under fire. Because of the special nature of the information available, this study of Communist China will deal most explicitly with the problem of ideology and the Chinese scientist.

We have seen how a state's ideology can shape and direct its science policy. The agrarian background of many of Israel's founding Zionists posed problems for the initiation of state involvement in science. India's goal of avoiding the "Japanese path" of monopolistic capitalism has made research cooperation within industry next to impossible. Yugoslavia's developing brand of profit-motive socialism has had a distinct effect on the funding and planning of its science effort. And in Communist China we find the strongest example yet of ideology's intrusion into the laboratory.

During the six years of ideological retrenching that followed the inception of the new Chinese state in 1949, scientists were able to conduct more or less free research. Scientists became more subject to centralized planning, however, with the establishment of the State Scientific Planning Commission in 1956, and the promulgation of the twelve-year "Longterm Scheme for Scientific Development." Although the complete text of this plan has never been released, we do know that suggestions were entertained from large numbers of Chinese scientists, and that the whole plan was then sent to Russia for approval, where it was reviewed by twenty-six research groups of some 640 Soviet scientists and technicians. The principal areas of emphasis in the plan were the development of the peaceful uses of atomic energy, of sophisticated electronic computer techniques, and of applications of jet propulsion.

With the 100 Flowers Campaign and some particularly vociferous "contending" by scientific researchers, the Academy of Sciences was branded as a stronghold for rightists, and those who disagreed with the twelve-year plan were liquidated.[33] The subsequent anti-rightist period brought an attempt at greater centralized control of science. "Henceforth, all scientific organs, including the Academy, had to obtain the approval of the State Scientific Planning Commission to initiate new research and establish new research institutes."[34] Finally, in 1958, the State Scientific Planning Commission was merged with the State Technological Commission to form the State Science and Technology Commission, an extremely powerful administrative unit. The merger reflected the emphasis given to applied science during the Great Leap Forward in 1958.

In sampling source material from Communist Chinese media, we should keep in mind the increasing politicization of the science establishment. After gaining power in 1949, the communists assumed an initial pose toward scientists which appeared tough but was actually conciliatory:

In the case of those scientists who are still working for the reactionaries, but are not adamant enemies of the people, providing they are willing to change their stand and admit their mistakes before the people, we should also win them over to serving the fatherland of the people.[35]

An attempt was made at first to give preferential admittance into science schools to students of peasant background as opposed to those from bourgeois or landowner families, but this was eventually abandoned as impractical at the time of the Korean War.

By 1956, the first years of prosperity had convinced China's leaders that science could be made part of a rational planning scheme:

The development of the natural sciences is basically determined by the requirements of the actual production goals. Separated from social requirements the natural sciences would be totally devoid of significance.

—TU JUN-SHENG, SECRETARY GENERAL
OF THE CHINESE ACADEMY OF SCIENCES, 1956

This was clearly a foreshadowing of the "Labor and Study Movement," the "peasant scientists," and the "worker engineers" of the 1958 Great Leap Forward. Notable for its poetry, this period saw the initiation of such programs as "March against Nature," "Reform the Deserts," and "Let High Mountains and Glaciers Contribute toward Socialist Construction." *The Red Flag* in 1958 called science "bourgeois science;" bookish knowledge, "a pile of garbage, to be replaced by proletarian science." Liu Shao-chi "described the intellectuals as maintaining a neutral stand but anticipated that manual labor would change all that."[36] While more than doubling the number of schools and research institutes, the Chinese effected a turnover of administrative personnel which was to lead to a large-scale fiscal and planning disaster:

The Big Leap put half-illiterate party members in charge of research institutions. In the Botany Research Institute of the Academy of Sciences, for example, all the forty-three persons in charge of administration were demobilized soldiers of farmer origin with no education.[37]

By 1961, however, after three years of severe agricultural failure and the withdrawal in July 1960 of Soviet experts and technicians, "the party began to modify its policy toward the higher intellectuals."[38] A party secretary was assigned to each research group, so that the science leader was no longer responsible for political and ideological work; cadres were warned not to disturb researchers for political training; the 5/6 Rule (initially, one out of every six hours per day, and then one day out of six workdays per week, was to be devoted to group indoctrination) was relaxed. In contrast to the attempted exclusion policy of the early 1950s, it was noted in 1961 that although Hsu Kuang-chu, a chemist, came from a merchant (small landowner) family, this "absolutely cannot be taken as a basis for praising or disparaging his academic achievements."[39] In June 1961, Chien Hsuih-sen, present head of the Chinese missile program (Chien was trained in America and returned to China in 1955), pleaded for more fundamental scientific research, and stated in a published article that the abolition of the teaching of "pure science" was absurd. On 28 December 1961, the editorial in *People's Daily* took a less collective stance: "In science, personal research will forever remain important."

Through 1962 and early 1963 the official line toward science, stressing the need to apply technology to large-scale agricultural problems, was conciliatory. The party's planning problems were openly acknowledged, and in a humble gesture expressing "ignorance of scientific matters on the part of the party," the editorial in *People's Daily* (29 June 1963) called for a leadership composed of the party, the masses, and the experts, and solicited the cooperation of "those who know."

Yet by April of that same year politics, ideology, and the cult of the peasant had once again crept into science officialese:

Our young scientists are now advancing in the direction of redness and expertness. They have profoundly realized that politics is the soul in this direction, that the cause of science is a part of the entire cause of Socialism, and that intellectuals must establish the attitude of making science and technology serve Socialism and production.

We oppose those who have acquired some knowledge and techniques with the support of the collective, and then use this knowledge and these techniques as capital for bargaining with the people.

We must learn from the workers and peasants, because science originates from practice. Workers and peasants, being direct producers, have rich knowledge and experience. This then requires that intellectuals go to the factories and farms to learn from workers and peasants, to absorb the rich knowledge accumulated by the masses in the long years of practice. . . .[40]

It is difficult to explain this shift back to a hard line. It might very well be a reflection of greater stability after recovery from the abuse of the Great Leap Forward. Yet by mid-1963 considerable progress had doubtless been made toward the completion of a nuclear bomb;

perhaps growing army influence was pushing the party into a stricter ideological position.

On 16 October 1964, the Chinese exploded their first fission bomb. (The explosion had been planned for 1 October but was delayed, as the Chinese apparently had intelligence information on Khruschev's impending decline. The blast was detonated six hours after the shakedown in the Russian leadership was announced by Moscow.) It was an implosive U-235 device, as was the second bomb set off on 14 May 1965, showing that the Chinese had indeed perfected an efficient gaseous-diffusion system for uranium-isotope separation—a feat the French had yet to accomplish though the Americans and Russians had been using the technique for a number of years.

In 1966, the coming hard line of the Cultural Revolution became progressively discernible in statements concerning science policy.

China trains postgraduates in its own way, with politics taking the lead, with theory and practice closely combined and collective training integrated with individual tutoring.[41]

By April, a meeting of an unidentified "committee" of the Academy of Sciences issued the following statement:

The world of science through all these years has been corrupted by the capitalist spirit. The cure in such a case is class struggle, go to the factories, engage in manual labor.

On 9 May the Chinese exploded their third nuclear device, this time testing a fusion triggering apparatus. The New China News Agency reported the event in the following way:

The complete success of this nuclear test was insured by the Chinese People's Liberation Army and China's scientists, technicians, and broad sections of workers and functionaries who, under the correct leadership of the Communist Party of China, and holding still higher the great Red Banner of Mao Tse-tung's thought, gave prominence to politics. . . .

It appears, then, that by 1966 the politicization of science had once again begun in earnest. Speaking on 3 July of that year, Chou En-lai said: "The Chinese Academy of Sciences will be turned into a Red, Red, great school of Mao Tse-tung's thought." Yet by August it was decided that at least some scientists should be protected. Item 12 of Mao's sixteen-point directive on the Cultural Revolution stated:

As regards scientists we should in the present moment continue to apply the policy "unity—criticism—unity." Special care should be taken of those scientists and technical personnel who have made contributions. Efforts should be made to help them gradually transform their world outlook and style of work.

This did nothing to remove the underlying problem—the apparent resistance of scientists to politicization along doctrinal party lines:

In the field of natural science a grave, acute, complex class struggle is going on . . . against those who do not admit that science and technology must serve socialist construction . . . who like to work in laboratories and are not involved in politics.[42]

Why such resistance was a real problem—or was singled out as such after Mao's August directive—is an interesting point for speculation. The shifting viewpoint probably reflects the party vs. army power struggle and the party shakedown just then beginning. As certain party cadres began to feel threatened, science and science policy perhaps served as a convenient rallying point for expressing criticism and thus proving their own ideological purity. This trend raised many complications for the even then unsure directors of the Cultural Revolution. The science establishment was too important—militarily, agriculturally, even economically—to be sacrificed to revolutionary zeal. This is essentially the content of the August directive. Yet after August, Mao had the difficult task of balancing and reconciling the ideological purifiers—whether overzealous Red Guards or "reformed" party cadres—on the one hand, and the army power center on the other.

On 27 October, China exploded its fourth nuclear bomb, this time at the tip of an intermediate-range missile. The fifth nuclear test came on 28 December, and Washington announced that it expected a full-fledged hydrogen bomb within a year. The army was probably gaining greater and greater prestige; while the ideological position of science was to become more ambiguous in the next year and a half.

A first compromise with reactionary party power came in early 1967 over a crisis at the Sinkiang nuclear testing area:

[The area] was garrisoned by eight divisions of troops loyal to Wang En-mao, military commander, First Communist Party Secretary of the region, and Sinkiang's recalcitrant anti-Maoist overlord . . . Wang . . . was reported to have threatened to seize China's nuclear stockpile and in February, Mao dispatched loyalist troops to Sinkiang to restore Peking's authority after Wang had reportedly occupied two nuclear ballistic missile plants. . . .

This dangerous situation was adroitly turned by the conciliatory Chou En-lai who "suspended" the Cultural Revolution in Sinkiang. At a rally in Urumchi in early March Wang was hailed as a great "proletarian revolutionary" once more. . . .[43]

The situation, though, was far from under control. On 10 April, representatives of the Revolutionary Rebels Unit General Headquarters of the Chinese Academy of Sciences in Peking launched accusations against academy supporters of Liu Shao-chi.

On 17 June, China tested her first megaton-range hydrogen bomb:

The successful H-bomb test represents another great victory for the invincible thought of Mao Tse-tung; it is another quick fruit of the great Proletarian Cultural Revolution; it marks a victory for Chairman Mao's Proletarian Revolutionary line on the science front.[44]

The army had apparently consolidated its influence over the science establishment. By 30 June, the Chinese Academy of Sciences Revolutionary Rebels Committee for Seizing Power had been established, including representatives of the People's Liberation Army, with Kuo Mo-jo, the "reformed" party man, still in power. The arrangement was referred to by Radio Peking in August as being based on "Mao's three-way alliance—representatives of the Communist Party, the army, and mass organizations."[45] (This troika should be compared with Mao's triple leadership of 1963 consisting of the party, the masses, and the experts.) The Liberation Army then moved into the academy and, finding that the scientist "rebels" knew little of Mao, began teaching Mao's thoughts and the sayings of Lin Piao.[46]

On 2 October, the New China News Agency announced that the "Revolutionary Masses and Cadres of the Scientific and Technological front have carried forward the glorious tradition of the People's Liberation Army," and on 6 October noted that as the great Proletarian Cultural Revolution enters the stages of decisive victory, Chinese scientists have completed a giant new transistor computer suitable for all purposes. The development of this "scientific news article" reminds one of the poetry of the Great Leap Forward.

> Whenever they encountered difficulties, scientists sought help in the solution of their problems in Chairman Mao's works such as "On Practice," "On Contradiction," and constantly read articles: "Serve the People," "In Memory of Norman Bethune," and "The Foolish Old Man Who Removed the Mountains."
>
> To express their infinite love, loyalty, faith and admiration of Chairman Mao, the makers built the computer in such a way that every time the machine starts, a portrait of Chairman Mao appears together with the words "Serve the People" in a facsimile of his handwriting. It also plays the tune "The East Shines Red, the Sun Rises, There Emerges in China a Mao Tse-tung."

In early 1968, the *South China Morning Post* reported that "China's scientists, long regarded as outside the stresses of the Cultural Revolution . . . have been officially criticised as having a cold and indifferent attitude toward revolution and research."[47] Noting a "cold and indifferent" attitude toward revolution is in keeping with the trend toward ideological purity, and such a notation might not be expected to have a great effect on subsequent science policy. Such a characterization of research, though, seems to renew the emphasis on applied work which was evident during the Great Leap Forward. Street posters began appearing on Peking walls in early April, attacking "Conservatism and Factionalism in the Committee for Defense Science and Technology" and "Bad Leaders of the National Defense Scientific Bureau."

By 4 May, posters were reviling Nieh Jung-chen, Minister of Science and Technology and regarded as the "Father of China's Atomic Bomb"; yet Nieh appeared as a guest at a Maoist reception for army cadres on 3 June. Nevertheless, events of the next few months seemed to indicate that scientists and the science establishment had lost the last vestiges of immunity to the Cultural Revolution. According to a July 1968 Red Guard publication from Peking, "The Information Bulletin of the Scientific and Technological War," five scientists, including three associated with China's nuclear program, had been arrested on charges of treason and spying for the Soviet Union.

The 22 July editorial of *People's Daily,* attributed to Mao, laid down the following guidelines for scientific work:

It is still necessary to have colleges—here I refer, in the main, to colleges of science and engineering. However, the period of schooling would be shortened—education should be revolutionized, proletarian politics should be put in command. . . .

Integrating themselves with the workers and peasants, and participating in productive labor, is the important way for young scientists to mold their world outlook and gain practical technical knowledge. Therefore we propose that college graduates should first work as ordinary laborers in factories in the countryside. They should get "qualification certificates" from the workers and peasants. . . .

These are nearly restatements of the Great Leap Forward ideas, which eventually lead to catastrophic excess. As a follow-up, the *Shanghai Daily* complained on 26 July 1968:

The situation in Science and Technology circles is not satisfactory. . . . Some people indulge in personal ambition, rely too heavily on foreign textbooks and conventions, and never move beyond the library or laboratory. In short, scientific and technology departments have become a hotbed for the breeding of revisionist intellectual aristocrats.

It seems, then, that Mao left the science infrastructure, or at least its military sector, safe and immune so that it might continue to produce the tools the regime deemed necessary for international prestige and psychological gun-rattling. To suggest that this protection was withdrawn as soon as the first failures occurred is perhaps to confound coincidence with cause. It was probably success rather than failure that undid the technicians. China now has made good its membership in the H-Bomb Club and demonstrated its incipient missile capability. It is of little real strategic importance whether China has effective ICBMs in three years, or five years, or even ten years. Barring a preemptive Russian strike it will have them sooner or later, and everybody knows it. The problem then becomes the continued reshaping of China, the ideology of which has convulsed the country since the inception of the Cultural Revolution. It appears that a large-scale attempt is once again being made to politicize the scientist. There will be more applied work, more visits to the fields, more advice from "peasant experts," more of the excesses of the Great Leap Forward; and yet, inevitably, more progress and, eventually, perhaps with Mao's death, some moderation.

V. PROSPECTS

Scientific research is a contradictory creature. To be effective it requires the proper climate of combination—generous funding, institutional support, trained manpower, and external pressures. The latter refer to forces outside the country which influence the direction and tempo of domestic scientific research, such as threats to national security from scientific discoveries abroad. Yet once established, scientific research must reach some sort of "hands off" relationship with the very institutions that nurtured it. We have seen how precariously the equilibrium is maintained, and how easily it is disrupted.

Economic problems, ideological concerns, and military needs conspire in India to hamper scientific growth. Money is tight; a vague, mythological commitment to "nonmonopolistic" socialism inhibits large-scale industrial cooperation; the threat of a recently hostile Communist China makes nuclear weaponry—though economically a disastrous priority—still a going aspiration. Moreover, a ponderous bureaucracy complicates planning and the gathering of information to the point of impossibility. The country has grave problems holding on to its scientific brainpower.

Israel, although relatively strong in its basic research capabilities, faces the problem of inadequately developed links between industry and scientific research facilities, and in fact acknowledges the lack of any overall plan for scientific development. Military R and D, however, seems to be quite productive, and might well initiate a new dependence on Israeli technology which would of course, be of great benefit to the country.

The course of Yugoslav science since the war underscores the variability of the factors that shape a country's climate of combination. An apparent decision to abandon the idea of atomic weapons will channel sorely needed funds into Yugoslavia's small but growing science infrastructure. Flexible application of socialist ideology and generous incorporation of the profit motive into applied research will probably encourage technological growth as well as foreign investment.

Our study of Communist China's political path to technology raises more questions than it resolves, due at least in part to the meagre and biased information available. Military and applied research have been obvious priorities; yet it is not clear whether basic research has suffered in consequence; and if so, to what extent. It appears that until 1966 pure science and the laboratory were insulated from anything more than formal ideological intrusions. That situation seems to have changed. It is too early to evaluate the fate of science and the individual researcher in this new society, but one thing at least is clear: China is succeeding brilliantly in its race to catch up with the West. Whether it will "pull ahead" in any significant way remains to be seen.

Any nation hoping to survive scientifically must acknowledge the right of the scientist, because he is a scientist, to indulge in basic research gloriously unrelated to any production goal. Such considerations are neither moral nor metaphysical, but are born of the practical facts of scientific life. Science grows through fundamental research, through accidental discovery, through the invincible pursuit of the general sought in the exhaustive investigation of the particular. Without this basic research, a country's scientific education facilities and research institutions cannot grow.

Countries grow through the successful application of foreign or domestic technology, through the progressive elaboration of the kind of science infrastructure presented at the beginning of this essay. One of the most crippling errors a developing nation can make is to confound a failure of the science infrastructure—ideally a coordinated, working entity—with a failure of specific scientific education or research facilities, only a part of that entity. To demand of a part what the whole has proved incapable of furnishing accomplishes nothing. Thus, to grow in science, a country must define the foci of its science infrastructure and establish real and long-lasting links among them. It must work to develop new institutions not at the expense of old ones, but for the benefit and enhancement of the entire climate of combination. Only in the taxing pursuit of such coordinated growth can a country hope to harness technology to advantage in confronting the staggering problems of underdevelopment.

NOTES

1. P. Maheshwari, "Indian Scientific Policy," *Minerva* 3, no. 1 (Autumn 1964): 99.
2. Soli K. Ghaswala, "Technical Education in India," *International Science*

and Technology, no. 68 (August 1967), p. 14.

3. Ibid., p. 14.
4. Ibid.
5. Council of Industrial and Scientific Research, "Report of the Third Reviewing Committee of the Council of Scientific and Industrial Research," *Minerva* 3, no. 3 (Spring 1965): 360–361.
6. Ibid., p. 361.
7. Ibid., p. 374.
8. "Orientation of Research on Practical Lines," *Economic Times of Bombay,* 20 November 1963, p. 5.
9. "Background Paper," *Economic Times of Bombay,* 20 November 1963, p. 4.
10. Ibid.
11. "Report on Seminar on Import Substitution," *Overseas Hindustan Times,* 3 May 1969, p. 5.
12. "Summary of Second Technical Session," *Overseas Hindustan Times,* 3 May 1969, p. 33.
13. This view was elicited during a personal interview with a ministerial employee in New Delhi.
14. Council of Industrial and Scientific Research, "Report of the Third Reviewing Committee," p. 363.
15. Shaul Katz, "Science in Israel 1968," abridged English translation (Jerusalem: Public Service of the Prime Minister's Office Information Services, 1968), p. 12.
16. *National Science Policy and Organization of Research in Israel* (Jerusalem: National Council for Research and Development, 1967), p. 25.
17. Shlomo Gonen, *Scientific Research in Israel 1968* (Tel Aviv: National Council for Research and Development, Center of Scientific and Technological Information, 1968), p. 15.
18. *Jerusalem Post Weekly,* 20 January 1969, p. 6.
19. Daniel Shimshoni, "Israeli Scientific Policy," *Minerva* 3, no. 4 (Summer 1967): 447.
20. The Weizmann Institute, *Science and Technology,* August 1966, p. 64.
21. Neville Brown, "Proliferation in the Balance," *New Scientist* 42, no. 646 (24 April 1969): p. 190.
22. *Jerusalem Post Weekly,* 6 October 1968, p. 10.
23. Ibid.
24. Branko Rakovic, "Scientific Policy in Yugoslavia," *Minerva* 3, no. 2 (Winter 1965): 203.
25. Mimeographed English translation and summary of articles from the Yugoslav press in the "Science" file in the office of the Science Liaison, U.S. Embassy, Belgrade. Articles were identified with the initials "E.P." and the date, here 8 June 1968.
26. E.P. (23–29 December 1968), p. 1752.
27. Rakovic, "Scientific Policy in Yugoslavia," p. 194.
28. E.P. (13–19 May 1968), p. 587.
29. Ibid.
30. Ibid.
31. Ibid.
32. E.P. (20 January 1969).
33. Chu-yuan Cheng, "Scientific Engineering and Manpower in Communist China: 1949–1963," NSF 65–14, Washington, D.C., 1966, p. 63.

34. Ibid., p. 38.
35. *Jen Min Jih Pao,* 18 August 1950.
36. *China News Analysis,* 458 (1 March 1963).
37. Unsigned memo, "Science 1957–67," in "Science Policy and Arms" file in the American Consulate library in Hong Kong, dated 16 February 1968.
38. Cheng, "Scientific Engineering and Manpower," p. 283.
39. Ching-chih Shieh, "The State of Science and Education in Communist China and a Comparison with that in the USSR," Union Research Institute, Hong Kong, August 1962, p. 23.
40. "Important Mission of Young Chinese Scientists and Technicians," editorial in *Cheng Kuo Ch'ung Lien Pao,* 9 October 1963.
41. *Jen Min Jih Pao,* 18 January 1966.
42. *Kwang Ming Daily,* 7 September 1966.
43. *Hong Kong Standard,* 28 June 1967.
44. *New China News Agency,* 19 June 1967.
45. Frank T. Halpin, *Peking Scientists Undergoing Maoism Test,* US Information Agency, Science Policy and Aims File, September 1967.
46. *Party Daily,* 22 December 1967.
47. *South China Morning Post,* 15 February 1968.

JOHN H. ZAMMITO

University of Texas

Why Doesn't India Make It?

So overwhelming is the misery endured by the people of India that one feels compelled to seek its source and solution. All the more pressing is this compulsion in the face of the prophesy of Thomas Malthus—a prophesy threatening fulfillment in the immediate future. However critical a role India may play in the political and military fates of Asia and the world, these pale before the imminent human catastrophe which stalks the subcontinent's 520 million inhabitants.

India has, over the past two decades, exerted tremendous energy in an attempt to reach economic maturity or at least some measure of progress toward it. At the present time, given the crippling population increments, the prospects appear dim. The inability of the

JOHN H. ZAMMITO *is a native of Laredo, Texas, and joined IHP from the University of Texas, where he was enrolled in the special honors program in the social sciences. John was a Junior Fellow in the College of Arts and Sciences at the University of Texas, and his interests were economics, poetry and other creative writing, and student government. John returned to the University of Texas after IHP, and graduated in 1970 as valedictorian, a member of Phi Beta Kappa, and a recipient of the Independent Study Award and a Woodrow Wilson Fellowship. After his graduation John married, and is presently doing research in the economic growth of the South for a brokerage firm in Memphis, Tennessee. He plans to attend graduate school in history.*

Indian social system in general and of the Indian government in particular to move the system from its ancient and deepening ruts is particularly disheartening. It is toward an explanation of this tragic failure that this essay devotes itself.

I. STRUCTURE

Sector analysis, while of great utility in disentangling the unmanageable whole of an economy, has in it a potential for distortion. Using subsystems to understand the process of the economic system as a whole, sector analysts too often fail to relate them. Yet these relations between the subsystems are critical to an understanding of the workings of the system in question. Without this understanding, serious distortions are introduced into the system by the planners which cause strains in the economy sometimes beyond withstanding. Table 1 presents a breakdown of the Indian labor force into occupational sectors.

TABLE 1
DISTRIBUTION OF WORKERS BY INDUSTRY (BY PERCENT) [1]

Industry	1901	1911	1921	1931	1951	1961
Agriculture						
Cultivators	50.6	49.7	54.4	45.0	50.1	52.8
Agricultural laborers	17.0	20.6	17.5	24.7	19.7	16.7
Mining, quarrying, livestock, forestry, fishing, hunting, and plantations, orchards and allied	4.3	4.8	4.5	5.1	3.1	2.8
Manufacturing						
Household industry	*	*	*	*	*	6.2
Manufacturing other than household industry	11.8	10.0	9.4	9.0	9.0	4.2
Construction	0.8	1.0	0.8	1.2	1.0	1.2
Trade and commerce	6.0	5.4	5.8	5.5	5.1	4.0
Transport, storage, and communications	1.1	1.0	0.8	1.0	1.5	1.6
Other services	8.4	7.5	6.8	8.5	10.5	10.5
Total	100.0	100.0	100.0	100.0	100.0	100.0

* No figures are available.

The most striking fact emerging from Table 1 is the static quality of the distributions in spite of programs for national development.

The massive percentage of population in agriculture—69.5 percent in 1961—and the correspondingly small percentage in industry—only 10.4 percent, including household industry—are the clearest overall indicators of the backwardness of the Indian economy. A more detailed analysis of these sectors might help to explain this phenomenon.

THE AGRICULTURAL SECTOR

In Asia, farming is not a business; it is a way of life. That is a common assertion, and its truth is beyond much question. But to the degree that farming remains a way of life, and not a business, the theoretical framework of economic development in the agricultural sector will be out of joint with reality. Because farmers aim only at satisfying their own small needs and not at increasing their profits, they are not a mobile sector of the economy and make little contribution to economic integration. It is particularly important, therefore, to understand the structure of agrarian society in India.

Traditional patterns of trade and economic activity have, in agrarian societies, been confined within relatively small geographical units which are nearly self-sufficient. This virtually cellular pattern is structured around subsistence farming and village handicrafts.

Subsistence farming is a system in which the farmer has relatively limited production and demand. The output he can achieve in a good season is sufficient only to ensure his and his family's continued survival. Though custom may lead the farmer to save for dowries, funerals, and the like, the amounts are so small as to merit only a mention. Such limited exchange in a subsistence economy is critical. Given the minimal marketing that it implies and the limited demand due to low income, the entire structure is operating very near stagnation. Any serious problem, flood or drought, infestation or disease, drives the farmer—and the entire local economy with him—toward ruin.

To alleviate this almost unbearable crush of difficulties, institutional remedies evolved within the traditional society. In the late Tokugawa and early Meiji eras in Japan, for instance, the use of land was a matter of village agreements, and not formal titles. Communal pastures were used for grazing livestock or as sources of grass to be dried for fertilizer. Cooperative efforts of the whole village at planting and harvest time overcame the often acute labor shortage of these peak seasons. And in the event of a bad harvest, the farmers could appeal to landlords to lower the rent; and the landlords were likely to comply. These patterns of interdependence within the local economies carried over as well to the village artisans, who were compensated in goods and services—usually around harvest time. The entire society, within the geographical area, depended upon the harvest, and the interactions of the society were adjusted to the success of the harvest. Such a description is remarkably applicable to China and to India as well.

Most of the commodities available within these local systems are produced and consumed on individual farms by the farmers and their dependents. Moreover, any articles not produced on the farm are usually acquired locally. In China during the 1920s for example, though neither families nor the village itself were self-sufficient, almost all market exchange took place within the same *hsien* (county). Only 8 percent reached distant markets. Three-fourths of all consumption goods were produced on the individual farms, and the remaining fourth, consisting mainly of such goods as oil, meat, sugar, and clothing, was produced and purchased within the area.[2] Commodities unavailable in some areas, such as salt or metals, reached even remote villages. Elaborate patterns of interdependence existed even in such subsistence economies, but only for a limited number of commodities. These items could affect the market only in terms of deprivation, rather than expansion, of their availability.

Local economies need not maintain such a degree of autonomy for the theoretical implications to be important. Any self-sufficiency in rural India will affect the degree to which prices can be manipulated and adjustments planned.

Looking into India's agrarian system will shed more light upon these critical questions. One need only repeat the fact that 70 percent of India's population works in agriculture to point up an acute pressure on the land. Nearly two-thirds of all farms are under 5 acres; nearly one-half are under 2.5 acres. The 25 million farms which make up these percentages take up only 15 percent of the cultivated land.[3] With such an excessive man/land ratio, most farmers have holdings so small that to feed themselves and their families (most of whom work at least part time in the fields) they must go into debt.

One begins to wonder what is meant by "marketed surplus." Leaving aside for the moment the case of the cash-crop farmer, the cultivators are producing in large measure (in some cases completely) for their own consumption. Indian farmers must work on an initially small plot, with debts mounting merely for items of consumption, to say nothing of fertilizer, seed, and so forth. They are subject to the vagaries of weather. Only 19 percent of India's cultivated area has irrigation facilities and even less is actually irrigated—the rest is subject to the monsoons. With next to no mechanization, little fertilizer, and few seed varieties, the harvest itself is desperately small, never quite enough to give the farmer any margin over debts, any exit from the continuing maze.

Inevitably, debts are incurred at exorbitant rates of interest, for the only source of credit is the usurer (supplying 86 percent of total agricultural credit); and so, more of the crop must be surrendered to meet the interest, and this marketed surplus, more forced than real, leaves the farmer short of the necessities. Sometime during the ensuing season he will again be forced to go into debt to purchase goods (and this at the precise time when scarcity bids up the price) similar to those he himself sold in the postharvest glut market.

The rural population is not homogeneous, moreover, and the classes within this population must be considered. Not all—indeed, not many—farmers own their own plot of land, however small. Most farmers are sharecroppers. Even those who may own a small plot take on other plots as sharecroppers to survive economically. And for these, the scant harvest must be divided between consumption and rent, to say nothing of interest and taxes.

More important still is the class of landless laborers who must purchase all their needs with wages. Their direct consumption takes in a good deal of the marketed surpluses from the other classes. This is also true of the village artisans and the rest of the nonagricultural rural population.

In describing this situation, particularly in India, two institutions seem critical in molding the present-day structure of the agrarian society. The first of these is the caste system.

The caste system has had a great impact upon rural society. The sharp distinctions of ritual purity and craft separation led to an elaborate and complex social hierarchy which overlapped, but did not necessarily coincide with, wealth or power hierarchies. Poverty was ubiquitous in the villages. Status was an independent quality. Caste and Hindu culture stigmatized manual labor. Though there were "farmer" castes, these avoided labor, and it was the *harijan*—the untouchable—and other low-caste people who did the work. (It must be said, however, that the caste system did solve the economic problems of allocating people to production within the traditional society.)

Historically, the second institution arose much later. In traditional India, as I have mentioned, the use of land was not often connected with any titular ownership. In different areas, different systems evolved. In areas ruled by a strong central monarch, a royal representative was invested with the right to collect taxes and supervise the use of the land. In other areas, the village owned the land, and the village chief was the arbiter of its apportionment. In some areas peasant proprietorship was not ruled by any more rigorous legal or institutional system than possession and use.

British imperialism brought with it the need of the colonial power to extract taxes from a definable legal entity. The British replaced the nebulous Asian concept of land ownership with the rigid definitions of European agriculture. Here arose the practice of *zamindari*: the former representative of the monarch, whose duty was merely to collect taxes, was now recognized by the British in many parts of India as the owner of the land. Where land belonged to the village, the village chief was given titular ownership; and where the peasant held the land, that land was given to him in titular ownership by the colonial administrators. Throughout, the result was the introduction of land ownership into the social structure. The distinction is not, however, between a "classless society" in a Marxian sense and private ownership. There was, previous to the colonial intervention, appropriate sanction for the use of the land, guaranteeing rights of cultivation and tenure, without resorting, in some cases, to any concept of titular ownership.

These two institutions, one indigenous, the other imposed, reinforced greatly one pattern of status—the ownership of property. It enhanced the status even of tenancy and sharecropping, while reducing the status of landless labor. Thus, peasants who owned title to the land would not give it up, and as generations passed, their holdings, given out to each of their male children, became smaller and more fragmented. The system of fragmentation soon resulted in holdings too small to support the families. Debts mounted, and

the land was surrendered to landlords or moneylenders. Some peasants, while retaining a small plot of land for the sake of status, took
to sharecropping or leasing land. Some peasants lost all their holdings and became laborers. This was exploited by the upper castes
and landlords, who developed large estates.

The resulting concentration of land in the hands of a few landlords, both in the areas where *zamindari* had developed and in areas
of peasant proprietorship, allowed the landlords to move to the
towns and cities, and absentee landlordism resulted. Rent and taxation began to be collected in cash as well as in kind, and the forced
surplus was extracted now by the landlords and the moneylenders
with a growing sense of commercialism. The frequent coincidence
of landlord and moneylender in the same person intensified this
process.

The farmers now had to sell their produce immediately after harvest, when the market was glutted and prices were low. They had
no means to store their crops and no income to tide them over. Often
they were compelled by contract to sell their crop to the moneylender, or were forced to settle upon a price before the crops were
harvested, at even lower prices.

Generally speaking, it is nearly impossible to increase agricultural output in Asia by simply raising prices. (There are exceptions.
The most important case is the cash-crop farmer, who will be discussed later in the essay.) Usually there is only the well-known problem, relevant to all farmers, of price reduction causing an increase
in production. To secure the same income the farmer must produce
even more, for this income is allocated toward what might well be
considered fixed costs—interest to the moneylender, rent to the
landlord, outstanding debts—as well as surplus. This further lowers
the price.

What the farmer takes to market is theoretically surplus over
necessary personal consumption. For most farmers, however, this
is not a substantial portion of the crop. An increase in price can
result in a reduction of marketed crops, because the farmer, again,
is sacrificing personal consumption of his crop for other commodities. If he can have his outside commodities for a smaller portion of
the crop, he tends to reduce his surplus to approximately the amount
of income necessary for the outside purchases and debts.

The question of labor productivity follows from an understanding of the slim margins over subsistence I have outlined. And here Gunnar Myrdal's suggestion in *Asian Drama*,[4] that agriculture in India is of an extensive rather than an intensive nature, is most penetrating. Though the actual area of cultivation might well be comparable to the clearly intensive patterns of Japan or China, the cultivation methods, especially in terms of labor utilization, are not. Indeed, in India, though participation in agriculture is extensive (70 percent of total population) and though seasonal unemployment is extensive as well, these facts do not lead Myrdal to conclude that the marginal productivity of labor is near zero, at zero, or below, as in the classic notion. Rather, he points out that India's labor utilization measured in terms of duration of work—by hours or seasons of the year—and labor efficiency was quite low. The caste prejudices against manual labor reinforced this situation. The actual pattern of labor participation is more aptly described as an adjustment to population increases within the agrarian sector by assigning more tasks to the larger work force. Participation in agriculture remained high, but the duration and efficiency of that participation remained quite low.

In this century, when Western practices of preventive medicine and public health have drastically lowered the death rates and caused the population surge that now threatens to justify Malthusian pessimism, the pressure of population upon the production of food has intensified. The difficulties caused by a bad harvest have become more severe. And yet, the vast rural population has eked out a living maintaining in most (though not all) crop years the slimmest margins over famine.

The growth of population and the surplus of labor created two trends in the rural areas. The first, as in agriculture, was to lower the work per individual, increasing the participation of labor by spreading the tasks among more laborers. But the second, more dynamic, response was a movement to the cities, a movement which was swelled with agricultural laborers as well. This exodus from the rural areas had little connection with any fresh demand for industrial labor.

The newly urbanized classes with their lack of industrial skills were unable to secure the few industrial positions made available through whatever industrialization might have occurred. This sector was too small, in any event, to absorb much of the labor force migrating to the cities. Rather, these migrants turned to "service" tasks of retailing, trading, hawking in the streets, or providing middleman services for goods shipped to or through the urban areas. For these tasks little capital or skill was required. The cheapness of laborers, and their low productivity, meant that workers were underutilized even in the cities. Urban population jumped from 11.4 percent of total population in 1921 to 18 percent in 1961, bringing to the great cities of India one of the world's greatest problems of urban congestion. It was hoped that industry could create jobs to take up this slack during the period of the five-year plans.

THE INDUSTRIAL SECTOR

The lines drawn between large- and small-scale industry are in some sense arbitrary. Nevertheless, there is an obvious difference between enormous and highly organized industries and the small household shops which sometimes lack even a power supply. Large-scale industry is heavy industry—iron and steel plants, engineering firms, chemical factories, and the like—and the output is destined for the raw materials market. On the other hand, small-scale enterprises supply whatever consumer goods are available in these societies, though subcontracting to produce capital goods—machinery and equipment used to produce consumer goods—is also relevant.

Large-Scale Industry. In India, five industries—cotton textiles, iron and steel, cement, paper, and sugar—employ about 60 percent of all workers, and their total proportion of value added is about the same.[5] Such concentration is precisely what is meant by large-scale industry, especially when iron and steel and cement are two of the five leading industries.

There is more that must be discerned in the nature of large-scale industry. First, it entails a heavy initial outlay of capital (3.5 billion rupees for a public sector steel plant), a high degree of mechanization, and all the other elements of modern mass production. Entry into such production is limited (particularly in iron and steel) by the prohibitive initial capital outlay. Once a firm is in the market, on the other hand, it enjoys a monopolistic position. Government awareness of this results in price control either in the market or through fixed rates of government purchases, which in a developing economy tend to be substantial.

Faced with a threatening exchange deficit, India, like most underdeveloped countries, raised import barriers against foreign goods, especially consumer durables and machinery, which had drained considerable sums. What resulted was, once again, a market where existing firms were assured of a monopolistic position. The monopolistic market allowed domestic firms large profits, and this in turn allowed for relaxation of efficiency and rising costs.

A significant effect of this situation was that the sources of credit for large-scale industrial investment were many and varied, both in the private and the public sectors. Returns on such investments are assured, given the market structure and existing or government-planned demands. In terms of a firm's expansion program, the relation between labor and capital is influenced by this availability of credit and government regulations concerning dismissal of workers.

After describing the developments in labor-management relations and the cost factors of the postwar period, George Rosen summarizes:

The net effect of all of these postwar changes—a reduction in the "area of control" of management, increasing downward rigidity of labor costs, higher real wage costs as well as much higher indirect labor costs in comparison to the prewar period, a sharp reduction in skill differentials—has been an increase in the demand for labor-saving machinery on the part of the industrialists.[6]

Capital and entrepreneurial skill in India during the colonial period and in the postwar years tended to be concentrated in the "managing agency" system, wherein many industries desiring skilled managerial administration gave over the direction of the firm to a central agency. The government's antipathy toward this concentration of economic decision-making and power is reflected in the following statement by Ashoka Mehta:

500 important industrial concerns of our country are managed by 2,000 directors. These directorships are held by 850 individuals. But 1,000 of these directorships are held by just 70 men. . . . At the apex of the pyramid stand 10 men holding 300 directorships, the supreme arbiters of the destinies of our industrial economy.[7]

Yet in the 1950s these managing agencies were still welcomed in the industrial firms themselves, and 80 percent of the industrial firms took advantage of their services.

Small-Scale Industry. Small-scale industries have grown considerably in India. Their development can be associated with the expansion of urban industrialization, the availability of raw materials and other factors of production around large industrial centers, and also the demand for consumer goods.

The main market toward which these enterprises tend is the consumption market. Myrdal describes the sector as follows:

Small-scale industry . . . is increasingly characterized by production of non-traditional, or less traditional, commodities sometimes using modern techniques. In India . . . such products as radio sets, electric motors, bicycle parts, sewing machines, machine-tools, and spectacle frames emanate from small-scale industry, if produced at all.[8]

A second area of evolution for small-scale industries, according to both Rosen and Myrdal, has been subcontracting. This has especially developed around Bombay. Yet these industries, whether producing final goods or components, are operated with very small reserves, and with little staying power or credit available in case of fluctuation in demand or delays, both of which are common bottlenecks in underdeveloped economies.

II. PROCESS

Political and social elements intervene in economics at the policy level in India as in every other country. In India, however, this intervention is particularly strong. Various reasons may be advanced: for instance, feelings generated out of the colonial period and the independence movement, the ideals of such figures as Gandhi and Nehru, and the forces of India's pluralistic society, with its strong regional polarities. Out of these elements, a policy emerges. Out of this policy, the process of economic change, articulated by the planners, enters and molds the social system. Policy and process are so inextricably merged that they must be dealt with together.

The Indian policy-makers have set as their main goal the establishment of a "socialist pattern of society." The meaning of this phrase should not be taken in strict Marxian terms, but rather in terms of greater equality in the distribution of wealth.

India has opted for planning economic development along frankly Soviet lines, of five-year plans and specific and concentrated investment in heavy industry. In this India parallels Communist China.

Establishment of a heavy industrial base is associated not only with the Soviet model, but also with the feeling on the part of many underdeveloped nations that the need for foreign capital and machinery inhibits foreign policy. Another factor in this situation is the exchange gap. The drain of exchange for the purchase of imports caused severe shortages. Strict curbs upon imports were established, and foreign investment and the purchase of foreign capital goods were sharply reduced.

Other values entered into the planning policy. First, an attachment to cottage industries and handicrafts (generated in part out of the independence movement, and held as part of an elaborate myth of Indian native industrial sophistication in precolonial times) drew protection from the government after independence. Second, the dominance of such institutions as the managing agency system in industry was attacked. The concentration of wealth in the hands of a few industrialists was considered an evil, as can be noted in the statement of Ashoka Mehta given above.

The preference for public-sector industrial growth in this context drew obvious support. After the highly successful First Five-Year Plan, the planners decided to emphasize industrial growth especially in organized industry and more particularly in heavy industry. The goal of such an emphasis was to expand the number of enterprises, production, jobs, and income, as well as national autonomy.

Government policies resulting from these goals had direct economic consequences. Some of these more important policies should be mentioned. First, in order to secure the vast capital needed for the planned expansion of large-scale industries as well as social overhead capital, the government had to engage in enormous deficit financing. Second, in order to control the flow of capital and credit within the industrial sector, licensing for expansion or for the establishment of a new plant was required. Such licensing would depend, of course, on the planned allocations to various industries. Third, as mentioned above, employment was a major goal, and labor legislation was imposed which made it extremely difficult to dismiss workers. Compulsory arbitration was resorted to when labor-management difficulties resulted in serious production lags. Finally, the tax structure—in very broad terms—was highly progressive in the industrial sector while light in the agricultural sector. This placed a heavy burden upon industry.

Policies which protected cottage industries against competition from large- or small-scale enterprises using more modern techniques, and policies which curtailed imports and conserved foreign exchange both impinged upon Indian planning. Government policy toward the cottage industry's difficulties at first imposed taxes, quotas, and restrictions on imported equipment for the new competitive enterprises, stifling their development.

In general, India's solution to the situation, consonant as well with the new realities of import restrictions, was a policy of import substitution. In this way, industries could expand without entering into competition with the cottage industries, and could take up an already existing market. This policy was introduced by P. C. Mahalanobis, the chief architect of the Second Five-Year Plan. Myrdal analyzes his approach as follows:

India's Second Five-Year Plan established as a major goal the rapid expansion of heavy industry turning out producer goods. It was part of the grand strategy of the plan to restrict the growth of larger industries producing consumer goods and to rely as far as possible on cottage industry to satisfy the needs of consumers. The main architect of the plan, P.C. Mahalanobis, later expressed this thought: "In India a dual strategy was adopted from 1956 in the Second Plan to expand, on one side, the strategic heavy industries for steel, metals, machinery, electricals and chemicals, etc. to build up the foundations of industrial progress, and at the same time also to expand the traditional cottage industries and small-scale production."[9]

There were serious weaknesses in this approach. Though markets for imported goods existed before the curbs on imports, those markets might not have been large enough to justify the expenditures involved in creating new, domestic production plants. Further, the need for foreign capital goods was not escaped by this policy; rather, with the special emphasis on heavy industrial production, this need was increased, and the competition among planned investment industries for the scarce foreign exchange was a problem for the planners.

As we have seen, the effect of the import restrictions and prohibitive cost of capital construction made the domestic market monopolistic and inefficient in terms of the cost/profit ratio. This also cast doubts upon the Mahalanobis model.

One factor which rarely enters into planners' considerations is consumer preference. When production of milled goods was curbed in favor of cottage industries, or imported goods were cut off to be replaced by domestic production, their capacity to fulfill the demand (or even to serve as adequate substitutes) was limited. There is a case for the position that some shifts in demand are irreversible. They remain a part of the demand structure, and the adequacy of substitutes is questionable. Some Indian examples are the replacement of *gur* by refined sugar, and of handwoven cloth by milled textiles.

The clearest manifestation of the planners' preferences is in the concentrated allocation of investment in heavy industry under the Second Five-Year Plan. Government investment (50 percent of total investment) was devoted almost entirely to capital goods. Of private investment, 65 percent was aimed at capital goods, including iron and steel, heavy engineering, chemicals, cement, and aluminum.[10]

This left little credit available for small-scale enterprises aimed at consumption goods markets, or for stimulating market demand. It withdrew the bulk of capital and credit not only from immediate but also from short-term production of consumer commodities. Moreover, it hurt the chances of more quick-yielding investment approaches by small or medium-sized firms. In other words, it weakened the potential effects of external economies by robbing the possibly responsive firms of the margins necessary for their expansion.

Finally, the high priority attached to industry in terms of employment is questionable. Population growth far exceeds the creation of industrial jobs. Two particular phenomena add certainty to this position. First, given the structure of capital allocation and credit availability, the pattern of industrialization will become increasingly capital intensive and mechanized.

The second phenomenon is the competition which evolved between the new industrial sector and the cottage industries, which has tended to force some of the traditional, high-labor firms out of business. Government regulation has aimed at halting this two-pronged process, but the twin goals of industrialization and preservation of cottage industries are not completely compatible.

We can see that the attempt to modify the economic structure had, by and large, negative effects upon balance in the industrial sector. The strong preference on the one hand for heavy industries and on the other for cottage industries, resulted in a drop in available funds for the development of small- and medium-sized firms aimed at producing consumer goods. This was known and sanctioned in the planning policy itself. It remains to ascertain what effect this system of resource allocation had upon the rest of the economy.

The institutions between heavy industry and agriculture form the channels through which industrial change motivates the whole economy to growth, according to the theory of industrialization as generative force. Expansion in industrial production, which theoretically expands not only output, but employment and income, has "spread" effects in the other sectors. The increase in output, primarily of producer goods, finds its way into greater production of factor inputs in the other sectors, such as machinery for small-scale industries, and fertilizers and tractors for agriculture. New jobs are created, with all the attendant benefits in income.

This theoretical model must be questioned, however. First, one must question the argument concerning the creation of jobs. It has been shown here that the increase in employment will be small in the initial stages of industrial development. Moreover, the expansion in industrial employment which does occur is a mixed blessing, creating demands which strain the market whose supply is relatively inflexible.

One must also question the hypothesis that the production of factory equipment and machinery increases the use of factor inputs like seeds and fertilizer and results in greater output. These factor inputs are often not available because of the long-term character of the investment. An indication of this is the frequent complaint concerning the waiting lists for tractors and other farm machinery. The same complaints concerning industrial machinery are voiced by small-scale industries.

Further bottlenecks arise in terms of inefficient transport facilities. In its allocation in this sphere, the government has concentrated upon railways, with only minor expansion of roadways. Rail transport, however, still involves considerable delays. Loss of perishable goods is common. Meanwhile, road transportation is hindered by state inspection of trucks and the widespread use of bullock carts to transport farm products to the cities. These delays in arrival of raw materials or production goods have detrimental effects, particularly on small-scale enterprises, whose deadlines and margins are tight. The facilities for storing goods, as well, are inadequate, particularly in agriculture.

There is, moreover, a lack of skilled personnel which results in "excess capacity" in some industries and "excess demand" in others.

Turning at last to wages, it is true there is an increase in income. The expansion of production in industry, both in producer goods and consumer goods, creates new jobs. There is an increase in the number of workers and the duration of employment. Wages, too, tend to rise. The problem with this rise in income, however, is that there is no supply to service the expanded demand. "The economic system as a whole has no slack from which increases in output can quickly be made available to match increments in demand."[11] There results a rise in prices.

A number of inflationary effects are present in the economy. First, import restrictions and the creation of large sums of money through deficit financing, beyond the growth potential of output, created an inflationary gap. Second, the low cost/profit efficiency of domestic industries in protected markets was inflationary. The inflationary pressures on the economy caused by increases in income without available consumption goods was also considerable. The pressure of the tax structure added more forced savings. And finally, the structure of the investment program, with long-term payoff projects absorbing much of the resources allocated, imposed high forced savings and reinforced the inflationary trends. Myrdal explains the process in this way:

> The ubiquity of bottlenecks gives rise to inflationary price increases, particularly for foodstuffs and for other staple consumption goods, soon after the first injections of additional incomes. When this has occurred, South Asian governments—and particularly the Indian government—have used direct and indirect controls to block the initiation of some enterprises, and thus checked forms of secondary expansion that might otherwise have taken place. This amounts to an unintentional killing off of spread effects. Underlying these measures of restraint is the concept of a "ceiling"—the height of which is rather rigidly determined—that limits the volume of aggregate demand the economy is thought capable of tolerating.[12]

The manifest conclusion is that in such a system, the degree of balance in the different types of production, the integration of the system, and the spread effects are stifled by bottlenecks and wasted by inflationary pressures. A closer balance between supply and demand is obviously required.

This entails the expansion of consumer goods production and of consumption. But theory holds that growth can emerge only from savings and investment. In terms of what has been found to be the case in India, I submit that this definition is questionable. In fact, I would suggest that for India (and other underdeveloped nations as well) consumption is useful in giving rise to productivity and output.

Table 2 shows the consumption patterns of India. These data clearly indicate that the proportion of the total budget spent for food and clothing (Engels' coefficient items) is very high. Taking

TABLE 2
PATTERNS OF CONSUMER EXPENDITURE (1963–64) [13]

	Per Capita Expenditure Per Month (Rs.)			Distribution to Total %		
	Rural	Urban	Cities*	Rural	Urban	Cities*
Foodgrains	10.05	8.36	8.21	45.06	25.35	15.79
Milk and milk products	1.61	3.08	5.41	7.20	9.36	10.39
Other food items	4.01	8.21	14.70	17.99	24.91	28.26
Total	15.67	19.65	28.32	70.25	59.62	54.44
Clothing	1.82	2.08	2.58	8.15	6.30	4.95
Fuel and light	1.48	2.08	3.10	6.61	6.32	5.96
Rent, taxes, and miscellaneous	3.34	9.15	18.03	14.99	27.76	34.65
Total	6.64	13.31	23.71	29.75	40.38	45.56
Grand Total	22.31	32.96	52.03	100.00	100.00	100.00

* Bombay, Calcutta, Madras, Delhi.

into account the nutritional value of the diet shown merely in these income figures makes a case for an increase in productivity with an increase in food consumption.

The marginal propensity to consume in the Indian market will clearly increase demand most in these areas of improvement of diet and living conditions. Moreover, other consumption goods as well, like televisions and radios, may not be wasteful or conspicuous in a harmful sense. These goods, on the contrary, act as stimuli to expand demands and hence production for income.

In taking up this position, it is never forgotten that the majority of consumers are farmers. Clearly the increase in demand for food and clothing will depend upon increased agricultural production. Along the same lines, if industrial growth is to occur, demand markets in the rural agricultural areas must be developed. Thus, the critical problem is how to increase demand and supply in the rural sectors.

III. MOBILIZING AGRICULTURE

How can agricultural output be increased? And how can the demands of the rural population be expanded? It is to these critical questions that we now must turn. To answer them, we must consider a different kind of cultivator. This is the cash-crop farmer. The reason for his separation from the other farmers is simple. Willy-nilly, the cash-crop farmer must market his produce; moreover, he has to compare his prices with those of other goods on the market. In other words, the cash-crop farmer is forced to pay more attention to market structure. He has developed methods of storage in order to avoid the postharvest drop in prices; and he has taken advantage of market competition for his produce by selling at market centers. One analysis dealing with groundnuts in western India claims that almost perfect competition exists in the market.[14]

Not only do these cash-crop farmers avail themselves of the market on the supply side; they are absolutely dependent upon it on the demand side. They must purchase food crops on the market. In this they are joined by a host of other rural consumers: share-croppers, agricultural laborers, village craftsmen, and middlemen, so that the rural market for food grains and food products is open to the expansion of demand given a rise in output.

The focus sharpens now on the food-grain farmers. Their subsistence approach to production is the critical bottleneck in the entire process of expansion in demand and supply that would signal growth for the entire economy. Stagnation in food-grain production means little progress elsewhere in the economy.

To move these farmers toward higher output, government resources have been allocated increasingly toward such agricultural production inputs as fertilizer. Relatively little is done in terms of stimulating their demand. But the farmer's general willingness to accept the additional inputs must be seen to rest upon an expansion of his desires. It must be remembered that increased inputs cost money, and that most farmers are already in debt at high rates of interest. The instability of harvest prices, the unpredictable weather conditions, and the strangeness of the new techniques all act against the investment. Farmers, given the cultural bias against manual labor, may not think the added risk and the added labor justified. Some effort must thus be made to demonstrate the attractiveness of these potential profits. One way to do this is to expand his demands —to instill in him the desire for material goods available from the industrial sector.

One difficulty presents itself immediately. The goods produced by industry (when they *do* emerge) are far too costly for the farmer.

This is especially true when the inefficiency in production in industry is marked, as is the case in India.

What of the input side of the question? This brings us to the prospects for a "green revolution" in agricultural production. With the shift in resource allocations in recent years to industrial production of such agricultural inputs as chemical fertilizers, tractors, pesticides, and the like, marked increases in farm production are expected.

Yet one point must be made concerning the new inputs. It is only when all the innovations are applied that production experiences a surge of radical proportions. New seed varieties demand not only more fertilizers and irrigation, but new techniques of farming, and greater protection from plant pests and diseases. To use new seed varieties without improving technology is pointless. In the same way, some seeds of the traditional varieties have low response both to fertilizers and to irrigation, and increments will thus fall below anticipated levels.

The expense of such an array of innovations must seem prohibitive to the farmer. New seed varieties cost more than traditional seed, fertilizer is scarce and expensive, and water rates can be quite high in irrigated areas. Some inputs might be scarce or completely unavailable in some areas. Moreover, the farmer may not be convinced of their efficacy.

Credit can be seen as the critical variable in agricultural production. Traditional sources could not finance the new investments. With the institution of cooperative market societies, some planners thought the problem would be solved. A large increase of funds was made available through these institutions to the agricultural sector. This new supply of funds, however, was limited by the exigencies of survival in the rural area of the cooperative societies to the very group which had adequate collateral to secure loans from other institutions. The small-scale farmer or sharecropper, who had little security to offer, was not likely to obtain any credit, and sometimes membership in the cooperative (which involved costs, as well) was required. The result was that farmers were left with only the traditional moneylender for desperately needed credit. All of this tends to cast doubt on the idea of a "green revolution."

Even so, production has increased. The demand for fertilizer exceeds the supply, and the waiting list for tractors is overwhelmingly long. The new seed varieties have achieved considerable use, and areas planted with them are increasing. Indeed, the seed industry is itself considerable. Sources of credit, traditional and modern, are being used, and there is reason to believe that businessmen (in response to government investment and tax benefits for agriculture) are buying land and investing in agriculture. These factors argue for the possibility of some increase in output.

IV. APPROACHING A BREAKTHROUGH

India depends upon a breakthrough in agricultural production if it is to achieve any significant economic development in terms of an integrated and sound system. This breakthrough is being approached through resource allocations and price controls. If we accept that consumption may well raise the productivity of labor, and that new demands may stimulate individual farmers, it seems clear that a reconsideration of government policy on consumer goods production and consumption is necessary. By stimulating demand in the agricultural sector, and by halting restriction on consumer goods production, supply can be stimulated both in industry and in agriculture, with attendant integral growth in the entire economic system.

NOTES

1. This table is based on data from *India: Pocket Book of Economic Information* 1967, p. 21.
2. W. W. Rostow, A. Eckstein, et al., *Prospects for Communist China* (Cambridge: Technology Press, of M.I.T., 1954); J. L. Buck, *Land Utilization in China* (New York: Paragon, 1937).
3. S. C. Jain, *Agricultural Policy in India* (Delhi: Metropolitan Book Co., 1970).
4. Gunnar Myrdal, *Asian Drama* (New York: Pantheon, 1968).
5. George Rosen, *Democracy and Economic Change in India* (Berkeley: University of California Press, 1966).
6. Ibid., p. 127.
7. Note, in Myrdal, *Asian Drama*, p. 1110.
8. Ibid., p. 1223.
9. Ibid., p. 1226.
10. Rosen, *Industrial Change*.
11. Myrdal, *Asian Drama*, p. 1189.
12. Ibid., p. 1190.
13. This table is based on data from *India: Pocket Book of Economic Information*, 1967.
14. Z. Y. Jasdanwalla, *Marketing Efficiency in Indian Agriculture* (Bombay: Allied Publishers, 1966).

JOHN A. ALMSTROM

University of British Columbia

Why the Military Steps In

Anyone who surveys twentieth-century history is bound to notice the great role played by the military in national politics. Indeed, the number of states which have experienced military rule in this century illustrates the point forcibly: Thailand, Pakistan, Egypt, the Sudan, Iraq, Spain, Portugal, South Korea, El Salvador, Paraguay, Nicaragua, Jordan, the Congo, Persia, Honduras, Indonesia, Argentina, Turkey, Brazil, Venezuela, Peru, Ecuador, Guatemala, Burma, Syria, Algeria, Japan, Germany, and France.[1] Outstanding in this list is the number of underdeveloped countries.

In the following pages I want to examine the causes, and the limitations, of military intervention in developing countries. This phenomenon will be approached in two ways: by examining the nature of military elites themselves, and by considering the dynamics of military intervention in civilian politics. Then, in the light of

JOHN A. ALMSTROM *is from Whitehorse in the Yukon, Canada. He joined IHP from the University of British Columbia at Vancouver, where he was enrolled in the history honors program and was an officer-cadet in the Canadian Air Force. Before IHP, John planned a career in either diplomacy, teaching, or federal politics. Following the journey John graduated with first class double honors in American military history and international relations from the University of British Columbia. He is now a graduate fellow at Rice University in Texas and also a first lieutenant in Princess Patricia's Canadian Light Infantry.*

my findings, I intend to deal with a critical question: Is military government an appropriate method for accelerating economic development?

I. THE MILITARY MIND

In underdeveloped countries the officer corps is an elite. Other ranks in the armed forces are simply not politically significant. To put it bluntly, they tend to lack the education and the political sophistication needed to handle the problems of leadership. Because the officers are among the highly educated in underdeveloped countries, therefore, they must be considered potential actors in the political drama.

The development of a professional officer corps is a recent phenomenon even in Western countries. This growth has been a concomitant of the industrialization, increasing specialization, and opening of careers to talent which took place in nineteenth-century Western Europe. In retrospect, the experience of Western countries would indicate that the separation of military and political elites is a hallmark not only of modernity, but of an emergent professional military ethic as well.

The military can be said to become truly professional when competence and specialization are introduced as prerequisites for officer status. Briefly, this development in Europe meant new entrance qualifications, new standards for promotion, and the necessity for broader, as well as higher, education. Aristocratic criteria were replaced by recruitment on the basis of examination and education. Mercenaries, hired out on short-term contracts, gradually disappeared. Promotion by purchase or political reward was eliminated, to be replaced by criteria of examination, seniority, and competence. Finally, education was formally introduced into the military structure not only in technical fields, but at staff level as well. In essence, the officer corps became a full-time profession, no longer a part-time feudal duty or a trade hired out by contract.

Entry into a profession often requires a liberal education supplemented by advanced technical training. Professionalism relies on expertise obtained through long training and kept up through continuing research. Furthermore, most professions have technical journals to facilitate discussion and to spread new information. By these criteria, officers are professionals. Officers spend at least a third of their careers in formal education and study, and specialize uniquely in the management of violence, while its application is the specialty of noncommissioned officers. Other professionals—engineers, doctors, ordnance experts, personnel administrators, intelligence specialists, and communication experts—also gain entry into the officer corps, though with less status.

Central to the military's claim to professionalism is a sense of social responsibility. Monetary motivation is considered secondary to a strong sense of duty. Professionals consider their function indispensable to the public. For this reason they think it unethical to strike. Professionals consider themselves pillars of society, and morally bound to accept personal sacrifice if necessary. These concepts are part of the military ethic, and are even more rigidly codified in the military than in other professions. Finally, professionals exhibit a strong sense of corporate identity, due to long training, a common milieu, and a common burden of responsibility. This corporate identity is strengthened in the officer corps by the separation of the military from civilian society, and by the physical and psychological hardships of the occupation.

Professionals tend to be politically active, unless employed by the state. To explain the relatively high political activity of the military (state servants) in underdeveloped countries, we must now examine the values and attitudes of officers which stem from their professional qualities.

The salient military value is nationalism. Like other military values, it springs from a professional background and from the special nature of the profession of arms. The German officer von Seeckt accurately described the military's self-conception as "the purest image of the state." In even the smallest of underdeveloped nations, some military organization is maintained, if only to symbolize national power and sovereignty. The whole purpose of the military is to advance and defend the interests of the nation. This military sense of responsibility for the survival of the nation, coupled with a sense of ability to direct the state in the event of a civilian government's collapse, is the prime cause of the military's political intervention in underdeveloped countries.

"Puritanism" is a ubiquitous military value, due both to a sense of self-denial arising out of the ethic of social responsibility, and to the severe demands of military life. Great stress is laid on bravery, discipline, obedience, self-abnegation, and relative poverty. In underdeveloped nations, these values transfer readily into a dislike of "effete and corrupt" civilian politicians, a feeling often underlying the military's sense of moral self-justification when it takes over power from a civilian government it considers inadequate. Such sentiments were vehemently expressed by Ayub Khan in 1959, and by General Gürsel in 1960.

Military officers also possess a strong sense of corporate interest, due to long specialized training and extended isolation from civilian life. This sense of corporate interest is accentuated in underdeveloped countries by the fact that the military offers a secure channel of advancement to ambitious young men from the lower middle class. Thus, the military can come to be, in underdeveloped countries, the political force of an aggressive, upwardly mobile modernizing elite, representing in fact an entire social class and force within itself. Middle Eastern armies are an excellent example of this development —they are the sole salaried career open to the lower middle class on the basis of ability. Regional, as well as class, predominance in an officer corps can make it a political force: witness the anti-Catalonian attitude of the Spanish army, or the control of the Pakistani army by western military families against secessionists of the east. The national identification of military officers, when coupled with a tradition of corporate solidarity, gives to officers in underdeveloped countries a strong liking for collective activity and communal self-abnegation which they often come to insist upon after seizing power.

The professional ethics of officers, as well as occupational peculiarities, create in them feelings of national patriotism, moral rectitude, and collective political interest which encourage them to intervene in politics when civilian governments fail. There are, however, other military values which tend to discourage political activity—particularly the strong sense of apoliticism inherent in the professional military code. This apoliticism is largely a function of intense professional specialization, which requires concentration on the execution of complex military duties and leaves the formulation of broad national policies to "the politicians." Moreover, the military sense of social responsibility draws upon the immutable primacy of obedience as the ultimate military virtue. Thus, officers have a strong desire and a strong penchant to identify civilian political supremacy with the best interests of the nation.

One factor which intensifies the latent apoliticism of officers, even in underdeveloped countries, is their sense of corporate identity. Officers, living a "complete" style of life, with a heavy accent on ethics and social grace, dislike the moral ambivalence and sordid interchanges of political activity. They wish to keep themselves and the military above politics. Furthermore, officers are never anxious to waste their men on police actions or internal security operations based on political intrigue. Only when a weak civilian government augurs the collapse of the whole nation is the military highly motivated to intervene in politics. Military intervention, then, usually seeks to fill an authority vacuum, and seldom to prosecute narrow class interests.

The attitude of the military toward society in general can best be defined as one of "conservative realism." In other words, little faith is placed in human "strength" or "virtue." Conflict is viewed as an inevitable and permanent phenomenon, due largely to human weakness and greed. This reluctance to admit the moral worth of the individual intensifies the military's faith in the group over the individual, with individual abdication to group interests a prime virtue and indeed duty. In underdeveloped countries, it is the military which often feels best able to inculcate the value of individual discipline and sacrifice into the society in order to facilitate development.

Such an attitude culminates in the nation-state, which is typically viewed as the highest level of human organization possible, worthy of all the individual's loyalty and affection. In addition, the military's strong attachment to the nation causes it to accent the permanent nature of war, and hence of national insecurity and the need to meet all conceivable threats, including inner weaknesses of economy, of social consensus, or of political administration. The military tends, however, to be very slow to commit itself to active combat, and dislikes "adventuristic" policies.

In sum, then, it seems quite clear that given a stable and effective civilian government, the military, far from desiring to intervene in politics, actually eschews involvement. This is due mainly to the intense effort demanded of officers to maintain their competence in purely military matters and their great hesitation to sacrifice time for politics. Usually, the officer corps is content to obey and merely advise civilian superiors. Apoliticism is further enhanced by a strong adherence to obedience as a way of life, and by an ethical distaste for moral ambiguity and self-indulgence. Finally, military elites recognize that political activity not only contradicts the spirit of a professional military ethic, but ultimately divides the officer corps, expends valuable human resources, and thus weakens the entire military apparatus. The military's political intervention, then, is probable only if the following forces combine to overwhelm apolitical inertia: a sense of cohesion, a sense of emergency, a sense of superior political power and ability, and a grievance against the civilian regime. When these factors do coalesce in underdeveloped countries, they often provoke military intervention on the grounds of national interest and progress. It is the role of the military governing elites in developing countries to which our discussion now turns.

II. CLOSING THE CULTURAL GAP

Gabriel Almond has defined effective government in underdeveloped countries as an organization that can ensure social integration in a stable political framework which accommodates change and facilitates development.[2] Here, "social integration" implies mass mobilization—a vital prerequisite for modernization which includes the political training of all citizens, their encouragement to articulate their political interests, and the synthesis of common national interests, all within a stable environment.

The obvious fact that these tasks are not adequately performed in underdeveloped countries is due largely to a general social bifurcation. Underdeveloped societies are actually split into two widely differing cultures: modern and traditional. And between these two cultures exists little communication.

Most people in an underdeveloped country are farmers. These masses (usually over 80 percent of the population) are illiterate, untraveled, and out of contact with national events. More important, sheer ignorance of the possibility of a better way of life has, over the generations, bred inertia. Such traditional forces as religion often serve to rationalize this passivity, and hence to intensify it.

Superimposed on the passive, ignorant, and impoverished rural masses is a small, modern sector of the population, living in cities and towns. These people tend to be literate, or at least in contact with the media. Such city-dwellers, due to their greater knowledge and more cosmopolitan surroundings, are more capable of expressing broad regional or national—as opposed to communal—loyalty. Inflated expectations are easily built up in the cities. So are increasing frustrations, as a backward agricultural economy is incapable of satisfying newly created wants. Cities, then, are sources of political unrest and violence in underdeveloped countries, as they combine the grievances of rural migrants and the frustrations of educated urban dwellers. Internal stability, essential to orderly government, becomes harder to maintain.

Underdeveloped nations, then, tend to be faced with an imbalance which is uncomfortable to all. On the one hand are rural passivity and ignorance, which block both agricultural and economic development. On the other hand are increasing demands by urban masses on inadequate resources. The only solution is to close the cultural gap—to modernize and motivate the rural peasantry; to promote agricultural development and then apply the increased wealth to industrialization; and finally to check unbalanced urbanization. The only permanent solution to this cultural gap is economic development, which would create a new, modern culture throughout the whole nation, and amalgamate the common interests which alone can guarantee national integration and stability.

It has been suggested that the military is an ideal group to bridge this cultural gap. One reason for this assertion is that the officer corps, although definitely a modern and Western institution, is ideologically much closer to the rural masses than are the civilian modern elites. Its members, mostly recruited from small country towns, lack an identification with traditional elites, and have an anti-urban outlook. It has further been asserted that military men are well suited to deal with traditional masses, because of their sensitivity to the role of tradition in social organization. Thus, the military is thought to be better able to develop traditional masses of communal loyalty into a rational, national, and modern way of life than are the urban civilian elites, many of whom have never seen a village.

As a westernized and technological institution, the military possesses many skills which can be applied to the civilian sector. This military distribution of Western technology reveals itself both through training of technical personnel who are subsequently released to civilian life, and through construction of certain infrastructures such as roads, communication nets, and public health facilities.

A large army with a high turnover of personnel plays a great role in national integration. Recruits are often for the first time indoctrinated in national loyalties, and exposed to a regulated, disciplined style of living. Often these effects are enhanced by postings away from home, by instruction in basic literacy in a national language, and by a code of discipline impartial to caste or regional origin.

Finally, any military officer has had sound managerial and administrative training. This ability, when combined with a strong sense of honesty and service to the nation, would appear to make the officer corps in an underdeveloped country a potent competitor to the civil service at its higher levels, as well as a threat to self-serving politicians. The officers in an underdeveloped country are usually ambitious, selected and promoted on the basis of ability alone, and devoted above all to national development and power. But is the military elite, competent and well motivated as it appears, really a viable alternative to civilian government?

That the military is incapable of directing a complex nation by itself is evident from the following civilian/military ratios of various post-coup cabinets: in Iraq (under Kassim), nine of the sixteen cabinet posts were filled by civilians; in Pakistan (under Ayub Khan), civilians held eleven of fourteen cabinet positions; and in Franco's Spain, twelve cabinet posts out of eighteen were held by civilians. The allied military occupation governments in postwar Germany immediately relied on civilian experts in all fields of government and administration. Obviously, military governments simply lack the breadth and depth of organization to penetrate through all layers of society, or to manage all branches of government. Thus, military rulers are forced to continue to rely on professional civil servants, contenting themselves with only the broadest direction of policy. In addition, it is clear that the military itself lacks the complex technical knowledge required to administer a whole society.

Because of such inadequacies, then, military governments are able to dominate only the highest levels of government; and even at the top, heavy reliance on civilian experts cuts into military power. Ultimately, the military tends to exist as yet another layer in the bureaucratic structure of an underdeveloped country, yet another step from the scenes of policy implementation, and yet another administrative hindrance to the very modernization it seeks to encourage.

At the top levels where political power is exercised, the basic nature of the military tends to lock it into a series of contradictions, the resolution of which lies only in a return of the control of government to civilian leaders. These contradictions are founded on the military's frequent unwillingness, or perhaps inability, to form a true mass base to legitimize its regime. Clearly, the military desires order and progress, but tends to stress order to the point where any disorder attendant on change is stifled, and change itself is suppressed. The outcome of the military's obsession with law and order is the stifling of protest, controversy, and initiative. The result in an underdeveloped country is that rural passivity remains untouched, and urban civilian elites are forced into active opposition to the regime.

A further limitation on military governments is that they seldom include all of the educated, modernizing elite. In many underdeveloped countries, there does exist an elite with modern goals and traits. Even under military government, as modernization progresses the size of this civilian elite grows, in the end forming a potent counter-elite to the military modernizers. The civilian modernizing elite, unlike the military, is willing to build mass organizations to back it up in its drive for power. For just as the military relies on infantry battalions and the monopoly on armed violence to seize power, so do modernizing civilian elites rely on mass organization and mass violence.[3]

In conclusion, it can be said that the military can hold power only in the absence of competent civilian control. Military intervention occurs most easily when existing civilian institutions are discredited or uncomprehended; when interests are deadlocked and prevent change; and when military intervention can appeal both to the masses who find a charismatic military leader easy to accept, and to the modern elite, who find the military's claim to be above petty politics refreshing.

What, then, should be the military's role in development? The essential role of the military in any society is to complement the efforts of civilian government. Admittedly, the high levels of command do provide excellent administrative training, but this can be put to political use by officers after they have left the military. Meanwhile, the military can make technical contributions to economic development and social integration. Finally, the military must be available to provide internal security at the request of the civilian government. The separation of civilian and military remains, however, the sole guarantor of the efficacy and efficiency of both organizations.

If the military's most useful role in an underdeveloped country is to remain complementary, but subservient, to increasingly participatory civilian governments (although officers with suitable skills can enter politics as civilians), then the objective of civilian-military relations must be one of limiting the political power of the military as an organized group.

III. A COMMUNIST ARMY UNDER CONTROL:
THE PEOPLE'S REPUBLIC OF CHINA

Party control is an effective way to eliminate the military's influence on politics. In the People's Republic of China, where one party has dominated, the political inactivity of the military varies inversely with the strength and stability of civilian government. Marxist thinkers tend to regard the military as the coercive instrument of the ruling class. Therefore, the military is maintained as a backup force to the police and as a national defense force. Any political activity by the military (such as indoctrination of the masses) is undertaken only by units so firmly under party control that ideological deviation is highly improbable.

In China, the People's Liberation Army (PLA) is considered by Mao Tse-tung as more than a defense force. It is the embodiment of his revolutionary concepts. To ensure ideological purity in the PLA, techniques of political control similar to those of the Soviet Union have been applied. Yet the political role of the PLA now is paramount.

Briefly, excessive political interference has hindered the development of a professional officer corps, which really began when the Korean War revealed the need for professional officers in modern warfare. The "communist vs. expert" dilemma has been resolved since 1960, when Lin Piao was made supreme commander. Essentially, officers have been allowed to develop professional skills, while the army as a whole has been mobilized to support Mao. It appears, however, that the Chinese officer corps itself supports Lin Piao, who has kept the party from interfering with operational efficiency.

The Great Cultural Revolution was Mao's attempt to reinstate his revolutionary concepts and personal power throughout China. The PLA supported Mao in his new revolution largely because the PLA supported Lin Piao, and Lin Piao supported Mao Tse-tung. The outcome of the cultural revolution has been the destruction of all previous civilian power structures throughout the nation. The PLA alone remains as a cohesive organization capable of governing. Thus its political power exceeds that of what is left of the party, and even that of Mao himself.

Thus, the PLA's political power was restrained largely by civilian competence. The army could be controlled by an omnipotent and omnipresent party, but the party's collapse enhanced the military's political power, and ultimately made it preeminent.

IV. INDIA: CIVILIAN COMPETENCE AND MILITARY RESTRAINT

The Indian army to date has provided an excellent example of self-imposed restraint on political activity. This has been due largely to the exceptionally intense apoliticism inherited from the Indian army's British background. All high-ranking officers were trained by the British, and recently produced junior officers seem to be molded in the same traditions.

Traditional professionalism alone, however, does not explain abstinence from politics. In fact, the Pakistani army, offspring of the same British organization as the Indian army, has held political power since the late 1950s. The original coup in Pakistan was necessitated by the total collapse of civilian government and popular faith in civilian politicians. Typically, military intervention on the subcontinent has varied inversely with the effectiveness and popularity of civilian governments.

That the Indian army has remained outside politics must be attributed to the relative competence of the country's leaders and civil servants. One explanation for the competence of India's government compared to that of other underdeveloped countries is the inheritance of the British-trained professional civil service. A further explanation is the relative abundance of opportunities for higher education in India—a result of British educational policy. The Indian army has no monopoly on educated personnel for top government positions (the only level where military intervention is an issue). Thus, there is no authority vacuum which the military feels compelled to fill. For now, Indian officers believe that the country can afford their absence from the political arena.

This is not to say, however, that the Indian army can continue to isolate itself from matters political. Much depends on as yet unpredictable trends in Indian politics. On the one hand, as urban unrest continues, the army may be called upon to attend to internal security matters. This will cost the army its political anonymity. Finally, Chinese pressure has made the military increasingly concerned with national security and stability. At present it can only be surmised that the Indian army will abstain from politics as long as civilian authorities maintain their present competence, and as long as the political system neither explodes into widespread communal violence nor denies the military the resources it feels are necessary to counter the Chinese threat.

Ultimately, it is the commitment of the Indian modernizing elite, including the military, to democratic values which makes a democratic government a possibility in India. And it is the growing politicization of the masses, as well as the existence of many political organizations, which makes rule by decree increasingly impossible. India's alternative, then, to mass participatory democracy is mass party totalitarianism. Military intervention in politics would solve nothing.

V. EGYPT AND TURKEY:
THE DYNAMICS OF MILITARY INTERVENTION

Between 1930 and 1961, the Middle East provided an arena for no less than twenty-three military coups. In 1961, the military ruled directly over Egypt, the Sudan, Iraq, Pakistan, and Turkey. During that year the main support behind regimes in Iran, Jordan, Lebanon, Saudi Arabia, Yemen, Syria, Afghanistan, and Algeria was the military. There has been no tradition of separation of civilian and military rule in Middle Eastern history. The strong have always automatically governed. Indeed, this theme is dominant in Islam, for the religion provides a code of ethics for rulers and the ruled. The Ottoman Empire, which controlled the area until this century, was ideologically divided between the military and their subjects, with the religious office of caliphate providing an institutional support for the sultan's rule.

Modern forces, surprisingly, have not altered the pattern of military dominance in the Middle East. In fact, they have intensified it. For the military in the Middle East is no longer a body of traditional warrior kings and their retainers, but the main profession for rising middle-class modernizing elites. The officer corps is the main employer of the ambitions. Middle-class moderns who do not find work with the military usually go jobless, eventually to turn in desperation to radical political movements. The military, then, has evolved from the top echelon of the traditional order—a sort of praetorian guard —to the vanguard of modernizing forces in the Middle East.

Finally, it is the nationalism of these middle-class officers that has spurred them to become the most dynamic modernizing elite. For modernization in the Middle East has been a defensive movement, an attempt to develop enough power to thwart interference from Europe. This trend, intensified by recent European colonialism and a series of catastrophic defeats at the hands of Western powers and small but modern Israel, has spread from the Ottoman Empire in the early years of the last century to all Middle Eastern countries of today.

In the Middle East, military intervention in civilian politics seems to follow a pattern. First, limited pressure is applied to civilian cabinets. Should the cabinets fail to respond to the demands, the military enters politics openly. At this stage, the military exercises power along with some political figures and their organizations. This stage —this "dual regime"—is not absolutely necessary, though; the military can proceed directly to complete political takeover if opposition seems slight.

It would appear, however, that military rule without civilian connections is doomed to impermanency. This is due to the military's inability to attain legitimacy in the eyes of civilian modernizing elites and the masses. Changes in top-level leadership, in the absence of mass mobilization, alter little. For the modernization which military elites seek, the masses must be motivated and mobilized to change their attitudes and their occupations. But because the military is incapable of organizing a mass party (it has little ideology save nationalism based on an external threat) for mass mobilization, it finds itself a vanguard of modernization without any followers.

Once the military recognizes the need to organize the masses, however, counterelites are liable to enter into the fresh political activity. Precoup political organizations reappear to compete with the military politicians. Ultimately the military is sucked into political engagements and forced to rely on repression to keep control over the situation. As soon as the military resorts to force to retain power, it alienates what support is available among civilian elites, and invites mass agitation. At this stage the officer corps usually splits into those who resent the dissipation of energy in politics, and those who find themselves politically engaged.

A military regime can attempt to settle an outbreak of political activity in two ways. One is to "withdraw to the barracks," leaving politics again the sole preserve of civilians. The alternative is to organize a mass party, to "civilianize" its image (drop military uniforms and titles), and to attempt to balance political control and political activity. This process is most effective when a charismatic officer can rally both urban elites and rural masses.

EGYPT

In 1936, the military academy in Cairo was opened to Egyptians. Because a military career was one source of employment open to educated young men, positions were soon filled. Among the early graduates was Gamal Abdel Nasser. The Egyptian officer corps rapidly became the institutional preserve of the rising middle class. People in other professions switched to military careers in search of security. General Neguib, for example, was trained as a lawyer.

This officer corps reacted bitterly to the humiliating defeat suffered at the hands of the Israelis in 1948. Nasser is reported to have stated that the battles were lost before they were fought, due to corrupt government in Egypt itself, and to the ignorance of the troops and the economic weakness of the country—all products of underdevelopment. An officers' conspiracy was organized which attempted to bring pressure to bear upon the civilian government for reform. A new cabinet under a civilian, Ali Maher, was engineered into power. Farouk was banished. The committee of officers interfered only casually with the new civilian government.

The period of indirect control ended when the Maher regime failed to deliver reforms, among them a new constitution. Dual military-civilian rule commenced when Neguib, president of the committee of officers, took over the prime ministership. Neguib hence controlled both the military, and the civilian Muslim Brotherhood and Wafd parties.

Direct and total military rule arrived on 9 December 1952, upon the elimination of all civilian political figures from office, and the liquidation of all parties. A revolutionary command council took over as a "transitional" government to restore national strength. On 9 January 1956, Neguib was eased out of power by a Nasser "mini-coup," and the total suppression of the Wafd, the Muslim Brotherhood, the press, and the intellectuals was enforced by the Nasser regime. Nasser, however, realized the need for mass mobilization if Egypt was to modernize. The Suez crisis gave him a good cause around which to rally support—the threat from foreign enemies. A plebiscite on a new constitution was passed, granting him great powers.

Has mass mobilization succeeded in modernizing Egypt? If not, it is certainly not for want of trying. Nasser evolved elaborate theories and even designed radio programs for the masses. The problem with mass mobilization, however, has not been so much with technique as with content. Anti-Israeli sentiment was a major force which kept Nasser in power. The civilian elites could have challenged him if national security were not so tenuous. An even greater difficulty for Nasser was that his nationalistic propaganda ran away with itself; the masses often demanded policies even more chauvinistic than he himself wished (the prelude to the 1967 war was a good example) to pursue. Nasser retained military backing because he separated himself from the army, and allowed the army to leave politics for professional pursuits. Political activity by the ex-military is carried out through the National Union, Nasser's attempt to organize a popular political base. No politically engaged officer holds an active command. Yet the military itself is strangled by the ignorance of its troops. It is questionable whether the military can afford to watch modernization fail. The possibility of another military coup may well increase in the future.

TURKEY

As long as officers remain in the party, we shall build neither a strong party nor a strong army.   —MUSTAFA KEMAL ATATÜRK

The military was the first institution modernized in the Ottoman Empire during the last century. Indeed, it was largely as an offshoot of military reforms that many other facets of Turkish life were opened to Western influence. Military instructors from the West brought new political attitudes, as did returning Ottoman military attachés. Technical education was spread into the middle class by military institutes. As Westernized Ottoman officers began to realize that the weakness of the empire was inherent in its backwardness and lack of modernity, the officer corps became the primary force for modernization, if only to develop the infrastructure to allow for proper military defense of the threatened empire. When the officers were unable to obtain reforms within the system, they plotted the seizure of power in such clandestine organizations as the Young Turks. The Young Turks (a clique of military officers) did finally manage to seize power in 1908. However, this group was too preoccupied with the impossible defense of a hopelessly decayed empire to effect development. The drive for modernity pushed on.

After Atatürk's revolution in 1918, one could see the benefits of military modernization spread throughout the nation. The Atatürk regime, especially in its early years, relied heavily upon the army as its agent of nation-building and defense. The leading figures of the early republic were military personalities.

Atatürk, however, wished no repetition of Young Turk despotism. Atatürk was a national charismatic figure. He wanted Westernization, and since the West appeared to separate the military from civilian government (with the civilians on top), measures were duly taken to limit the military's political activity, military police powers were terminated. No political figure was allowed to hold a military office. All officers who wished to indulge in politics were forced to resign their commissions. Mass mobilization was conducted through the civilian People's Party.

By separating military and political activity, Atatürk avoided many of the dilemmas attendant on military seizures of power. The military was able to remain above politics, and hence was better able to defend the regime. The military, more importantly, was free to develop professional prowess—the excellence of which was demonstrated in Korea thirty years later. The only role of political significance played by the military was in national integration, by the indoctrination and education of rural recruits during their compulsory service. In the process of modernization in Turkey, then, the contribution of the military per se was to introduce the middle class into positions of power. And this role of the military has remained essential to this day, for the army under Atatürk became in effect the guardian of his revolution and of his principles.

In 1950 the opposition Democratic Party came to power, largely on the basis of a rural support which appears now to have been a backlash against Atatürk's attacks on traditional attitudes. As the ineptitude of the Democratic regime pushed the country into economic chaos, and as the regime's ambivalence to modernization and especially secularism (due to its rural votes) became more obvious, the modern elites in the cities became increasingly dissatisfied with this government headed by Adnan Menderes. The Menderes regime, in turn, felt obliged to enact harsher measures to deal with urban unrest. In May 1960, the army—although alarmed by the regime's incompetence and its opposition to modernization and the values of the Atatürk revolution—was ordered to suppress opposition parties and student riots. On 4 May 1960, General Cemal Gürsel sent a letter to Menderes demanding reinstitution of civil liberties. In return, the general received another order to enforce internal security. On 27 May the military Committee of National Unity seized power, and jailed the Menderes cabinet.

Among the reforms obtained by the military cabinet was a new constitution which limited the possibility of a president's usurping power ever again. A state planning organization was established to improve the economy and speed its modernization. A labor party was permitted for the first time. Finally, foreign policies were reaffirmed, and efforts were made to balance budgets and check inflation.

The Gürsel regime in its early days was popular, at least among the urban dwellers. It is doubtful, however, that the regime was ever able to break the farmers' almost idolatrous affection for Menderes. Military popularity, in fact, began to wane as the regime felt itself obliged to try to punish all offenders against the constitution and the principles of Atatürkism, and to exterminate the Democratic Party. The prime weakness of the Gürsel regime was that it did not act in a political vacuum; strong civilian institutions survived the coup, including the Democratic Party's infrastructure. Attempts by the military to discredit or eliminate any civilian political organization only robbed the military of its cloak of impartiality. The military, furthermore, was never able to break the charisma of Menderes, nor could it produce another Atatürk. In a nation as split as Turkey, charisma is perhaps the only force which can unite divergent urban/modern and rural/traditional interests.

After 1950 the army contained little of the middle-class, educated, and modern talent in the country. In fact, a middle class had grown up in the cities which was capable of competing with the military in leadership ability. Finally, the original cabinet split into two distinct groups. One group was composed of young men below the rank of colonel who favored holding power for a considerable length of time and forcing wide reform. The dominant group, however, was composed of middle-aged men above the rank of colonel who favored relinquishing power at an early date to a competent civilian regime which could be trusted to prosecute reform. Six months after the coup, fourteen radical members of the clique were expelled. In October 1961 a civilian government under Gürsel took over, already plagued by the popular reappearance of the Democrats under the guise of the Justice Party. Two coups by radical military men (February 1962 and May 1963) were attempted, and were followed by the dismissal of great numbers of officers.

The officer corps finally split when some officeholders turned out to be of lesser rank than their military commanders. The regular military resented such a mockery of status and the loss of efficiency due to factional splits over political issues. In the end, a "return to the barracks" was demanded, and obtained.

Some of the Gürsel regime's military reforms survived the subsequent civilian era. In the long run, however, the coup solved nothing. Turkey continues to be split along urban-rural lines. Policy continues to waver between modernization and resurgent traditionalism. Should Turkish politics continue to deteriorate, there is no guarantee that the military will not feel compelled to intervene once more —nor is there any likelihood that their success will be any greater, due to increasing political awareness and a growing civilian modernizing elite.

VI. TOWARD A SOLUTION

We have seen the central importance of civilian competence and military restraint in separating military elites from active politics. More obvious has been the fact that this "civilian competence + military restraint" formula is valid only when both elements are functioning. The Indian army, highly professional, stays out of politics because the civilian government is relatively competent. In China, on the other hand, the People's Liberation Army is paramount because the civilian political party is defunct. In underdeveloped countries it is, however, the incompetence of civilian governments which provokes the military to seize power (Turkey, Egypt, Pakistan).

The impermanence of military rule, especially in a country where development is increasingly demanded, is due basically to the military's inability to bind a diverse society together, and to the military's reliance on civilian elites which end up forming counter-elites. Military rule is not a viable form of government in underdeveloped countries. It presents neither a durable alternative to civilian totalitarianism (communism) nor to civilian democracy.

NOTES

1. I refer here to the "generals' revolt" which took place in Algeria in defiance of the metropolitan government in 1961.
2. G. Almond, ed. *The Politics of Developing Areas* (Princeton, N.J.: Princeton University Press, 1960), p. 5.
3. The phenomenon of civilian modernizing elites and mass organizations is the main topic of Lasswell and Lerner's *World Revolutionary Elites* (Cambridge, Mass.: MIT Press, 1965).

Chapter Four | Changing
Ourselves

Late one May evening in Paris two IHP students were discussing the experiences they had been through together. Asked by her friend in which country she had been the happiest, the other student deliberated for a while and then responded: "I suppose I would have to reply by deciding which of the countries was least painful."

Such was the nature of IHP. The nine-month global study trip particularly challenged our ability to separate rational interpretations of experiences from emotional ones. It was a trip in which we confronted some of the world's most complex issues—overpopulation, militarism, women's rights, social change—and attempted to assess them analytically, while at the same time we were barraged with sensory impressions which defied all but subjective reception. Were we to convey our feelings on the urgency of economic development in India in a statistical treatise on economic growth? Or in a literal description of a village of mud and grass outside Delhi?

The dilemma was a real one. Neither reason nor feeling alone seemed adequate to convey the breadth and depth of the problems we faced. And when reason and feeling were both called upon, their conclusions often conflicted.

The long journey was for many of us a search—a search for happiness, cooperation, equality, humanism, truth, for that unidentifiable quality missing from the American social fabric. But we found no panacea—only disparate clues which will take a lifetime to decode. Japanese tranquility was disturbed by the country's cacophonous consumption; the Indian philosophical tradition was shattered by the inhumanity of the country's social elite; and Swedish stability was broken by its citizens' political apathy. We arrived in the country of our birth in despair, frustrated because we knew the world's great problems but not their solutions. Indeed, the hardest part of the search was coming home, for once home we reflected on the scope of what we had seen, and felt its impact. Amid what seemed the superficial queries of relatives about our health and our photographs, we struggled to convey the state of the world—the poverty, the war, the hunger, the inhumanity—when we talked. We were newly endowed with an international perspective, and the voice and vision of the nation-state seemed then—as they still do—strident and myopic.

The essays in the following section, then, describe the world of our birth through the eyes of writers changed by a worldly education. Vidar J. Jorgensen describes his impressions of a war we have watched on our television screens ever since we can remember. John H. Zammito, in a valedictory address at the University of Texas, questions this democracy which has allowed itself to become so confused by the men of rhetoric that it has blindly sacrificed its sons in the same war. "A Portrait of the World by a Young Man" further examines American society, comments on its comparative level of achievement among the civilizations we studied, and warns against dehumanization in the corporate state. In "A Letter to a Sophomore," Mark Gerzon writes to a young friend, sharing his own reflections on what college can and cannot teach its students about the "global village." Finally, Candace Slater's poem photographs the kaleidoscopic scenes that still materialize in thirty-two young minds.

This section, then, is a statement of what we saw and felt. It is written for our friends here who wonder why we are not like we were before, and for our friends around the globe who, perhaps, know.

VIDAR J. JORGENSEN

Harvard University

Vietnam

On the Air Vietnam flight from Bangkok to Saigon I felt more like I was returning to a familiar land after a long absence than like the complete stranger I was. The writings of Bernard Fall and David Halberstam in particular had left me with firm preconceptions of what I would see during my eight-day visit. But the impressions created by the solemn prose of these two writers were already being challenged in my conversations with some of the passengers on the crowded and almost festive plane. When I remarked how similar this plane seemed to the average convention-bound domestic flight, I learned from a passenger that most of the group were delegates to a week-long International Anti-Communist Conference that was to begin in Saigon the following day. Anti-Communists from all over the world were descending on Saigon to draw inspiration from a star-packed program that included such luminaries as Nguyen Cao Ky and Ellsworth Bunker.

VIDAR J. JORGENSEN *is from Shelby, North Carolina, and joined IHP from Harvard University, where he was a government major. At Harvard, Vidar was interested in the problems of mass communications in specific cultures, and was active in sports and political activities. After IHP, Vidar returned to Harvard, graduated in 1970 with honors, and founded the International Summer Ecology Program for students who wish to travel around the world and study environmental problems. He has recently started his own business.*

.After being herded through fairly efficient customs stalls, the prosperous-looking conference delegates piled into taxis for downtown hotels and I wandered off into the warm night on foot in search of a local press office to which an American soldier had directed me. In a giant warehouse of a building, clearly inspired by Pentagon architects and labeled "Allied Command Headquarters" by nostalgic World War II veterans, I met an officer who offered me his car and Vietnamese driver to get downtown. This generous gesture gave me a taste of the problems involved in running a major American military operation in a country where considerably less than one percent of the population speaks English and still fewer of the military personnel speak Vietnamese. The ten-minute drive to Saigon took forty minutes—since every time I uttered a word, the driver, who would rather be late than wrong, drove me back to the Command Headquarters for a translation. After two round trips I caught on and kept quiet.

Saigon looked garish at night. The streets were brightly lit, and decorated with flags and overhead banners. The banners, curiously enough, were in English: THE DMZ—THE BERLIN WALL OF ASIA, or COMMUNISM—TERROR OF FREE PEOPLE EVERYWHERE. At first I suspected these banners were Saigon's way of demonstrating its resolve to visiting American congressmen, but I later learned they were for the benefit of the delegates to the International Anti-Communist Conference. The site of the conference, the Majestic Hotel, was especially brightly lit and heavily guarded. Being a white man, I could walk past the guards and into the hotel lobby without being checked, while Vietnamese were searched and required to show identification papers. After much snooping around I decided the hotel itself was much more interesting than the delegates it housed. The grand stairway of the French colonial building had been gouged with a big, ugly, open elevator that the times seemed to demand; but the rooms with their sixteen-foot ceilings, giant wash basins, and slowly turning fans seemed straight out of a Humphrey Bogart movie.

The streets outside were crowded with Vietnamese and, due to army regulations, lacked the roving groups of colorful GIs that were so prominent in the R & R cities of Bangkok and Hong Kong. The Hondas, bicycles, and three-wheel taxis that dominated the roadways were frequently rounded up into small groups by Vietnamese policemen checking identification papers in their constant search for draft evaders. In the darker corners of the lesser-traveled streets, solitary people or whole families were already bedding down for the night on pieces of cardboard or whatever else was available. On every street corner were formidable concrete bunkers lined first with sandbags and then with rolls of barbed wire. Since the fighting in Saigon during the Tet offensive in 1968, many of the major streets have been lined with coils of barbed wire so that they can be quickly closed off.

After talking with some American soldiers standing guard outside the press liaison office, I was given a free bed for the night in a hotel that was being used to house soldiers needed for support operations within Saigon. The plastic and formica decor of the over-air-conditioned hotel, complete with poker-playing and whiskey-drinking GIs in every room, was a welcome change from the strange, hot, muggy world outside. In addition to a feeling of security, the soldiers provided background information on Saigon luminaries who rarely make the wire services back home: Pappa Willie—a Vietnamese communications aide who can get you *anything* in exchange for *Playboy* and similar literature; and Mamma Ho—a mysterious cleaning lady everyone suspected was a Viet Cong agent since she never offered to rent out her attractive daughters. The soldiers here, who called themselves Saigon Warriors, were fighting a very different war from the one fought by soldiers I was to meet later in the field.

The next morning was spent clearing press credentials with American and Vietnamese military officials. The procedure earned me no fewer than seven identification cards, including one in Vietnamese to inform the Viet Cong of my rights if captured. Other fringe benefits included PX privileges, access to officers' dining facilities, the option to purchase one complete field outfit including combat boots —and, most important, access to military transportation of all sorts.

Access to military transportation is no small favor, because it is the only means of getting around beyond any of the larger cities served by the expensive and undependable commercial air service in Vietnam. It is this privilege, more than any other, that a writer must consider carefully before taking issue with the Vietnamese government or the American military; for there are clearly understood limits on what can be said without threatening that privilege. There is little overt censorship of foreign correspondents in Viet-

nam, but press credentials expire from time to time and applications
for extensions can be delayed or forgotten.

It was difficult to take Saigon seriously enough to give it a coherent description. Saigon is a bastardization of what seem to be the
least noble aspects of Vietnamese, Chinese, French, and American
cultures: sidewalk black market shops, bars, brothels, motorbikes,
and bicycles—all crowded into grand avenues linked with preten-
tious French colonial architecture. What can one say about a smiling Chinese merchant peddling a wide assortment of multicolored
aluminum Christmas trees in the hot Saigon sun in the middle of a
crowded boulevard with bright English anti-communist banners
flying overhead? The Chinese district of Cholon reminded me of
Hong Kong, and the wealthier residential districts with the large
homes within high walls looked like parts of Kowloon, but the
whole area was dominated by crowded refugees and military personnel and equipment of every description. My reaction was to leave
on the next available military flight for the central city of Hué, where
a semblance of Vietnamese culture still survived.

It was from the cave-like belly of a C-130 military transport
headed from Saigon to Phu Bai that I first began to realize what the
figures of 500,000 men and thirty billion dollars a year meant in
visual terms. In one morning I was treated to aerial views of military
installations at Tan Son Nhut, Bien Hoa, Na Trang, Pleiku, Da
Nang and, finally, Phu Bai, just south of Hué. From the air these
installations looked like cities of 50,000 or so that I had seen from
planes in the United States, and it was difficult to believe that these
and many military cities like them had been built up largely in the
last three years by people and material from a country ten thousand
miles away.

At Phu Bai I was met by a press liaison officer who had been in-
formed of my arrival; then I was driven to the press offices at the
Marine base there. After stowing my backpack under the bed of the
press cabin they offered me, I was briefed by a second press officer,
shown around the base, and then briefed by a third officer on current
military operations in the northeast province of South Vietnam. I
made it clear that I had come north only to photograph the remains
of the Imperial City of Hué, and yet I was being treated with a cour-
tesy one would expect was offered only to visiting members of the
House Armed Services Committee. The attention reached embarrass-

ing proportions until I began to understand more clearly the amount of energy devoted to intraservice competition for favorable publicity. Press Liaison Office is the military term for Public Relations Office, and the maintenance of public support is clearly an important part of any military organization's operation.

The Phu Bai Press Club is worth at least a paragraph in any article on modern Vietnam. Here, in the middle of a crude (by army standards) Marine encampment only fifty miles from the DMZ, a reporter can sit comfortably in a wood-paneled, air-conditioned room drinking Pabst Blue Ribbon beer and eating Planter's salted peanuts while listening to the Supremes in stereo and staring at a blank television screen. There was, unfortunately, no television broadcasting in the Hué area, but if the bars in America had television receivers, the Phu Bai Press Club must have one too.

While it was easy to smile at the sight of aluminum Christmas trees and formica hotel rooms in Saigon, there was something pathetic about the Phu Bai Press Club. In Saigon, the big guns guarding the city were barely audible—a polite reminder that there was in fact a war going on. In Phu Bai, the big guns were much closer and their thunderous rounds shook walls, rattled glasses, and stopped all conversation. The Press Club was not just a monument to Marine vanity or an escape from boredom; it was also an attempt to avoid the unavoidable fear and loneliness that always accompany life so close to drawn-out wars far away from home. While the Saigon Warriors drank with an air of festivity and talked of local girl friends, the Phu Bai soldiers drank somberly and talked of girls back home. In Saigon, they counted the days until they would return home; in Phu Bai, they counted the hours. In Saigon, journalists made the trip from the bar of the Caravel Hotel to the afternoon press briefings dressed in nifty Ramar-of-the-Jungle shirts made by the local French-inspired tailors. Out in the field, journalists could be distinguished from the fatigue-clad soldiers only by the battered cameras that hung from their shoulders or the unusual hand weapons they carried.

Life in the forward camps was even less bearable than life at Phu Bai. Their nights were constantly lit by the eerie glow of flares dropped from continuously circling helicopters; and the constant drone of the helicopters was accented from time to time by intermittent machine-gun fire from nervous guards. Many soldiers slept with their boots on so that they could dash to the bunkers if the hostile rocket fire got too close. As the dangers of attack increased, the soldiers grew closer to the memories that were important to them back home. Without my asking they told me about their parents and grandparents, their wives and children, and the personal dreams that seemed threatened by this bitter war. Natural daylight drove away the fear, but the intense loneliness remained.

Most of my time was spent wandering through the ruins of ancient Hué and the majestic tombs in the surrounding countryside. "Speaking of Hué, people are wont to conjure up in their mind images of poetical scenarios, stately palaces, moss-grown vestiges of ancient eras." This description was taken from a travel brochure given to me at the bombed-out branch of the Vietnam National Tourist Office. Today, most people remember Hué as the city that was partially destroyed during the 1968 Tet offensive and immortalized by the American officer who later declared of the battle: "In order to save the city we had to destroy it."

One year after the Tet offensive the city had barely begun to make repairs. Whole walls and roofs were still missing from some buildings, while piles of rubble remained where other buildings once stood. For the ancient Imperial City itself, most of it built in 1802 by the Emperor Gia Long, the Tet offensive was only the latest and most destructive of a long history of battles. The grand outlines of the surrounding walls and moats are still intact, but the buildings within have been heavily damaged by war and neglect. Sacred shrines with altars and statues askew sit covered with dirt and dust. Marble floors once known only by royalty now stood exposed to the weather and the play of refugee children.

The gradual destruction of these remnants of imperial grandeur was somehow less moving than the accumulation of refugees in the already crowded centers which had sprung up just north of the imperial walls. Row upon row of corrugated steel houses resembling rural chicken coops housed Vietnamese peasants who had been driven from their homes by a combination of Viet Cong harassment and American saturation bombing. This refugee influx, called "urbanization" by scholarly American advisers, is welcomed in Saigon since the inhabitants of central Vietnam are often particularly uncooperative and are more easily controlled in crowded refugee ghettos. During a Buddhist-supported uprising against the largely

Catholic Saigon government in 1966, the University of Hué was closed; two years later, many of its student leaders were still in jail, in hiding, or fighting with the Viet Cong. The local officials who had shown sympathy toward the students and Buddhists were replaced by officers from Saigon. The university had reopened and was struggling to maintain Hué's reputation as the cultural capital of Vietnam. A day spent with a group of student volunteers helping to restore long-abandoned farmlands convinced me that there was among students and intellectuals little support for the Saigon government, which they described as a direct extension of French colonial rule. The student rebellion in 1966 was, according to them, a continuation in the independence struggle of Phan Boi Chao, a Vietnamese intellectual who died in Hué in 1940 after spending most of his life fighting French colonial rule.

The task of resettling the refugees seemed hopeless. The long-neglected fields needed plowing badly; while most of the area's water buffalo had been killed, and American aid money for tractors rarely filtered past punitive (and possibly corrupt) officials in Saigon. More serious than neglect is the practical implication of America's policy of saturation bombing of free-fire zones which turn out to include most of rural Vietnam. One's mind is easily dulled by meaningless accounts of daily bombing raids, but it is quickly brought to awareness by the sight of endless acres of former ricefields so pitted with bomb craters that the terrain now seems more lunar than terrestrial. For Americans accustomed to building Hoover Dams across ravines and cutting Interstate Highways through mountains, these craters are not impressive in size (four to six feet deep, twenty to thirty feet across)—there are just a lot of them. But to a Vietnamese farmer with or without a water buffalo, they can be insurmountable obstructions. The aerial view of these craters brought to mind President Johnson's statement about turning the Mekong Delta into a Tennessee Valley, and I wondered if he had thought to have the RAND Corporation interview a few peasants to see if the Tennessee Valley was exactly what they wanted.

The open lack of respect for things Vietnamese by the American military is best illustrated by the widespread use of the term "gook." The word was distasteful to me during my first few days in Vietnam; but after hearing it everywhere it began to sit more easily with me and I began to feel self-conscious about my constant use of the word

"Vietnamese." I felt like the uppity Southerner in the 1950s who tried to use the word "negro" to describe what everyone knew was a "nigger." Of course, officers were usually careful to avoid the term "gook" when talking to newsmen, but the word "Vietnamese" was a bit too much and they seemed to prefer to talk about the "locals" (as the cultured Southerner gradually compromised with the term "nigra"). It is, of course, difficult to suppress racial and cultural biases; and with some liquor inside them, or during a heated discussion, even officers would drop all pretense and tell us "what the Gooks are up to now." When it came to racial slurs the South Vietnamese (our allies) fared no better than the Viet Cong or the North Vietnamese.

Vietnamese are used extensively by the American military for menial labor of all sorts, including officially sanctioned prostitution. At five o'clock each day, long lines of Vietnamese form at the exit gates of military installations, where they are checked for proper identification and searched for stolen goods before being released to go home. Civilian white folks like myself could walk right by. Some military officers justified this widespread use of Vietnamese labor in terms of economic efficiency: "Why should we bring over more American boys to do what the gooks will do at one-fifth the cost?" Other officers explained that washing dishes and scrubbing floors for Americans helped the Vietnamese develop a sense of national pride or at least a sense of participation in the war effort. The political cost of this practice cannot have been studied sufficiently by the Pentagon's social scientists; for when this war is over it will probably be the daily abrasions with Americans that the Vietnamese civilian will most bitterly remember. By slipping so smoothly into the life-style of the French colonialists, the American military has created with its small but inevitable insults more deeply felt ill-will than the terror of the Viet Cong or its own indiscriminate use of firepower. Most apolitical Vietnamese—and in the fight between the United States and the Viet Cong most Vietnamese seem to be apolitical—have been threatened with violence by Americans and Viet Cong alike; but they have worked as gook servants, pimps, and prostitutes only for the Americans. It is like the difference between being slugged and being spat upon. Chances are the physical wounds will heal long before the humiliation of a racial slur has begun to subside.

Take for example the Vietnamese woman I saw digging deeply into a garbage pail for scraps of steak that had been discarded from the plates of American soldiers. Now any good American boy who has been taught from birth how to wash his hands before meals and to hold his knife and fork and who then sees some gook digging through a trash can with her hands is going to first kick the lady in the rear to get her attention and then swear at her in English so that she understands what she has done wrong. This is exactly what a passing medic did at Quang Tri; yet who is to blame for the resulting ill will? The Vietnamese woman probably saw the meat discarded directly from the soldier's plates as an excellent supplement for her family's basic diet of rice, and the medic may have overreacted in his concern for the woman's health without thinking that her system could probably handle much tougher bacteria than those found on discarded meat.

Incidents like this one do much to explain the bitterness and tenacity of the Viet Cong and the North Vietnamese against the over-whelming military superiority of the United States, for they lay bare the fundamentally racist assumptions behind all the tedious political and military excuses for the American involvement. From the perspective of America, even the domino theory, if repeated often enough, begins to take on an air of respectability—especially if graced with the terminology of loyal intellectuals. From the perspective of the day-to-day activities of the American military in Vietnam, respectable concepts like self-determination, rapid urbanization, and democracy not only lose their respectability: they become laughable. The interesting question is no longer the political one of whether or not the war in Vietnam is predominantly an American colonial war; it is rather the social and psychological question of what makes Americans think they are in any way significantly different from traditional colonial powers.

Considering the traditional assumption of racial and cultural superiority behind the American involvement in Vietnam, it is easy to understand the feeling of weariness and futility that accompanies any discussion of such secondary issues as the legal significance of the Geneva accords or the integrity of the Tonkin Gulf Resolution. A discussion about the legality of a colonial war seems to create about as much interest as a discussion of the legality of slavery.

As I left central Vietnam for Saigon and a connecting flight to

Phnom Penh in Cambodia, I thought about the big country far to the north characterized as the Yellow Peril from time to time in the United States Congress to smooth the passage of large military appropriations. Even if the Communist Chinese are the terrible people we have said they are, the Vietnamese may possibly prefer domination by them to humiliation by us. The Chinese, after all, have been quite gracious, for their criticism of America's aggressive foreign policy has been limited to its economic basis—and greed, even communists agree, is still a forgivable human shortcoming. A policy of officially sanctioned racial and cultural superiority, especially after the events of World War II, is today much less forgivable.

JOHN H. ZAMMITO

University of Texas

Humanism!

I have thought long about what I might say to you, how I might awaken in your minds a new spirit. But I feel like the psychiatrist Ronald Laing: "If I could turn you on, if I could drive you out of your wretched mind, if I could tell you, I would let you know." But I fear I can't reach you.

I tell you only there will be a revolution—not in the many but the few—a revolution which will restore beauty and hope to the soul of man—rescue him once more to the promised land which was not Canaan nor yet America, but his own soul purified of illusion and disillusion, inheriting only earth, the taste of earth, bitter but real, and the strength of his human soul.

It is too easy to forget the human spirit. We are too often and too easily trapped into categories. We lose our sense of common humanity, dividing human life into camps of the old, the established, the youth. There is no youth, there are only children. There is no Establishment, there are only parents. We must remove the blinders from our eyes. There is nothing but deceit in that which turns parents and children against each other. We must throw off the blindness of

This speech was delivered as the valedictory address at the University of Texas during graduation exercises in June 1970.

righteousness, of silence, of rhetoric. We have allowed ourselves to
be marshaled into camps of hatred and to abide our exile in silence.
We wrap in anonymous labels those who are our flesh so that we
may hate them.

Historical righteousness blinds the parent. He remembers the De-
pression and World War II. He remembers the age of annihilation,
of Auschwitz and Hiroshima. He remembers days of hunger and of
struggle to survive. He knows the harshness of historical necessity.
He is concerned with his labor and the practical business of the moment. He has little time to dream, and he has been stripped of his
ideals. He relishes his material possessions, for he labored for them.
He relishes American Power, for he fought for it. He respects the
government and the laws, for they do not seem repressive to him. He
trusts the men in power, for he cannot believe they would lie to him.
He thinks they know so much more than he or his children. And so
he silently obeys. And he is certain that he is right.

Moral righteousness blinds the young. They see around them pollution and death. They sicken of politics and the rhetoric of deceit.
They see cities of cold and horror, they see wars of domination for
profit, they see lies before cameras from men in highest office, they
see the burning engines and the radiant bombs of our civilization.
They cry out against the inhumanity of man against man. Their cry
is one of justice, but it resounds with accusation. They often condemn out of the purest moral idealism. They condemn the blindness
of their parents to the evils around them and hold them guilty for the
state of the planet they must inherit. In their fervor they do not
understand historical necessity or that the guilt must fall on all humanity. They are as blind as their parents.

And the man who profits from their blindness is the man of
rhetoric—he who appeals to the notion of necessity to pervert the
old, and the notion of principle to pervert the young. He who lies
to hold power. This parasite has blinded us all. He wears different
costumes in the different camps, but he feeds always on the same
blood. He tears sons away from homes to sacrifice to a war god. He
uses the blood of man to wet the gears of his industrial society, and
he argues political necessity. He burns and preaches destruction of
the entire civilization without any understanding of its fragility and
the labor of centuries and millennia to build it. He reduces a man's

vision until he cannot see that his son must die and that it is not necessary. That he has been betrayed.

Agamemnon, in Greek mythology, was offered the following choice. He could have great political power and fame if he would sacrifice his daughter. He killed his own child, turning bitter everything else in his life because he betrayed what was most precious to him. He killed his own child! Do you wish to kill your own children? The Sophists say it is necessary. Is it? The Sophists say you are not qualified to judge. Who is more qualified to judge whether a child should live or die than his parents? They tell you they know more—they have secrets of grave importance. But there is enough truth already for you to judge. Is your comfort worth your child? Does this civilization demand that you drink your children's blood to remain free? Were you so endangered that forty-five thousand *sons* had to die? If you are a sovereign people, why have you allowed this ghastly ritual?

And we, the young, have we so completely forgotten the love and care of our parents? Have we forgotten our origins? Are we to believe those who tell us to hate them or to ignore them? Are we so free from guilt? They faced historical necessity as we face it today. We must bear their guilt. There is no escape in the shabby rhetoric of violence. There is nothing in shouted principles without human understanding.

Only when we understand that we are theirs and they are ours and that this is the only truth—only then can we turn to the restoration of hope.

THOMAS A. HIATT
Wabash College

A Portrait of the World
by a Young Man

I. THE WORLD AND AMERICA FROM ABROAD

As I moved from Southeast Asia through India and the Middle East
to the Soviet Union and Europe, my weltanschauung gradually became more complete. Three impressions stand out clearly above the
rest.

The first: For all the diversity of culture and language on earth,
people throughout the world have largely congruent interests and
desires. In Lahore and Hong Kong, in Moscow and Tokyo, in
Helsinki and Delhi, women push their husbands out of bed in the
morning and try to get them to work. They worry about what their
children eat and where they go to school. Husbands fight congestion
to get to work and complain about taxes. Students everywhere listen
to records and study or talk politics. Whatever the political system,
most people share the same personal interests and inclinations.

The second: After living in Asia and in both communal and
communistic societies in Israel, Yugoslavia, and the Soviet Union,
I decided that the physical comforts of the industrial society are
many. It became obvious to me that, however elusive psychic hap-

A speech before the Wabash College student body in April 1970.

piness may be, it is not overabundant in traditional societies where people battle disease and discomfort and often work behind a plodding ox sixteen hours a day to die at the age of fifty.

The third: As a result of my contact with other societies, I concluded that I was a champion of the Western industrial middle class and that I championed the economic system that made that middle class the world's richest. This does not mean that I champion their values, or that I am against change. It means simply that from a distance I came to respect the great comfort that the majority of the people in Western industrial societies had attained. America from abroad looked like some sort of technological wonderland where everyone had his own car, where gas was cheap, and where one could buy good-tasting toothpaste and a plastic comb. It looked sort of homey and comfortably affluent.

II. AMERICA FROM WITHIN

America from within is strangely different than I had remembered it or than it had looked from Asia. Once I had penetrated the country's borders I was no longer impressed by the comforts but distressed by the cacophony of consumption. The seller's society screamed BUY! from every building, billboard, and neon light, and I found it hard to look at a large American car, or at all the garish filling stations with ragged flags, or at a shiny tin can full of foamy pop without feeling slightly disgusted. Entering the United States from Europe I noticed not the affluent but an effluent society. Approaching Kennedy airport from the sea I saw below me the smokestacks of New York billowing yellowish smoke into an ashen sky. While living in New York I have observed tugboats pulling large barges heaped with trash down the Hudson River and out into the Atlantic to be dumped. Circling over the city in an airplane, I have noticed the thoroughfares clogged with automobiles and the countryside scarred and sooty from the area's industry. Journeying from New York City to New Jersey, I frequently travel down streets littered with trash and garbage. I ride in a bus with dirty windows to a subway station that looks like a pit of hell, enter a grimy underground train which, compared to the subways of Paris, Moscow, and Stockholm, looks like a World War I reject, and clatter to the train station and board a dirty rickety train that would have been obsolete in most of Western Europe ten years ago.

Were these the only shortcomings of American society, one could smile indulgently and leave to the lumbering bureaucracy the job of providing more adequate services. Unfortunately, the problem appears to be more than just inefficiency. The whole American social fabric seems imperiled by technological advancement without proper guidance or control, and the moneyed minorities seem to have dangerously and disproportionately great power in charting the country's course.

News Item 1: When Chevron Oil Company was drilling recently in the Gulf of Mexico, one of its rigs caught fire and oil poured out of a hole in the ocean floor for two weeks before the well could be capped. A fifty-square-mile oil slick formed and floated out to sea. The tragedy could have been avoided with an $800 device.

News Item 2: The Department of Agriculture pays the Salyer family in the San Joaquin Valley, California, $1,700,000 annually in farm subsidies. It also pays more than $4,000,000 to the J. G. Boswell Land Company, which has farms in Arizona and California and land interests abroad. Comments Dr. Bishop, agricultural economist and vice-president of the University of South Carolina: "The Department of Agriculture has helped create a class of wealthy landowners while bypassing the rural poor—and that means forty percent of the poor people in this country."

Fact: In America, twenty-four children of every thousand born alive die before they are a year old. Approximately twenty nations in the world, including the newly developed Asian power Japan, have an infant mortality rate substantially lower than ours. Sweden's rate is half ours. A major reason that health care has lagged behind in the United States is because the interests of the American Medical Association want to keep the supply of doctors limited and their salaries high.

Fact: In America, twenty-four children of every thousand born percent of all tax money spent by the federal government—goes for defense and the payment of wars past and present.

Many Americans harbor the mistaken impression that America is the most advanced society in the world. These people should visit Sweden, a country which, with the world's third highest per capita income, has obliterated poverty, ghettos, and pollution. To those ethnocentrists who retain the notion that the highest per capita income denotes the highest level of human advancement, a polite sneer.

Unfortunately, the negative by-products of the technological society are not confined to these systematic aberrations. The technocratic society seems directly to threaten the very liberty and existence of the individual himself.

This society is convulsed with violence. Part of the reason for this is the easy accessibility of firearms. Arthur Schlesinger notes in *Crisis of Confidence* that together England, Japan, and West Germany are, next to the United States, the most heavily industrialized countries in the world. Together they have a population of about 214 million people. Among these 214 million there are 135 gun murders a year. Among the 200 million in the United States, there are 6,500 gun murders a year—*about forty-eight times as many*. To thank for the easy accessibility of bazookas, machine-guns and grenades, we have the untiring efforts of the national lobby for civil murderers and the Minutemen—the National Rifle Association.

The Chicago Conspiracy Trial has left in our minds grave doubts about even the quality of American justice. The government of the United States succeeded in prosecuting seven organizers of the demonstration in Chicago during the Democratic Party's convention. On trial was not Mayor Daley, whose refusal to grant a parade permit and whose aggressive police contributed more directly to disruption than did the sleepers in the park. On trial were protesters who attempted to bring some representation to an archaic method of selecting presidential candidates. The prosecution of these organizers appeared a foregone conclusion, for both the FBI and the local police force had undercover agents disguised as student radicals at the convention demonstration, and this is documented in the transcripts of the Conspiracy Trial proceedings.

If this bizarre morality stopped at our borders, the tragedy might be tolerable. Unfortunately it does not and is not. Since the successful coup d'état in Greece in 1967, the career army officers in power there have carried out mass arrests, imposed censorship on the media, incarcerated suspects for sedition, and tortured them—all on the pretense of saving the country from a communist take-over and with the intent of bringing it around again to Christian morality. The officers have not only jailed newspaper editors; they have also banned certain books and some Greek songs. The present military government of Greece has been kicked out of the Council of Europe by the other European countries for denying its citizens basic human rights. Most European countries have also recalled their ambassadors. The United States not only retains an ambassador in Athens but continues to supply the country with military aid. It is tragic that a former revolutionary democracy now supports a neo-fascist dictatorship in the birthplace of democracy. This paradox is symbolic of the present American malaise.

This nation's sanctimonious attitude toward the recognition of the People's Republic of China and of Cuba, and the country's support of the landed aristocracy and quasi-military governments of Taiwan, Brazil, Haiti, Paraguay, and the Dominican Republic are further indications of an ethnocentric foreign policy that sanctions only the politically expedient. In Vietnam, the First Infantry Division of the United States displayed its colors by carving a 1½-mile-long and 1-mile-wide swath of jungle into the shape of the First Division's emblem—a big numeral one. The infantry's exercise took six days to execute, and three men were wounded in the operation. An army photographer had to fly at an altitude of 6,000 feet to get the entire emblem in his camera viewfinder. This scar in the jungles of Vietnam reflects the mentality with which much of American foreign policy is being implemented throughout the world. The United States has shown little regard for the others who live on this earth, and less respect for their ideologies.

The United States seems to be tripping on its own technology. The sellers' society, through its advertising, is creating within its children feelings of psychic and physical inadequacy, nurturing them on a competitive rather than a cooperative ethic, educating them in a mediocre fashion, denying them a political role, and then asking them why they feel unhappy and alienated. The country seems to slight humanism at home and almost ignore humanity abroad.

III. CHANGE

Is change imminent? If I interpret the mood of the Silent Majority correctly, it seems that the country is moving not toward liberalism but toward a repression of liberalism. A new intolerance pervades the society, one which opts for silencing young people who organize moratoriums, challenge corporations, and occupy university buildings. The prevailing mood of the country was summed up by a woman juror in the Conspiracy Trial who said on a national television interview: "We've got to teach these kids some respect."

The national paradox is that we now have the technological means of shaping a world without hunger, disease, cancer, or toil. The mind of man which can navigate the heavens can surely create an environment without crime, poverty, conflict, or pollution. Instead of planning the elevation of humanity, however, we seem to be plotting its extinction. Our government spends billions on atomic bombs, MIRVs, gases, bacterial agents, napalm, defoliants, asphyxiating agents, and ABMs. It has dropped fifty percent more tonnage—some 2,948,057 tons—of bombs on Vietnam than were dropped on Japan, Germany, and other enemy territories during the last world war.

While millions starve in the streets of India, while 400,000 in Japan are homeless, while Chinese peasants live in their huts and harvest their crops as they have for centuries, while the Red Guard expounds the thoughts of Chairman Mao, while a systematic liquidation of Black Panther leaders seems to be occurring, while cities decay, while nations struggle and our environment spoils . . . the greatest crime of all is ignorance. Activists must remember that the numbers are not in their favor, and that blind destruction of property invites denunciation and decimation. The greatest follies are counter-violence or apathy; such responses are blind *reactions* to a dehumanizing society, not autonomous *actions* toward its transformation.

A rebirth of humanism must save man from the lumbering technological machine that threatens to destroy him. Man must realize that until the primeval force which rules the endless stretches of the universe makes its identity known to him, he is god. Man is in charge of society's destiny and his actions must channel change with a recognition of his own sanctity. Guard against infringements on your liberties and begin spreading the humanism that should have nurtured young gods like you.

MARK GERZON

Harvard University

A Letter to a Sophomore

April 5

Dear Harvie,

Got your letter yesterday. When you can feel spring being born, but you feel like you're dying—I know, man, that's really the bottom.

Sophomore year was like that for me, too. First year and a half at Harvard, I just gobbled up all there was around. I did too many things: courses, lectures, people, sports, drugs, the McNamara thing, reading, draft work. I feel like I did more in that year than in the rest of my life put together.

But then it starts happening, doesn't it? You called it the feeling of approaching an "invisible barrier." You know what you want to learn, you can practically taste it. But you can't get at it. There *is* a barrier. Whether it's ec, or phil, or soc rel, or international relations or history and lit, you feel like everything that's coming to you is selected, predigested, and delivered to you.

So now you sit there at home, back in good old Indianapolis, wondering why you should even come back. Thank God your intuition is still working, that it tells you there's more to learn than professors, or drugs, or reading lists, or SDS can tell you. I had that feeling, too, as a sophomore. Amorphous, fleeting, irritating. I knew Harvard provided the best education, but what did that mean? It meant it was simply the best filter on what was happening, the best job of selection, prepackaging, and delivery. I also shared your feeling, Harvie, that yet another year of second-hand experience would be too much, that it would deaden me to the point of insensitivity and blind fury—and neither quality makes for a good revolution.

But here's where we differ: you figured the problem was Harvard's completely. The structure of the institution, the content of the courses, the housing question, their faculty hiring and student admissions—you thought there was the entire problem. *That* was the barrier. *That* was what had to be changed.

Of course you're right but you don't go far enough. Of course Harvard doesn't teach a radical economic critique of our social system; of course it doesn't convey an accurate image of Third World circumstances; of course its philosophy is dry and sterile; of course soc rel is bourgeois titillation. Sure, this grand old institution needs renovation.

But Christ, Harvie, look what you're asking of the old pile of bricks! You're asking it to bring the whole world to you through a funnel, a nipple, and force-feed you. Or perhaps you suckle willingly. You're saying: "Offer me Mao, convey the dynamism of epic struggles, show me poverty fermenting into revolution, transport the sons of workers (and eligible, pill-taking women) right into my dorm, teach us to tame the technological beast we inherited, identify the pathology of American affluence, inspire me to align myself with the forces of liberation, translate the chaotic trauma of our time and give it meaning and unity . . . do not deceive me at this moment of my greatest need."

Remember how when we were little we'd run over to old lady Dowling's drugstore and watch the TV there because our parents hadn't gotten TVs yet? We thought we'd see the whole world by watching those flickerings on that screen. The world's history was being distilled electronically and brought, just for you and me, to Dowling's drugstore. How betrayed we felt, didn't we, that day we saw that big fireman pull those limp but living bodies from the flaming old people's home, and ran to Dowling's to watch it on the tube since we were part of history. But all they had was an interview with the fire commissioner.

Whose fault was that Harvie, the TV's or ours? And whose fault is this second-hand experience, Harvard's or yours? Don't your expectations of Harvard need to be changed just as much as Harvard itself?

My head was just where yours is at about this time sophomore year when we saw this ad in the *Crimson*: "Travel around the world. Study and live with families." So we wondered what the catch was. But it turned out the only catch was Harvard. It was the old syllogism that kept our generation under this university's skirt: (1) the draft was on your tail; (2) you needed credit to get it off; and (3) Harvard wouldn't give a full year's credit for work done away from Harvard. (Harvard did give credit, so I understand, for summers on the playing fields of Oxford.)

What most people don't know is that the Big H dropped the rule after we petitioned the ad board. This particular program (called International Honors Program: IHP) gets one or two students from about twenty universities and pays for everything beyond what a year of college normally costs. You go from September to June, living for about a month in each of eight countries. Two professors accompany and instruct the group of students and, in conjunction with professors, journalists, politicians, and others from the local country, lecture on their own work. My year the focus was on sociology and politics, but it's different from year to year. The students are always free to direct their reading and thinking to the area that grabs them most. Birth control studies, the role of the woman, American propaganda, children's art, resource allocation to scientific research, radical politics: everyone was on his own trip.

Beginning in September in San Francisco, the time of year when normally we'd be setting up our stereo or restringing our squash racket, we were torn from our academic womb. We had to digest not the youth culture placebo but the world itself. Indigestion followed: our sanitized stomachs were not prepared to cope with real food. Radical, preppy conservative, or that sexless breed "the neutral observer"—none of the student types in our group survived the Orient. For those who had breath left, India knocked it out of them. The deafening silence of India's poverty, and the bizarre and seemingly hopeless class and caste antagonisms, were no longer a saccharine *Time* article (followed inevitably by a full-page English Leather ad) nor a boring lecture delivered from a Harvard Hall podium. It was our entire environment. Rapidly developing schizoid tendencies were aggravated by the Middle East leg of our trip. The Israeli argument, especially when delivered with *kibbutznik* fervor by an old Polish émigré with whom we were working the orange groves, clashed explosively in our heads with the pro-Arab views of our Istanbul families. (We could not go to Egypt because of our State Department, nor to Ankara because the American ambassador had recently been stoned by "anti-American students.")

Yugoslavia, that small, pugnacious little David who dares openly to curse the Soviet and American Goliaths, delivered the final blow to any self-assuredness which might have remained. My Yugoslav "father," a revolutionary from the Thirties and an architect of the Yugoslav economy, rubbed communist salt into my New Leftist wounds with which I had left America a half-year earlier (Chicago, August 1968: remember?), and left me bewildered and impressed by an ideology which the USSR enables us too easily to dismiss.

Thus initiated into a brand of communist thought of which I had been almost wholly ignorant before (although as a sophomore in Leverett Dining Hall I could have been heard wisely advising a "Titoist" form of communism in Vietnam), we were Aeroflotted into the tourist mouth of totalitarianism, Moscow. After "well-supervised" tours, rifled baggage (they stole my Trotsky *Diary in Exile,* those bastards), and a few frigid confrontations with our young "guides" (the girls looked like they were taken right out of *Vogue*; the guys right out of Fort Dix), we were off to Leningrad where by some circuitous route someone learned about an occupation of University Hall or something.

Sandwiched in a Radio Free Europe broadcast between reports of an oil-tank explosion in Vienna and an Arab guerrilla attack, we could give the Cambridge episode no more than a second's thought, for we were on our way to the long-awaited confrontation, we and a group of Komsomol members in free discussion.

Having intellectualized about capitalism and communism for all the months since our intensive exposure to Mao's experiment, the departure from Russia's salad-less meals, colorless streets, and robotish guides made Stockholm quite sensual. Mere hours after escaping the iron cage, we were in paradise. Or were we? Yes, there was Donovan singing, beautiful girls in short lavender dresses, street dances, and wonderful vegetable markets with no long queues. Yet my first piss in the Free World, after a feast of salads, cheeses, and wines like Russia has never seen (except for those Politburo bashes, I suppose), was in a Stockholm University john with a three-foot hammer and sickle painted in red on the white-tiled wall.

The American vibrations, which had for so long been stilled, began to echo in my head once again.

Can't you see, Harvie, just from this drop-in-the-bucket retelling of our year away from this place, that to come back here to find students demanding all this from stodgy, vested, pocket-watch Harvard appears absurd? No matter how many student-faculty committees are formed, or how many revolutionary courses are established, you are bound to remain dissatisfied. You are reaching for living experience within the domain of immobile, institutionalized education. Within the sandbox of the campus, you wish to climb mountains.

I'm not saying you should leave the place the way it is. But please learn *first* what education can give you and what it can't. It can feed you information but not its proportions; it can give you access to knowledge but it can't tell you its relative importance. In *The Making of an Un-American,* Paul Cowan's powerful political autobiography, he makes the same point after he left Harvard for Peru, Cuba, Israel, and the American South:

In college classrooms it had been difficult for me to understand the meaning of phrases like "the impact of technology on poor societies," even after I had taken sociology courses devoted to that theme. Now, when I watched the sixty-five-year-old woman at whose house I was living struggle to understand the workings of the dial telephone that had just been installed, I understood that her look of confusion reflected the same sense of displacement as the lost expressions on the faces of old Oriental men in Israel, who listened to Doris Day songs on their transistor radios as they grazed their sheep near Abraham's caves.

I'm certainly not giving any broadly applicable answers, Harvie old friend. All I'm really saying is that because we left this place we learned what we did not know. We learned not to ask education to give us that which only life itself can provide. We learned how shallow it was to say that *America* was fucked up, that *they* didn't know the answers, that the *establishment* was parochial. We learned that, when you take away our stereo, our drugs, our posters, our existential novels, our weekly Fellini flicks, our dorms and dining halls, and all our fellow well-stuffed know-it-alls with whom we spend our time, when you throw us out on our asses into the world, *we* are fucked up, *we* don't know the answers, *we* are parochial.

And that, Harvie, is what you can't learn here. That is ultimately what Harvard can't teach you. It can't teach you what you don't know. It can grade you on what you know you know. But it doesn't accomplish the far more important part of life: teaching you what you don't know.

Since Harvard has changed its foreign study rule, quit using the draft as the excuse for not weaning yourself from the academic bottle. Get into this program, or another one, or organize one, or even do a Peace Corps thing. I got no prescription except that for a while, just for a while: get the hell out of here.

CANDACE SLATER
Pembroke College

Returns

1

. . . October 4. Thumbs of the sausage tree poke
through the darkness. A band of blue, then
violet, rings around the moon. On the terrace
of the Japanese Consulate of Hawaii, Messrs.
Rappoport and Poffenberger gulp fine wine.

. . . October 16. Morning in Roppongi. Sun slides
over ripe persimmons and butters frozen mud.
A woman with bad teeth, men's pants, and long,
white apron, fries noodles underneath a string
of flags.

. . . October 22. Frail boats. Kites mate above the lotus.
Spiders weave light above Tokyo Bay.

CANDACE SLATER *is originally from Floral Park, New York, and left her work in English and in human studies at Pembroke College, Providence, Rhode Island, to participate in IHP. At Pembroke, Candace's major interest was in writing, particularly poetry, and she has published a book for children. After IHP, Candace returned to Pembroke. She graduated in 1970 and was named a Danforth Fellow. She is presently enrolled in the Ph.D. program in English at Stanford University, and has spent recent summers studying Spanish in Mexico and doing research in Chile.*

. . . November 24. Old Chinese village. The main
canal has withered. At the Coca-Cola stand,
a water ox with flies as thick as fur.

. . . December 4. Hong Kong Opera. The cymbal and the
tambourine glitter in the air. Children
gobble chestnuts, pickles, ice cream, grapefruit.
Smiling, wet the benches. Nobody cares.

. . . December 11. Peng Chau. A house on toothpicks.
One dead, delicate, blue-white squid.

. . . December 19. Jane's Lapidary, Bangkok. The
jeweller adjusting a phalanx of tin shields.
A fat man with a mole, he prods an errant ruby.
The light that looks like orange ice is hot, so hot
that the American lady spilling sapphires from a
handkerchief sweats as much as does the jeweller whose
chest flames kiss.

So on and on, now a year later, now in Providence, Rhode Island, each
day's an anniversary.

2

Could this be instant replay?
Chinatown, San Francisco. The grocer shaving ginger
fades out to Matthew Fu. Through the dusk, a dragon
projects a vague resemblance to a cousin or an uncle or
a brother in Kowloon.
Omnipresent tailors. Jade windows crammed with ivory.
Grotesque bodhisattvas. The squawk of Cantonese.
The smell of melon frying impinges with the darkness.
Re-run? No. No re-runs here.

3

Nothing more than details.
Sites and crises, voices . . .
Hours in preservative. Salted into words.
But what's crystallized evaporates.
It's easy to forget:

rain and purple flowers bursting over Nazareth
historian Raychaudry reading *Time* magazine
bracelets like manacles; men pulling men through
Delhi.
noon on Ben Yehuda Street . . . cold, thin, air.

4

Snakes leave skins.
Snails, shells.
But the iris is no more.
The lemon slips from green to yellow without warning;
after harvest, is the juice, becomes the tea.
In Chinatown, in Fong Fong's, we sip our cups of steam
as the shadows part then mingle in the nervous breeze.

Appendix I:
The Guest Lecturers

HONOLULU

LANGUAGE AND SOCIETY

Dr. Elizabeth Wittermans (Senior Program Office, Institute of Advanced Projects, East-West Center)

Dr. Joan Rubin (Assistant Professor of Anthropology, George Washington University)

Dr. Jyotirindra Das Gupta (Assistant Professor of Political Science, University of California, Berkeley)

Dr. Ernesto Constantino (Chairman, Oriental Languages and Linguistics, University of the Philippines)

SOCIAL VALUES AND CHANGE

Dr. J. Milton Yinger (Professor of Sociology and Anthropology, Oberlin College)

Dr. Thomas Poffenberger (Consultant in Social Psychology, Ford Foundation, New Delhi)

Dr. Ki Suk Kim (Director, Student Guidance Center, Seoul National University)

Dr. Noel Gist (Professor of Sociology, University of Missouri)

MAN AND HIS ENVIRONMENT

Dr. Roy A. Rappaport (Assistant Professor of Anthropology, University of Michigan)

Dr. E. A. J. Johnson (Professor of Economic History, Johns Hopkins University)

Dr. Aprodicio Laquian (Deputy Director, Local Government Center, College of Public Administration, University of the Philippines)

Dr. William Vitarelli (High Commissioner's Representative, Trust Territory of the Pacific Islands, Saipan)

LAW AND POLITICS

Dr. Lloyd D. Musolf (Professor of Political Science and Director of the Institute of Governmental Affairs, University of California, Davis)

Dr. Jean Grossholtz (Associate Professor of Political Science, Mount Holyoke College)

Dr. Yasumasa Kuroda (Associate Professor of Political Science, University of Hawaii)

Mr. Naseem Mahmood (Member, Directing Staff, Pakistan Administrative Staff College)

ECONOMIC DEVELOPMENT

Dr. Harry Oshima (Professor of Economics, University of Hawaii)

Dr. Shao-er Ong (Regional Agricultural Officer for Asia and the Far East, Food and Agricultural Organization of the United Nations, Thailand)

Dr. Youngil Lim (Assistant Professor of Economics, University of Hawaii)

Dr. Shujiro Sawada (Professor of Agricultural Economics, Kyushu University, Japan)

TOKYO AND KYOTO

Dr. Takeo Doi (Psychoanalyst): *The Japanese Psyche*

Dr. Takeo Sofue (Professor of Anthropology, Meiji University): *Recent Changes in Japanese Culture*

Mr. David Osborne (Deputy Chief of Mission, American Embassy in Tokyo): *Japanese Politics*

Mr. Barger (Minister of Economic Affairs, American Embassy in Tokyo): *Economic Growth of Japan*

Dr. Morley (Special Assistant to the Ambassador, American Embassy in Tokyo): *Japanese-American Relations*

Dr. George Hodel (Director-General, International Research Association): *Reader's Digest Asia Survey*

Dr. C. Nakane (Professor of Sociology, Tokyo University): *Japanese Sociology*

Dr. H. Kato (Kyoto University): *History of Kyoto*

HONG KONG

Dr. Frederick T. C. Yu (Professor of Political Science, Columbia University): *The Background of Communism in China, Chinese Culture and Personality, Mass Communication and Recent Events in Mainland China, The Chinese Minority in Vietnam*

Mr. Tsu (Director, Union Research Institute): *Communist China*

Group from University Services Center: *Chinese Politics*
Mr. Sun (Federation of Hong Kong Industries): *Economics of Hong Kong*
Mr. Robert Elegant (Foreign Correspondent and Columnist, *Los Angeles Times*): *China-Watching*
Dr. Maria Yen: *Chinese Personality and Politics*
Dr. Mitchell: *Urbanization Problems of Hong Kong*

NEW DELHI

Dr. Ratna Dutta (India International Centre, Council on Social Development): weekly lectures as liaison professor
Dr. Charles Loomis (Research Professor, Michigan State University; Consultant to Ford Foundation in India): *Interpretations of India: Marx and Weber*
Dr. Prodipto Roy (Research Director, India International Centre, Council on Social Development): *Social Change and Social Development*
Dr. Romila Thapar (Reader in History, Delhi University): *India to 1947: The Historical Background*
Dr. Kirit Parikh (Professor of Economics, Indian Statistical Institute): *India since 1947: The Four-Year Plan*
Dr. T. N. Madan (Professor of Social Anthropology, Delhi University): *Caste and Class*
Dr. Douglas Ensminger (Ford Foundation representative in India): *India's Problems: Past, Present, Future*
Dr. Thapan Taychauduri (Professor of Economic History, Delhi University): *Evolution of the Indian Economy*
Mr. D. K. Tyagi (Commissioner of Mass Communications for Family Planning): *Family Planning in India*
Mr. M. N. Kapur (Principal, The Modern School): *Education in India*
Dr. Ashoka Mehta (Member of Parliament): *Socialism in India*
Dr. M. N. Srinivas (Professor of Sociology, Delhi University): *Religion in India*
Mr. Romesh Thapar (Director, India International Centre): *Intellectuals in India*
Mr. M. L. Sondhi (Member of Parliament): *Indian Foreign Policy*

JERUSALEM

Dr. Michael Gurevitch (Hebrew University): weekly lectures as liaison professor
Dr. Louis Guttman (Director, Israeli Institute of Applied Social Research): *Current Israeli Research and Methodology*
Dr. Nimrod Raphaeli (Lecturer in Political Science and Public Administration, Hebrew University): *Administering the Arab Territories*
Dr. Aron Antonovsky (Israeli Institute of Applied Social Research): *Ethnic Relations in Israel*
Dr. Emanuel Gutmann (Lecturer in Political Science, Hebrew University): *The Israeli Political System*

Dr. S. N. Eisenstadt (Professor of Sociology, Hebrew University): *Conservatism and Innovation in Israeli Society*

Dr. Moshe Lissak (Senior Lecturer in Sociology, Hebrew University): *The Role of the Army in Israel*

ISTANBUL

Dr. Şerif Mardin (Professor of History, Ankara University): *The Historical Context: From the Ottoman Empire to the Turkish Republic*

Dr. Feza Gürsey (Professor of Physics, Middle East Technical University): *Science and Development in Turkey*

Dr. Derek Price (Professor of History of Science, Yale University): Seminar with Doctors Gürsey and Mardin

Dr. Anlagen (Assistant Director, Hittite Museum): *The Ages of Man at the Gordion Digs*

Dr. Oktay Yenal (Professor and Dean of Economics, Robert College): *The Turkish Economy: Problems and Prospects*

Mr. Talat Halman (Poet, Critic, Journalist): *Poetry and Society: The Turkish Experience* and *Political Parties and Social Issues in Turkey*

Dr. Necat Eczacibasi (Industrialist): *The Private Sector in Turkey*

Dr. Paul Mojzes (Professor of Religion, Lycoming College): *Religion and Politics: Turkey and the Balkans*

Dr. Ilter Turan (Professor of Political Science, Istanbul University): *Major Themes in Turkish Foreign Policy*

Dr. Robert Kerwin (Ford Foundation Representative in Turkey): *Sources of Social Frustration in Turkey Today*

BELGRADE

Dr. Paul Mojzes (Professor of Religion, Lycoming College): weekly lectures as liaison professor

Professor Nicola Balog (Professor of Law, University of Belgrade): *Self-Management and the Communal System in Yugoslavia*

Dr. Leo Mateš (Former Ambassador to UN and US; Director, Institute of International Politics and Economics): *Yugoslavia's Foreign Policy*

Professor Ljubiša Adomović (Professor of Economics, University of Belgrade): *Economic Development and Social Change in Postwar Yugoslavia*

Professor Bernard Rosen (Professor of Philosophy, Ohio State University; former IHP faculty member): *Marxian Ethics*

Bishop Danile Krstić (Bishop of Serbian Orthodox Church): *Christian-Marxist Dialogue in Eastern European Countries*

Professor Branko Pribicević (Chairman, International Politics Department, University of Belgrade; Secretary, Belgrade Communist Party): *The Ninth Party Congress in Belgrade*

Professor Aleksandar Nejgebauer (Professor of English, Novi Sad University): *Contemporary Yugoslav Literature*

Dr. Miljenko Zreleć (Chairman, Belgrade Secretariat of Education and Culture): *The Educational System of Yugoslavia*

STOCKHOLM

Dr. Dag Norberg (Chancellor, University of Stockholm): *Problems of Higher Education in Sweden*

Mr. Jan Sture Karlsson (Secretary General, National Union of Students): *The Organization of Swedish Student Unions*

Dr. Berthil Saunel (Cultural Geography Institute and Scandinavian Institute of Town Planning): *City Planning in Stockholm*

Dr. Gunnar Myrdal (Distinguished Professor, University of Stockholm): *Sweden and America: A Comparative Analysis*

Mr. Peter Syndaarg (Chief, Third Section, Swedish State Department): *Sweden's Position in the World*

Dr. Karin Busch (Swedish Opinion Research Institute): *Sex and Welfare in Sweden*

Seminar on labor-management relations with four leaders of national employers' and labor organizations

PARIS

Dr. Otto Klineberg (Professor of Psychology, Sorbonne University): *Student Attitudes, France vs. America*

Dr. Jean Stoetzel (Professor of Psychology, Sorbonne University; Director, French Public Opinion Institute): *After De Gaulle, What?*

Mr. Claude Bourdet (Editor, *Nouvel Observateur*): *The French Referendum*

Professor Bertrand de Jouvenel (Professor of Political Economy, Sorbonne University): *The Study of the Future*

Appendix II:
Group Activities

HONOLULU

Full schedule of all-day seminars on orientation
One-day bus trip to Sea Life Park and nearby beaches

TOKYO

Orientation meeting with local representative, Mr. Ishii
Visit to Bridgestone Tire Factory
Evening at Japanese theater: *Noh* drama performance
Attended tea ceremonies and visited Nikko Park with host families
Sayonara dinner party with host families
Rode Tokaido Express train to Kyoto

KYOTO

Visit to temples at Nara
Sightseeing in Japan's first capital

HONG KONG

Visit to New Territories; view of Mainland Chinese border and visit to small
    spinning factory and village farm
Visit to plastics factory
Swimming in Big Wave Cove
Thanksgiving party at Professor Frederick T. C. Yu's home

BANGKOK

Visit with touring students from St. Olaf's College; debate between their leader and Dr. Lerner on *Westernization: Church vs. the Media*

NEW DELHI

Orientation meeting with host families and Experiment in International Living officials
Christmas Eve dinner party at India International Centre
Birthday parties for three members of group by host families
One-day bus trip to Agra (Taj Mahal)
Tea and talk with American Ambassador Chester Bowles
International Centre panel discussion with Delhi University students
Factory visits to Delhi cloth mills (textiles, chemistry, and industrial management), to Escort tractor assembly plant (industrial production), and to automotive supply manufacturer
Evening of Indian music and classical dance at The Modern School
Farewell tea with host families and Experiment in International Living officials

JERUSALEM

Orientation meeting with local representatives Michael and Pat Gurevitch, student counselor Yael de Haas, and research adviser Naomi Keyes
Visit to nuclear reactor in Tel Aviv
Visit and lecture at Israeli Institute of Applied Social Research
Three-day bus trip to Galilee and coastal areas, including Caesarea, Nahariya, Safad, Tiberias, Nazareth, West Bank, and Sebastia
One-day bus trip to Masada and the Negev
Nine-day period of working on kibbutz
Shabbat dinners with host families

ISTANBUL

Orientation meeting with local representative Nur Ener and Liaison Professor Şerif Mardin
Visit to Eczacibasi Pharmaceutical Factory
Four-day bus trip to Ankara, Gordion, King Midas' Tomb, village of Balgat, Middle East Technical University campus, Hittite Museum, Atatürk Mausoleum, and Citadel
Group exchanges with Turkish students at Robert College, Istanbul University, and American Cultural Center; also with Peace Corps volunteers
Güle-Güle farewell party with host families at American Officers' Club

BELGRADE

Orientation meetings with Student Travel Service, Fulbright officials, and American Embassy officials
Two-day bus trip to Dubrovnik, including tour of walled city
One-day bus trip to Novi Sad
Half-day bus tour of Belgrade and environs
Passover Seder at Jewish Community Center

Easter services in Catholic and Orthodox churches
Visit to cotton textile factory
Soccer game
Folk music and dance performances
Dovidjenja farewell party with host families at American Club

MOSCOW

Briefing at American Embassy by Messrs Cook and Richmond
Lecture: *The Economic Reform*
Group sightseeing: general bus tour, visits to Moscow State University,
Lenin's Tomb (on day of 100th anniversary of his birth), monastery at
Zagorsk, GUM Department Store, subway system, Dretzikoff and Pushkin
and other art museums; tour of Kremlin
Party with young engineers and students of Agricultural Research Institute
outside Moscow
Bolshoi Ballet performance
Variety concert at Palace of Congresses
Sabbath services at local synagogue

LENINGRAD

Group sightseeing: general bus tour, visits to Peter and Paul Fortress, Mu-
seum of the History of Leningrad, Piskarevskaya Cemetery, Hermitage
Museum, Pushkina Summer Palace
Round-table discussion with Russian students
Round-table discussion with foreign students studying in Leningrad
Kirov Ballet performance
Sabbath services at local synagogue
Visit to apartment house

STOCKHOLM

Arrival supper party with host families and local representative Yngve Lith-
man
Bus tour of city, suburbs, and Old City
Conference on Swedish factories with Mr. Per Alsberg, manufacturer
May Day student capping festivities
Walpurgis Night parties
American Embassy briefing with Political Consul Borg, Economic Secretary
Bowen, and Cultural Affairs Officer Tressider

PARIS

Au Revoir party